I0793701

IMAGES
of America

LOVES PARK

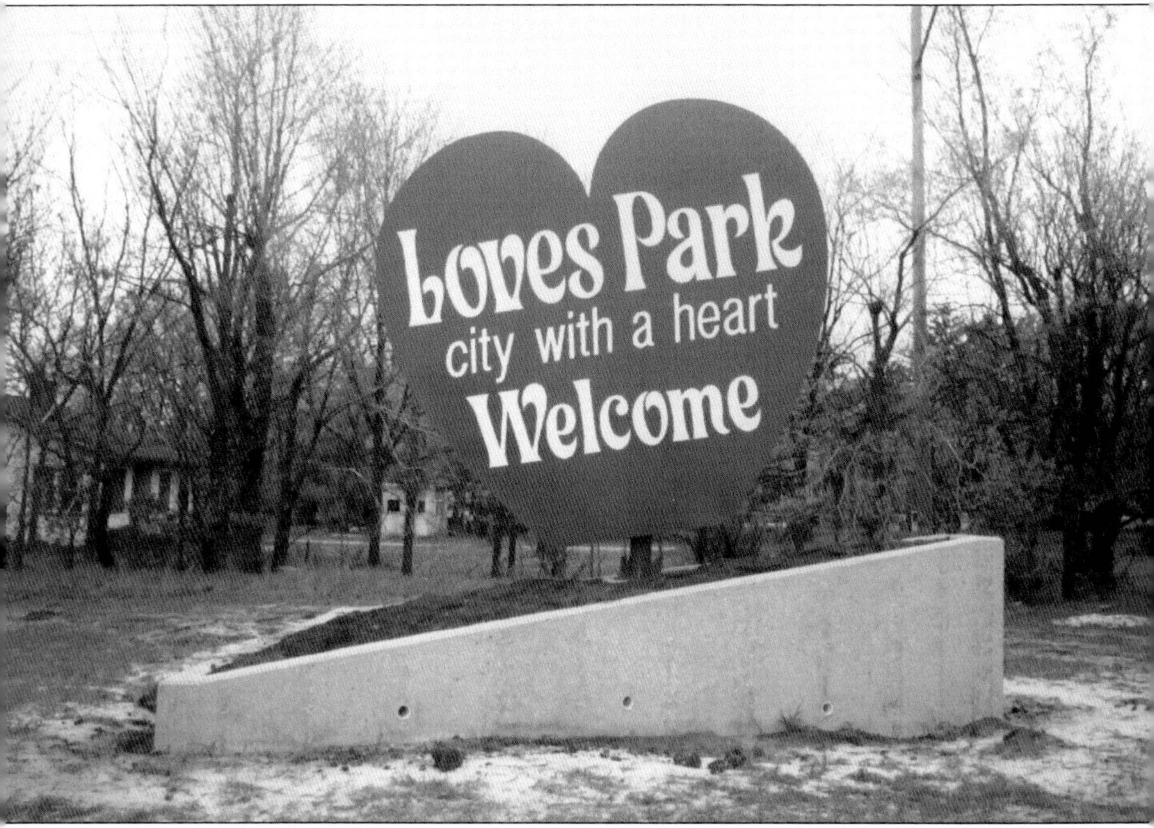

This 1989 photograph shows the sign that welcomes people who enter the city of Loves Park from the south via North Second Street (State Route 251). (Courtesy of the North Suburban Library District Local History Collection.)

On the Cover: In this c. 1969 image, the Phantom Regiment poses in front of Geri's Hamburgers at 5518 North Second Street in Loves Park. Geri's was a popular hamburger chain with locations in southern Wisconsin and northern Illinois. The last Geri's—located in Beloit, Wisconsin—closed in 1999. The Phantom Regiment is a famous drum and bugle corps based in Rockford. (Courtesy of Midway Village Museum, Rockford, Illinois.)

IMAGES
of America

LOVES PARK

Nicole C. Lindsay

ARCADIA
PUBLISHING

ISBN 978-0-7385-9093-6

Published by Arcadia Publishing
Charleston, South Carolina

Printed in the United States of America

Library of Congress Control Number: 2012944848

For all general information, please contact Arcadia Publishing:
Telephone 843-853-2070
Fax 843-853-0044
E-mail sales@arcadiapublishing.com
For customer service and orders:
Toll-Free 1-888-313-2665

Visit us on the Internet at www.arcadiapublishing.com

Contents

ACKNOWLEDGMENTS

Although my name appears on this book's cover, much of the credit belongs to the current and former residents of Loves Park who so graciously shared their photographs and memories. In addition, thanks to the city's churches, businesses, parks and other organizations for allowing me to look through their archives.

I would like to especially thank Tammy Tucker and Ann Martin, local history librarians at the North Suburban Library District, whose help, week after week, made this book possible. Unless otherwise indicated, all images appear courtesy of the North Suburban Library District Local History Collection.

In addition, I would like to thank Jean Lythgoe, librarian assistant in the Local History and Genealogy Room at the Rockford Public Library, and Robert Lindvall at the North Suburban Library District for helping me solve some puzzling questions that came up during this project.

Special thanks to Robert Burden (city clerk) and Steve Thompson (deputy director of community development) with the city of Loves Park for the information they provided regarding essential residents to contact.

I am also grateful for the counsel and encouragement of Craig G. Campbell, author of *History of Loves Park, Illinois*, which was published in 1997 to celebrate the city's 50th anniversary.

I am indebted to Dr. Catherine Forslund, department chair and professor of history at Rockford College, for her contagious love of history that is apparent to all of her students. I was fortunate to have her as a teacher.

Finally, I would like to thank my family for their love and support throughout this whole project, and although my parents did not live to see the finished product, I know they would be proud.

Introduction

As early as the 1830s, settlers were claiming and purchasing land in what would one day become Loves Park. These first settlers were primarily farmers, but in the decades that followed, the area began to grow, and with the growth came the establishment of businesses, schools, churches, and other organizations.

Although the city is named after Malcolm A. Love, he died in 1930 and therefore was not around to see its incorporation. Love and his wife, Rose (Stites) Love, did not play a significant part in the development of the city; however, the city bears the Love name because of the couple's purchase of 236 acres on the east bank of the Rock River in 1901—an area that came to be called Love's Park (and sometimes Love's Grove). The area became a popular gathering place, social center, and, eventually, the site of what was referred to as the city's "first subdivision," which consisted of 95 lots created from a portion of the Loves' land. The Interurban rail line, built in 1902, allowed for the growth of Loves Park, as it connected Rockford, Illinois, to Janesville, Wisconsin, stopping at all points in between.

In the early 1900s, the area was referred to as Love's Park, with an apostrophe in the name. This was changed to the current spelling of Loves Park, without the apostrophe, when area journalists decided to omit it around 1925. When the city incorporated in 1947, that spelling was used as the official one.

The path to the incorporation of Loves Park was neither quick nor easy. For over two decades, the community debated whether annexation with Rockford or incorporation was the best way to move forward. Finally, on April 30, 1947, residents voted in favor of incorporation, and the city of Loves Park was established. It was and is the first municipality north of the city of Rockford. Shortly after incorporation, the Loves Park (Riverside) Toll Bridge was built across the Rock River, which further connected the city to Rockford.

Throughout the years, many businesses have come and gone. Well-known places like Top Hat Restaurant, River Lane Outdoor Theatre, and Bredsteen's Pioneer Grocery Store are no longer open, but others—such as Blume's Garage, AW Anderson Agency, and Woodward, Inc.—are still thriving.

Some of the area's churches, including Grace Lutheran, Forest Hills Evangelical Free, and Bethany Presbyterian Church, date back to the early days of the city. Generations of residents have been members at these places of worship and have held christenings, weddings, and funerals within their walls.

Any introduction to the city would not be complete without mentioning Harlem School District No. 122, which is now shared by Loves Park and nearby Machesney Park. Harlemites, or "Huskies," as they are often called, have been educated in the district since the Harlem Consolidated School was completed on March 6, 1911. Loves Park Grade School has educated younger children since it was built in 1916. The schools have continued to grow along with the city, and additional district schools have opened throughout the years.

According to the 2010 census, Loves Park now has a population of 23,996 and a total land area of 16.03 square miles. Often, residents who live in Loves Park work in and visit Rockford and vice versa.

The community is well known for its annual Memorial Day Young at Heart Festival that began in 1972 as a way to celebrate the city's 25th anniversary. It still attracts visitors from across northern Illinois. In addition, Loves Park is home to the Rockford RiverHawks Frontier League baseball stadium built in 2006, the Rockford Speedway (which celebrated its 65th anniversary in 2012),

Rock Cut State Park (which contains over 3,000 acres), the nationally known Ski Broncs show, Sand Park Field of Honor Veterans Memorial, and numerous other recreational sites.

Of course, due to its proximity to the Rock River, the city has had its share of floods and other natural disasters, such as tornadoes and blizzards, through the years. However, the resiliency of the city and its residents continues to prevail.

Loves Park has had eight mayors since 1947; the current mayor, Darryl Lindberg, took office in 1997. The Loves Park motto is "The City with a Heart," and heart symbols can be seen all over town—from the welcome sign to the water towers.

One

The Early Years

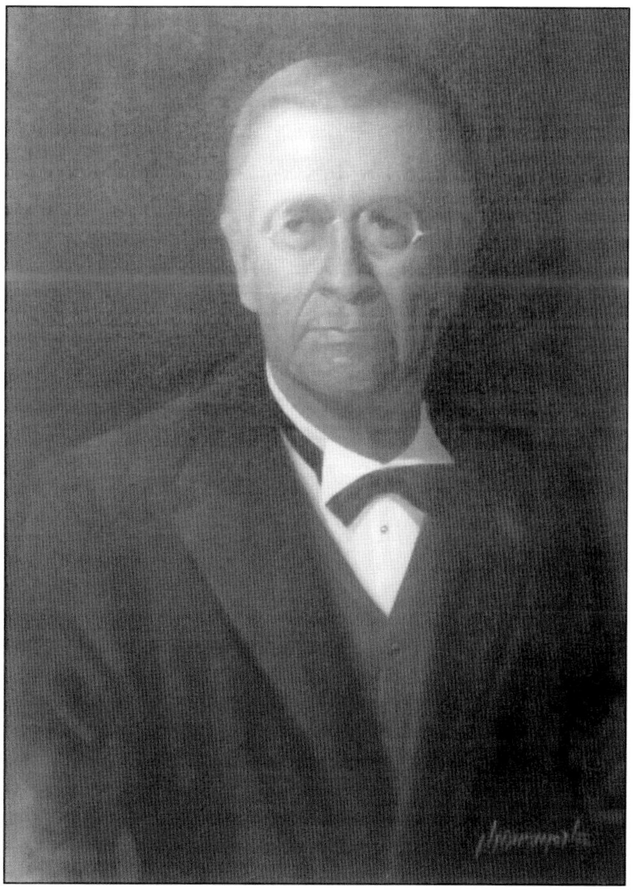

Malcolm A. Love was born in 1859 and died in 1930. There are no known surviving photographs of him. This portrait was commissioned by Arthur W. "Art" Anderson in 1995 and painted by Vince Chiaramonte using a picture printed with Love's obituary. The portrait now hangs in the Loves Park City Council chambers. (Courtesy of Nicole C. Lindsay.)

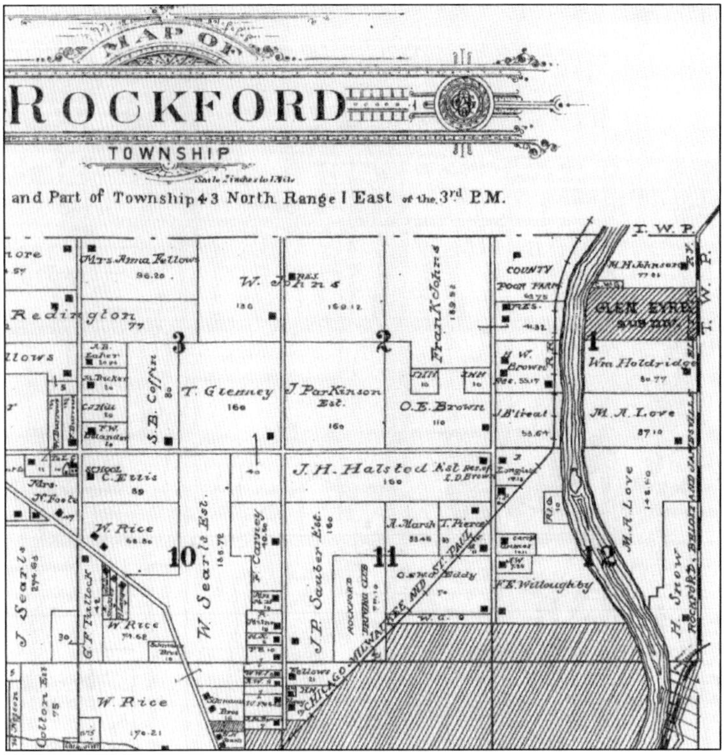

This 1905 map of Rockford Township shows the property owned by Malcolm A. Love along the east bank of the Rock River in Sections 1 and 12. The image also shows the properties owned by William S. Holdridge in Section 1 and Hiram Snow in Section 12; the Holdridge and Snow families were also well known in the area. (Courtesy of *Combined Atlas of Winnebago County, Illinois.*)

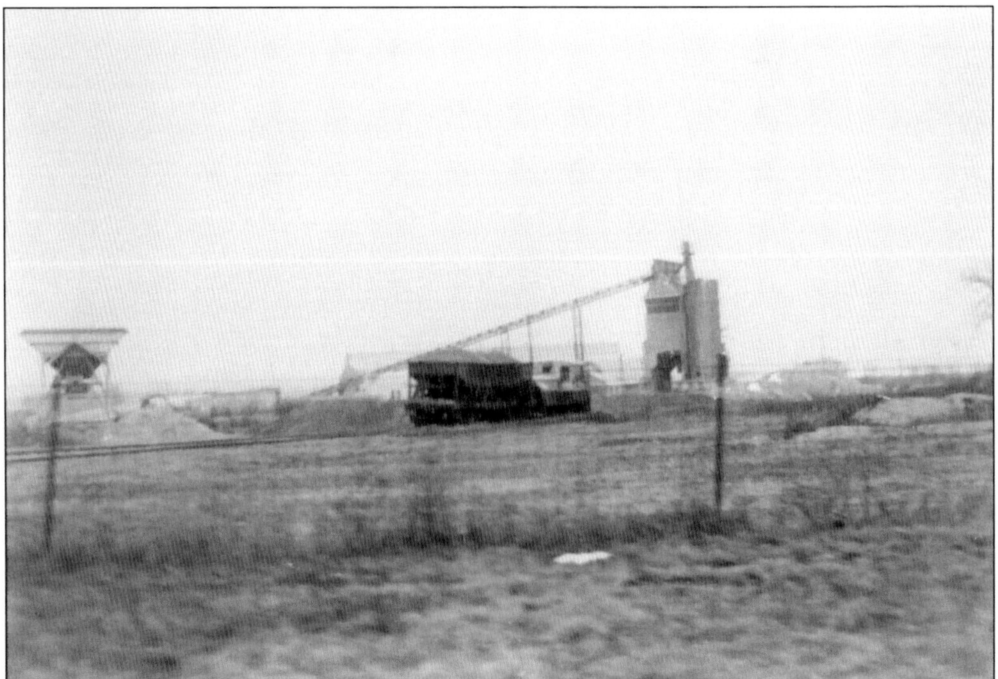

The Larson Sand and Gravel train is pictured on March 18, 1958, near the southeast corner of the intersection of Alpine and Windsor Roads. Larson Sand and Gravel is no longer in business, and the area where this photograph was taken has been completely developed.

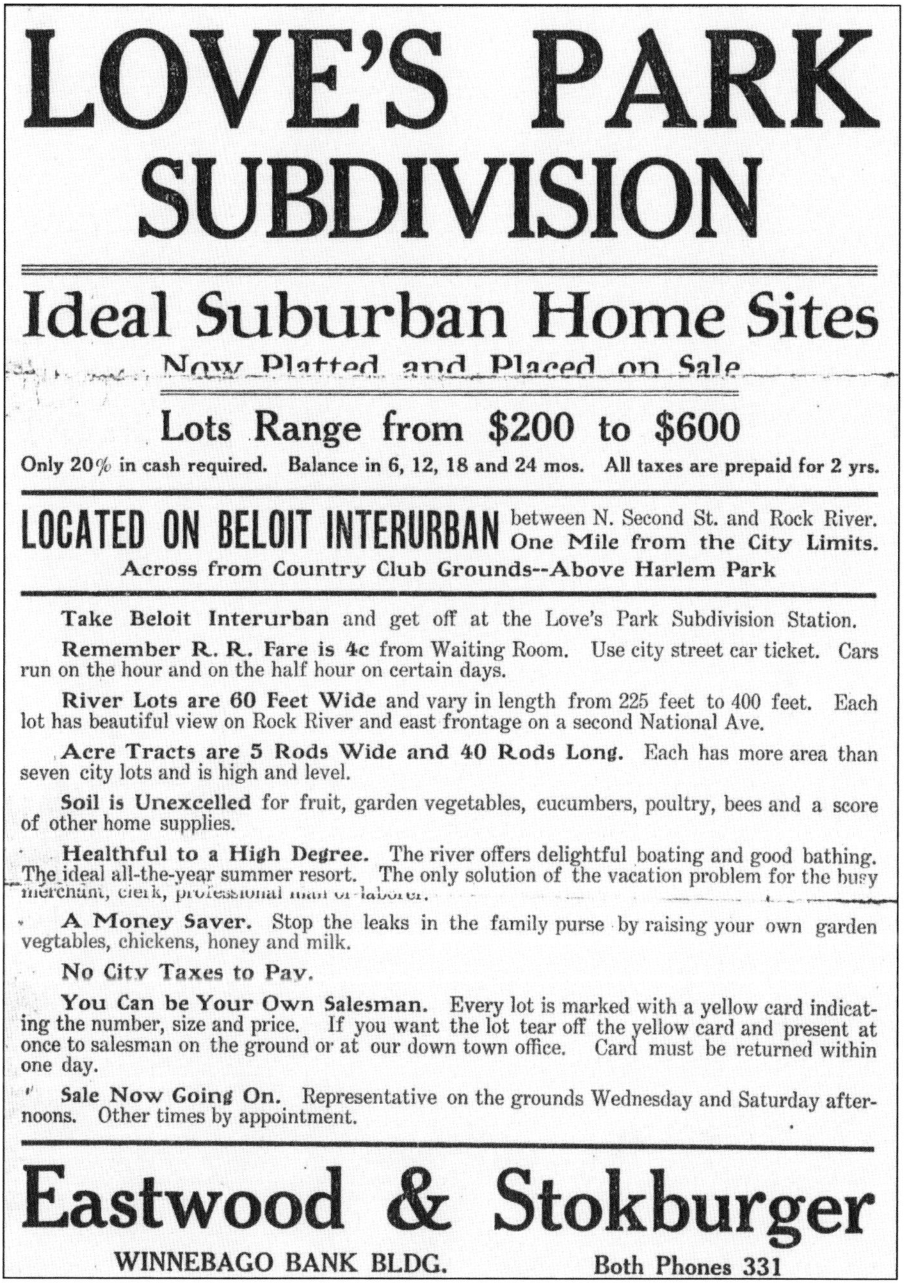

This flyer, which circulated around 1909, advertises "Ideal Suburban Home Sites" located on the Interurban rail line—the sites were available for between $200 and $600 and only a 20-percent cash down payment. Notice that Loves Park was spelled with an apostrophe at this time. Also notice that the telephone number for Eastwood and Stokburger is only three digits—331. The flyer touts the healthfulness of Rock River and its offers of "delightful boating and good bathing." It notes the soil is "unexcelled" and perfect for growing a garden and that by doing so, a family would save money. Another perk was that there were no city taxes to pay. The reverse side of the flyer shows a map with the layout of available lots. The development of this subdivision helped establish Loves Park and started the area on the road to its eventual incorporation in 1947.

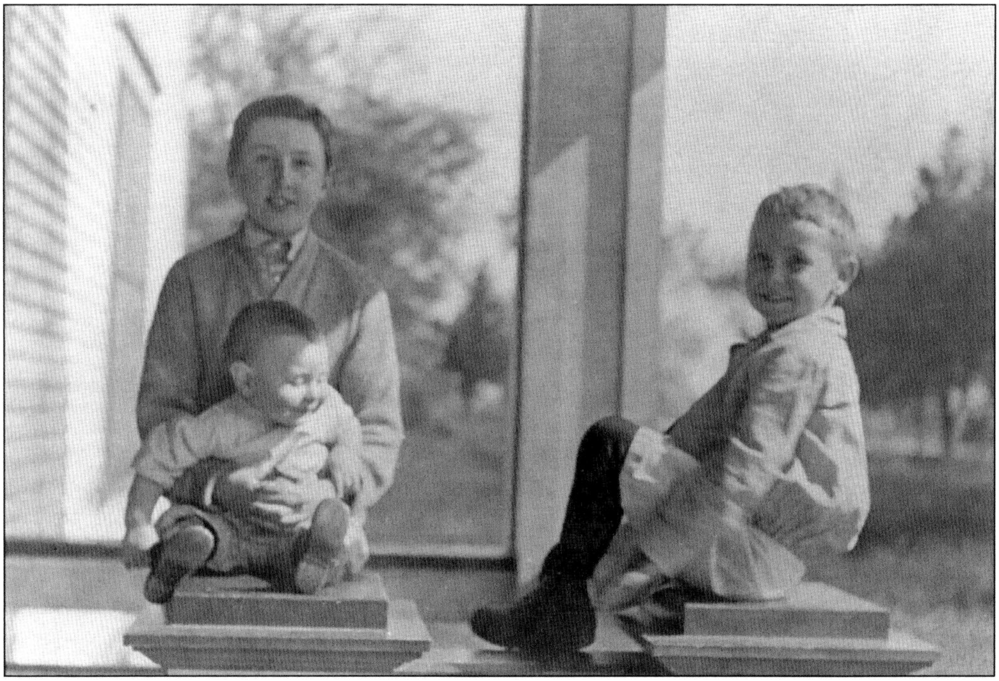

Pictured above in their younger years are Hiram (standing), Harry (seated, left), and Kenneth Snow. In 1881, Hiram Snow purchased 106 acres in Section 12 (see map on page 10) and later opened a pickle business named Snow's Rockford Pickle Works. The plant was located in what is now the 4600 block of North Second Street. The front part of the plant was two stories tall and made of brick; the plant also had a wooden water tower and a single-story storage building. In 1903, Hiram's son, Junius C. Snow, took over the business and added the "J.C. Snow" sign visible in the picture below. (Above, courtesy of Craig G. Campbell.)

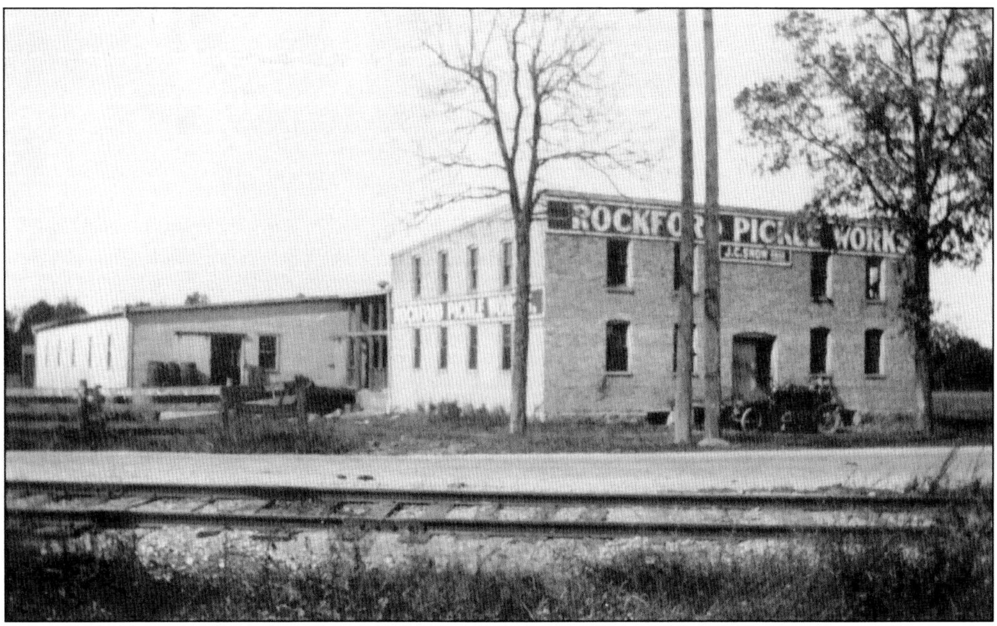

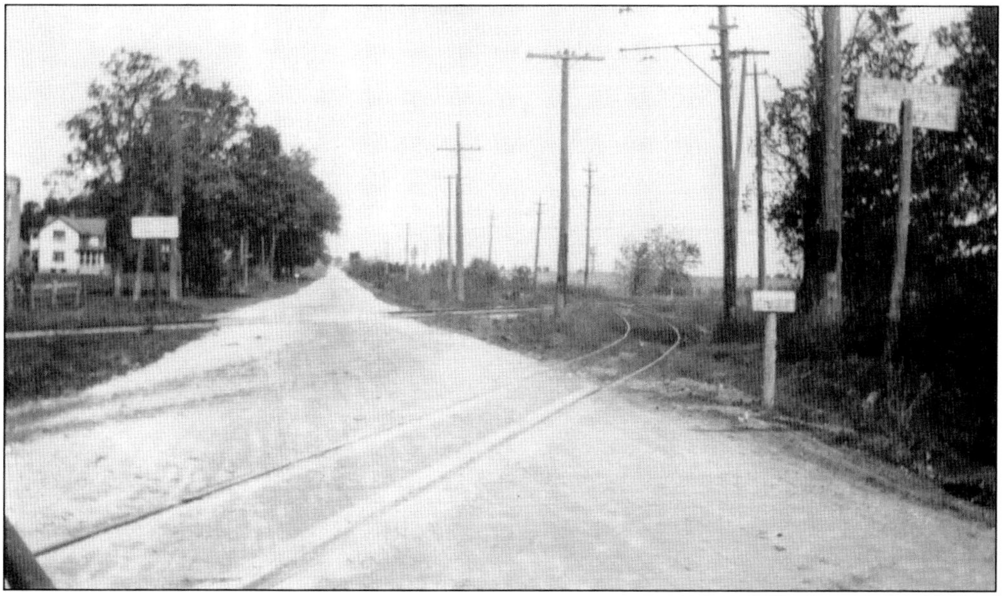

This photograph shows Snow's Crossing around 1915 or 1920. The corner of Snow's Rockford Pickle Works plant is visible at left, and the white house at left was the home of Junius C. Snow. This is where the Chicago & North Western Railroad tracks in the back and the Interurban rail tracks in the front cross.

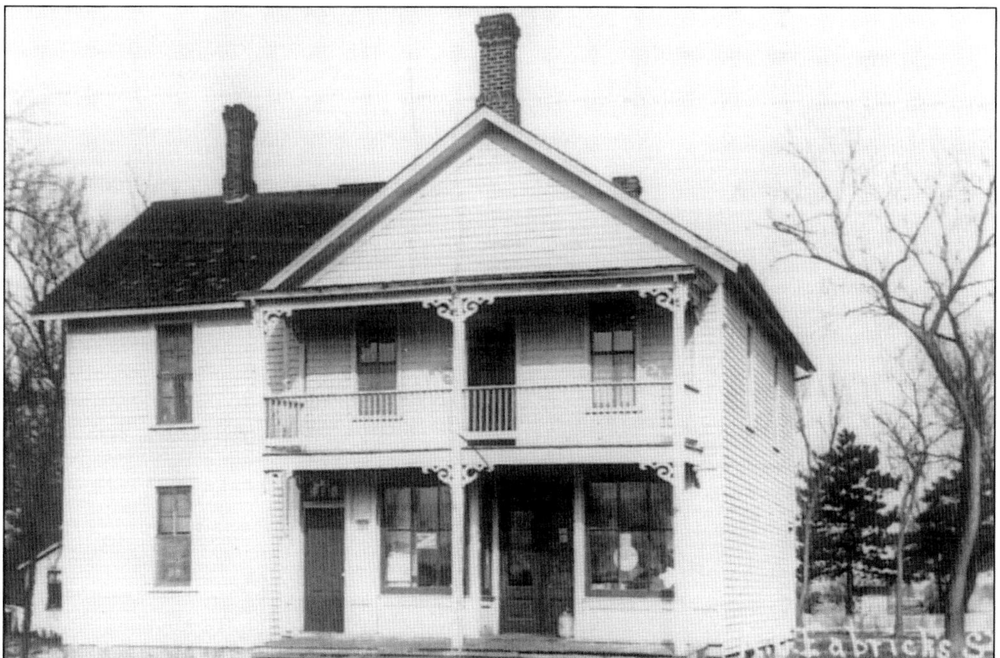

Lewis Andrew "L.A." Fabrick established the Fabrick Store in Harlem Village, which he ran along with Isaac Swartout. This photograph is believed to have been taken between 1900 and 1910. The store burned down in 1928 and was rebuilt in the same location. It was later purchased by Frank Rogers.

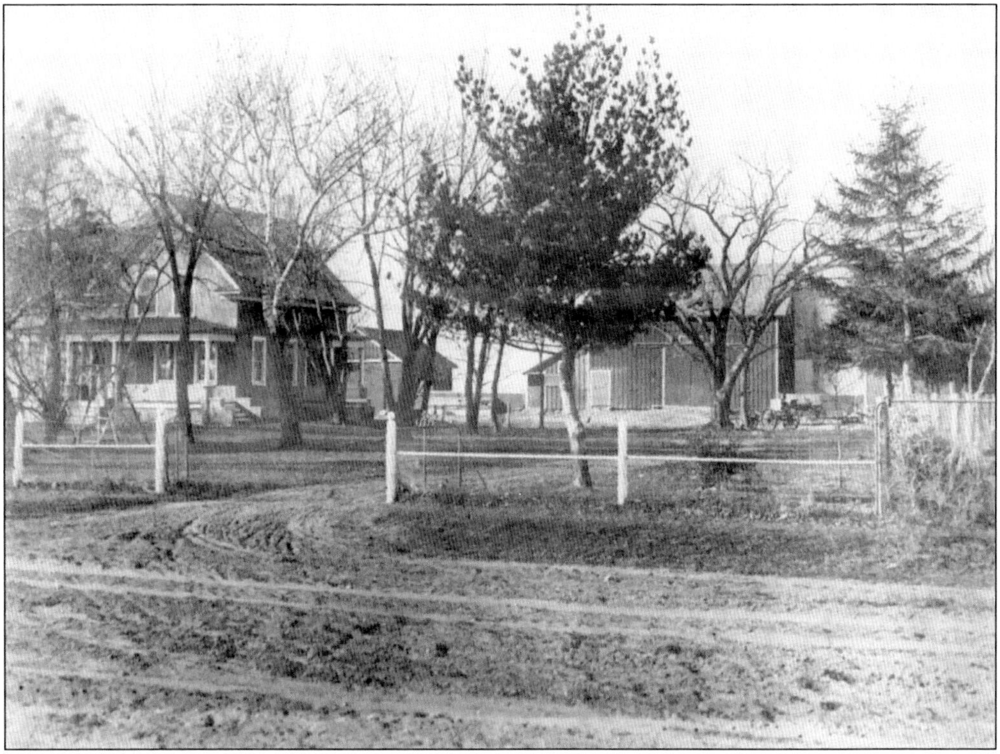

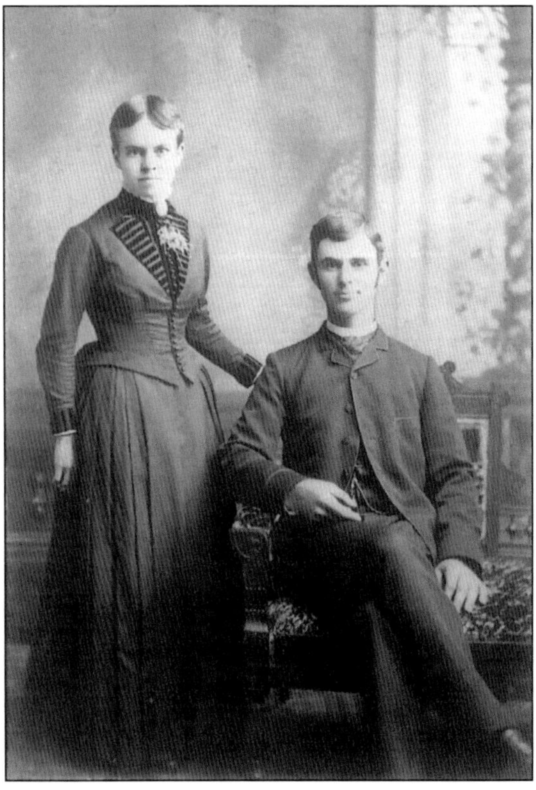

The 1915 photograph above is of the William S. Holdridge house and farm. The family's property was located in Section 1 east of the Rock River, but west of where North Second Street is now (see map on page 10). Holdridge was born on July 4, 1867, and married Hattie Anders in 1886; their wedding photograph is at left. They had four children—Edna, Eugene, Robert, and Ruby. William was a farmer who often delivered milk to area residents, and Hattie was known to be an excellent cook. The back of their farm contained a lagoon in the present-day location of Martin Park.

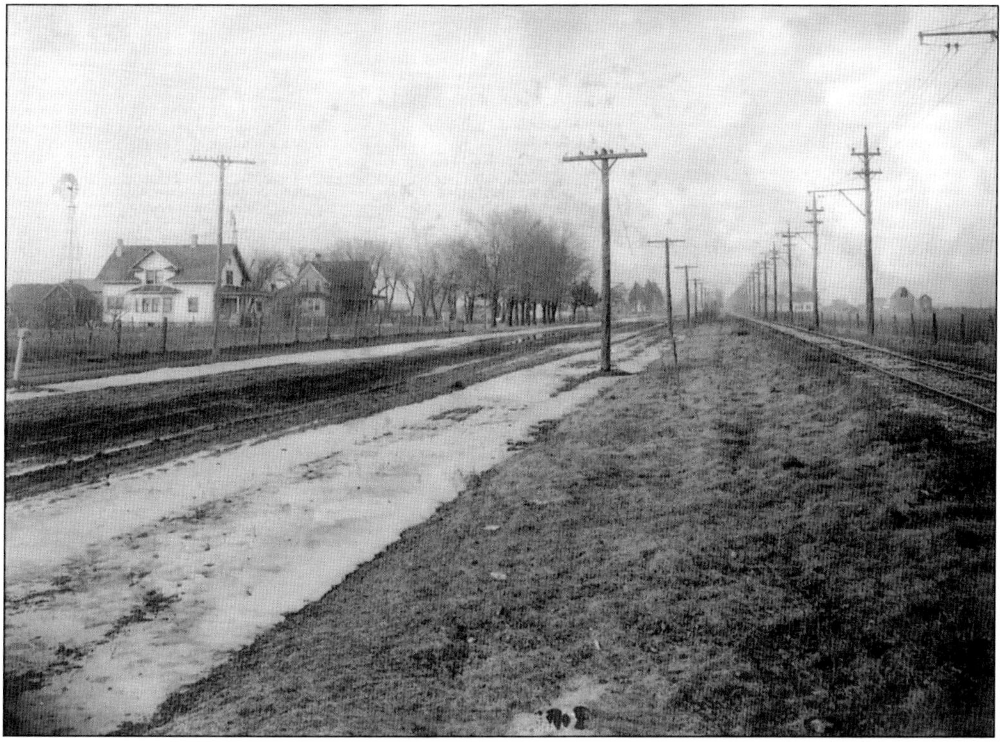

This February 20, 1915, image offers an early preview of the intersection of Riverside Boulevard and North Second Street. In 1915, this was still a dirt road. The Interurban rail line tracks are visible at right, and the William S. Holdridge farm is the second house from the left.

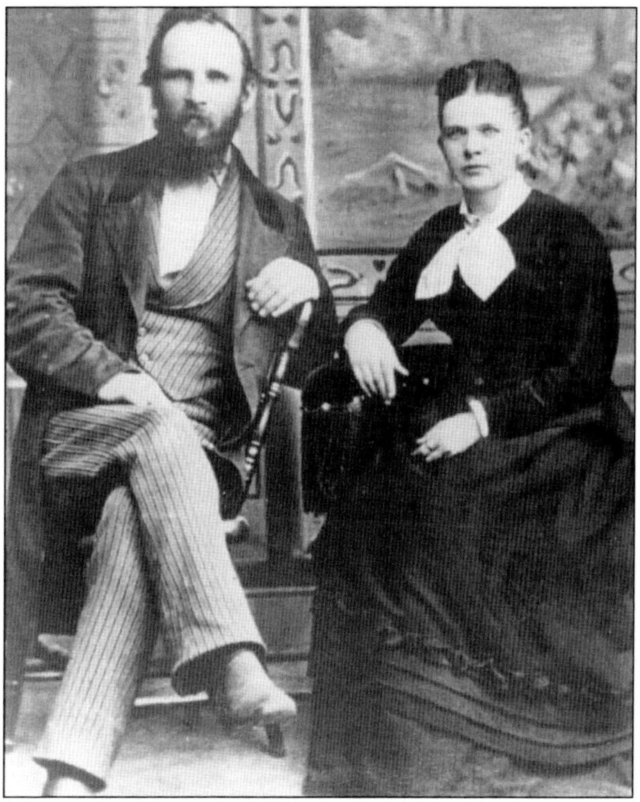

David W. Evans and his wife, Emma, pictured at right around 1880, owned a farm that included land from present-day Harlem Road to the north to Evans Avenue to the south. Their home was located near the present-day intersection of North Second Street and Sycamore Lane.

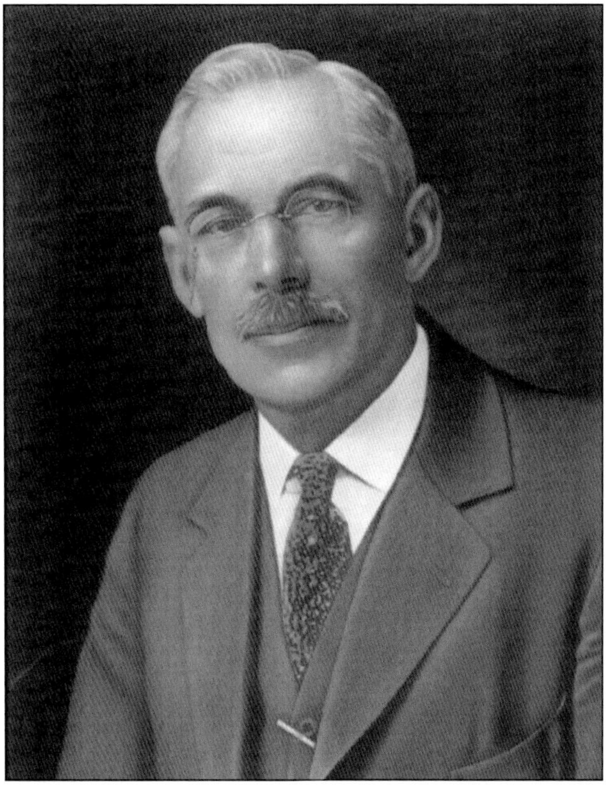

This is a portrait of Nathum Cobb Bement, a Loves Park resident who started his own tractor company—originally Bement Tractor Company and later Rock Valley Tractor Company—in 1919. The business specialized in direct drive differentials. In 1947, Bement donated two lots of land and sold a third lot to the city of Loves Park for construction of the city's first municipal building. His plant was demolished in 1949. Bement was 100 years old when he died in 1961.

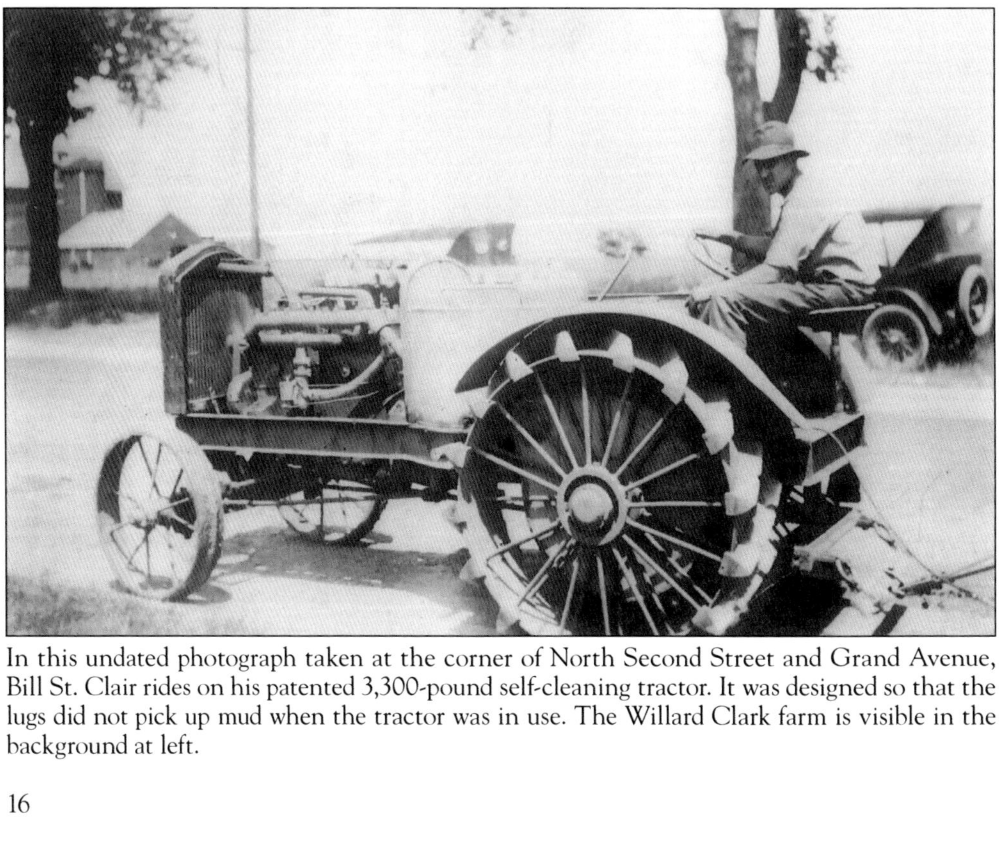

In this undated photograph taken at the corner of North Second Street and Grand Avenue, Bill St. Clair rides on his patented 3,300-pound self-cleaning tractor. It was designed so that the lugs did not pick up mud when the tractor was in use. The Willard Clark farm is visible in the background at left.

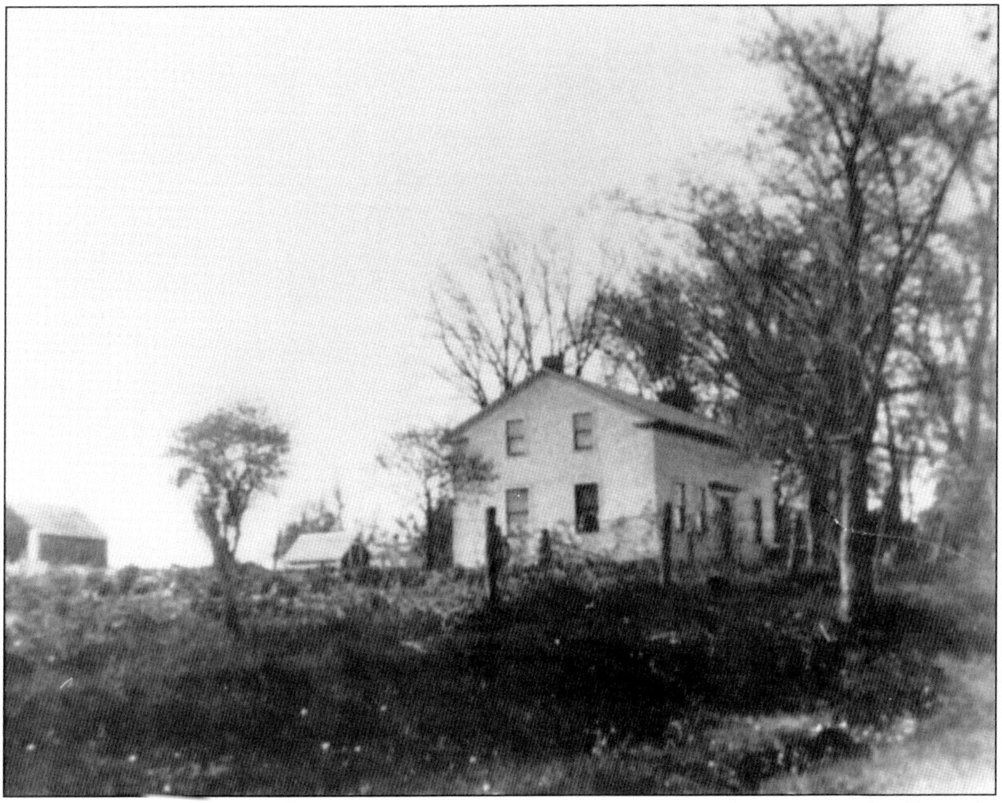

The farmhouse of Warren Paulson and Helen (Hull) Paulson was built in 1854 and still stands; it can be seen on present-day Paulson Road, which runs between Harlem Road on the north and Riverside Boulevard on the south. The Paulsons lived on the farm for approximately 46 years—from 1943 until they moved to a home in nearby Argyle in 1989. The above photograph is undated and was taken looking to the north. In the 1944 image below, Jim Reid operates a tractor in a bean field on the Paulson farm. (Both, courtesy of Warren Paulson.)

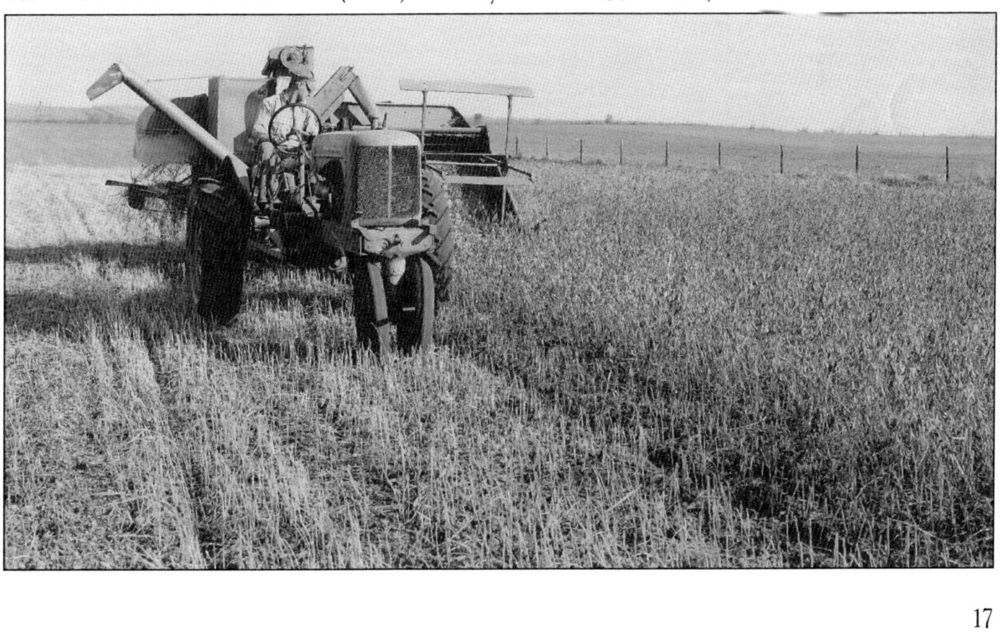

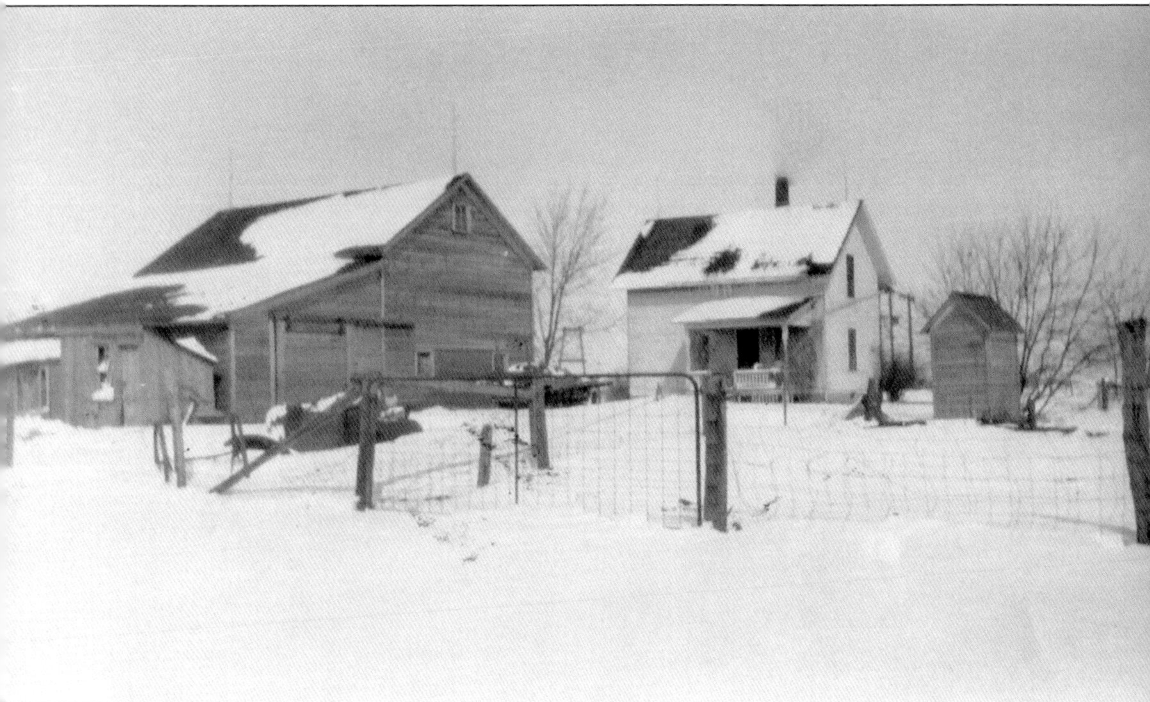

The farm of Robert H. and Margaret (Johnston) Burden was in the 1200 block of Windsor Road in suburban Loves Park. The future Elm Avenue was eventually built to the left of the structure at left in this 1910 photograph. The small wooden building near the right side of the photograph is an outhouse.

Two

Around the Town

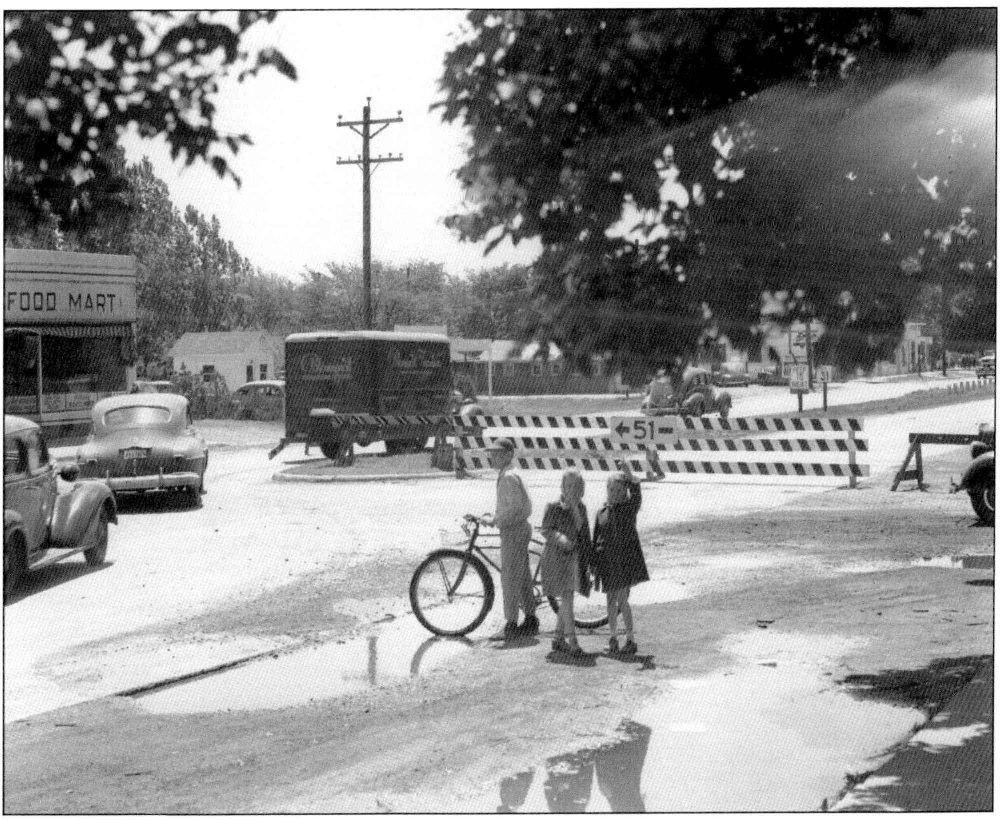

In this 1947 photograph, unidentified children stand in the 5400 block of North Second Street. A portion of the Parkside Food Mart building is visible at left, and the street has been barricaded for sewer construction. Note that this picture was taken when North Second Street was still US Route 51, whereas today it is State Route 251.

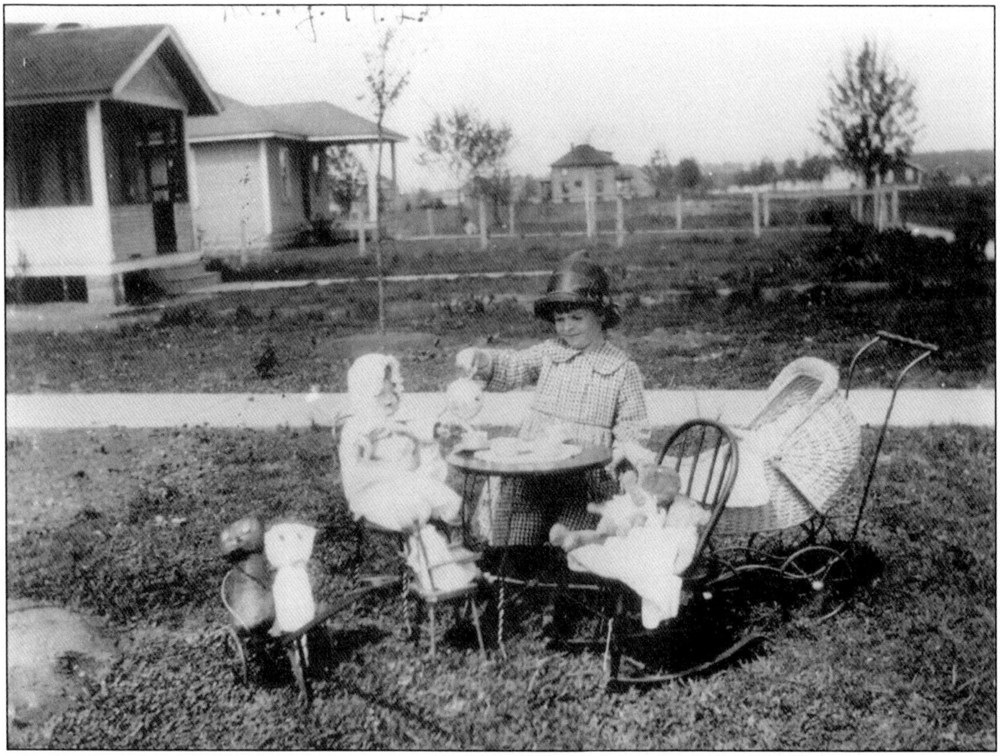

Elaine D. Peterson, daughter of Eric and Winnifred Peterson, holds a tea party in her backyard in this May 1920 image. The Peterson home faced north and was located at 407 East Riverside Boulevard. Eric worked in Rockford and took the Interurban rail line to and from work each day. (Courtesy of Craig G. Campbell.)

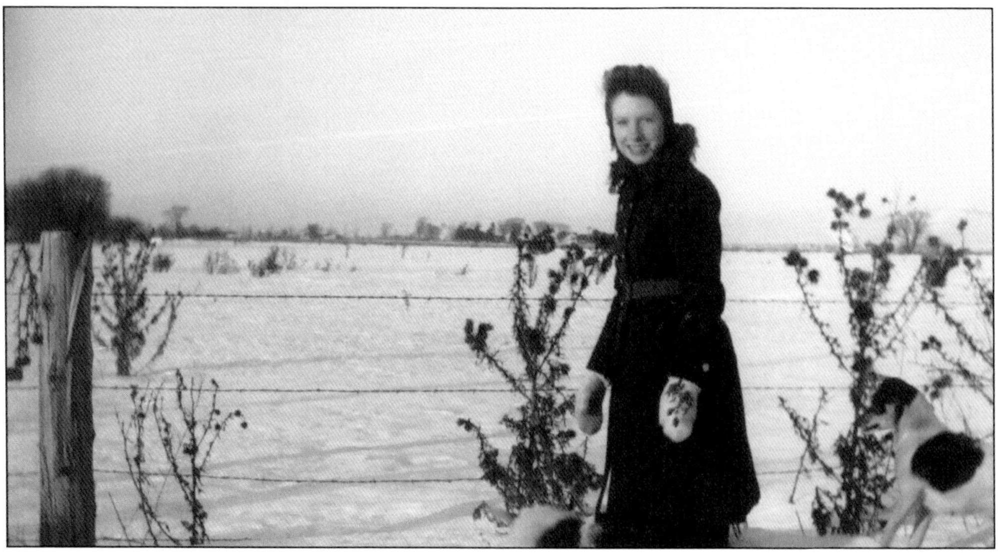

Bell Larson poses for a picture near a field of deep snow during the winter of 1942; Larson was a teenager at the time. She is standing on Clifford Avenue looking towards Walker Avenue. Today, Clifford and Walker Avenues are developed areas full of homes, businesses, churches, and parks.

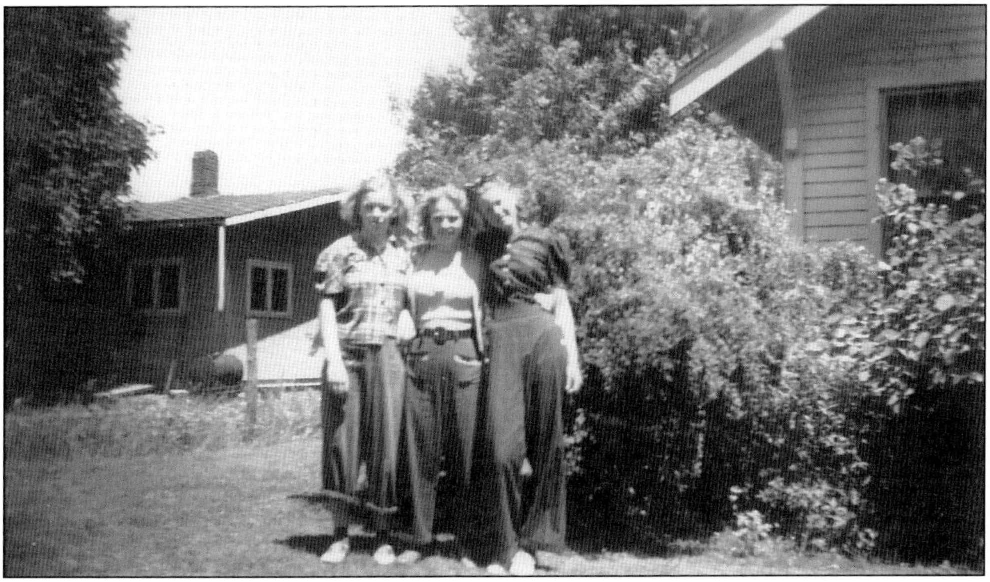

Mary Timmis (left), Dorothy Alfred (center), and Helen Hull pose for a picture in front of the home of Mary's parents, Daniel "Dan" and Mabel Timmis, at 5540 East Drive. The photograph was taken in the 1930s. Dan was the mayor of Loves Park from 1957 to 1969. (Courtesy of Mary Timmis Miller.)

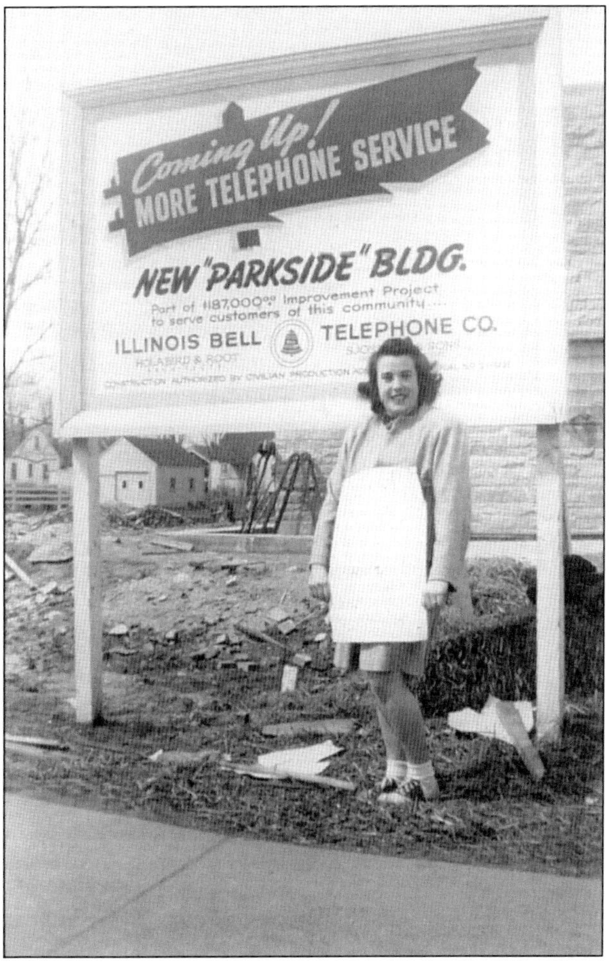

Betty Mayhew stands in front of a sign advertising the new Illinois Bell Telephone Company Parkside Building under construction at 5128 North Second Street. Mayhew was participating in a telephone operator's strike. The photograph is believed to have been taken between 1945 and 1948. The Parkside Building now houses Minuteman Press.

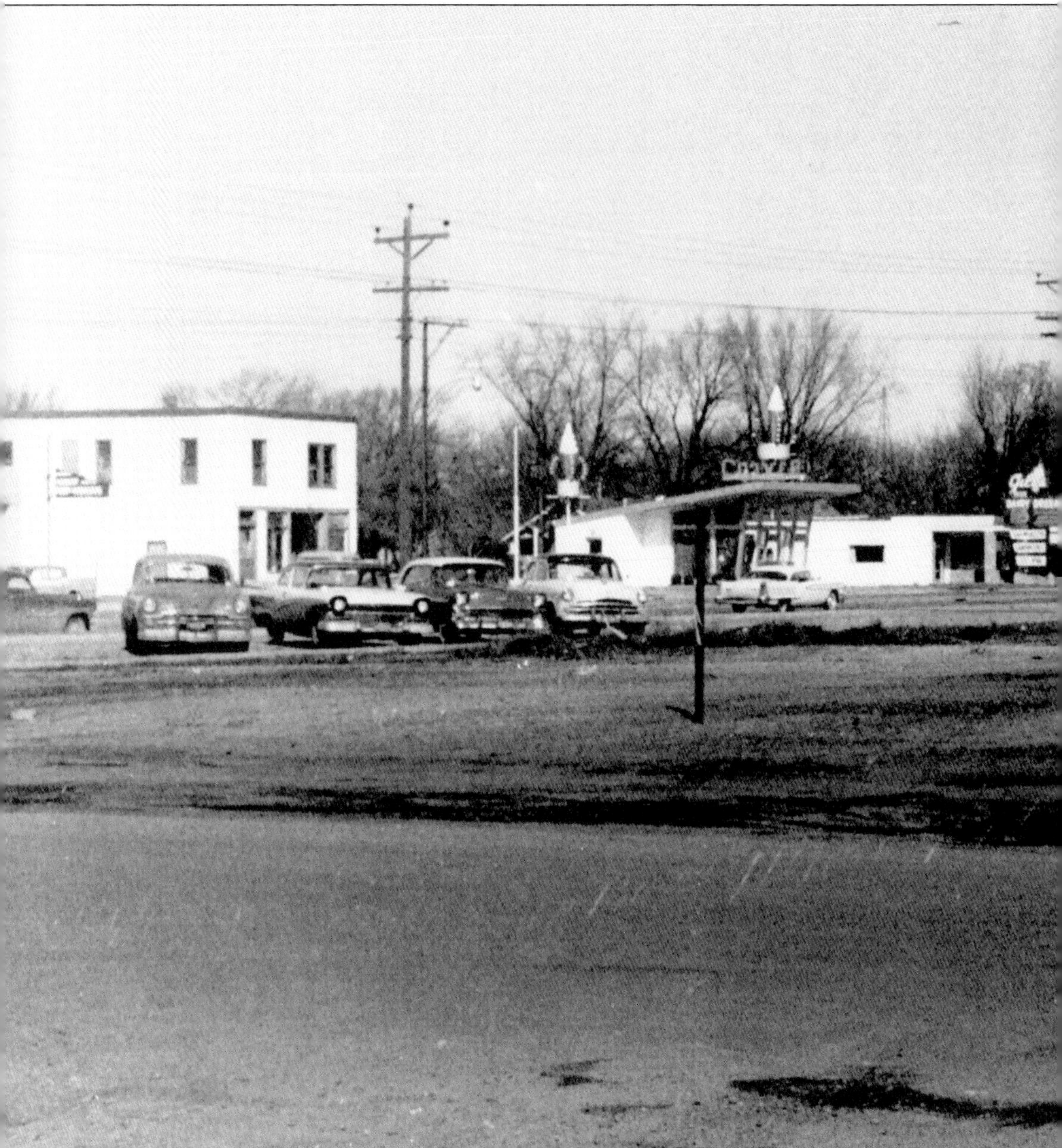

This late-1950s panoramic photograph was taken near the intersection of North Second Street and Loves Park Drive looking north. At left is the Carvel ice cream shop, which was located at 5704 North Second Street near the intersection of River Park Road. Miner Pump is in the white

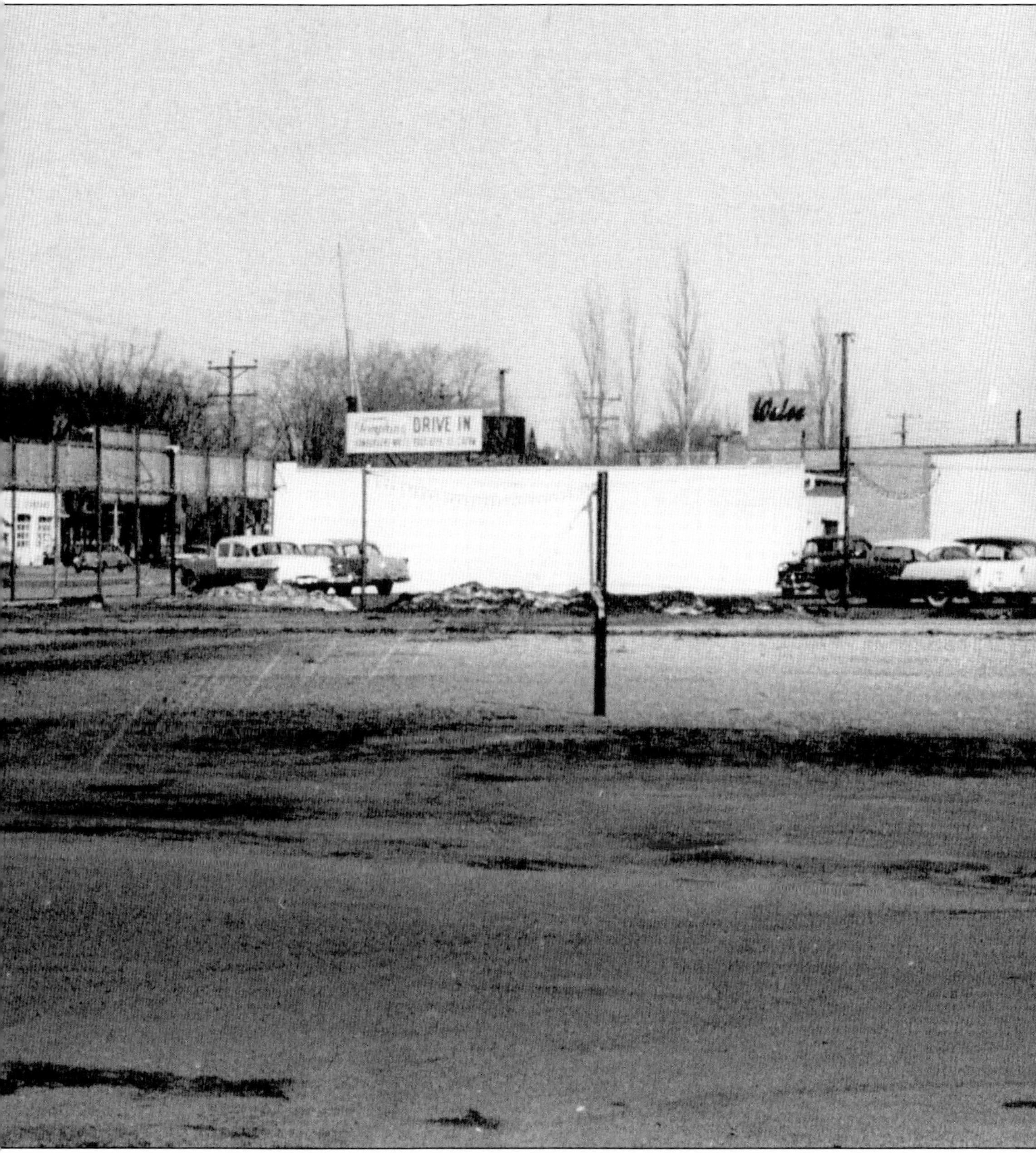

building at far left. In the center are Gill's Dairy Dreem and Hull's Standard Gas Station. At right is Tompkin's Drive In, with Weise's Department Store at far right. The cars on the left side of the image are parked on Jenson Drive.

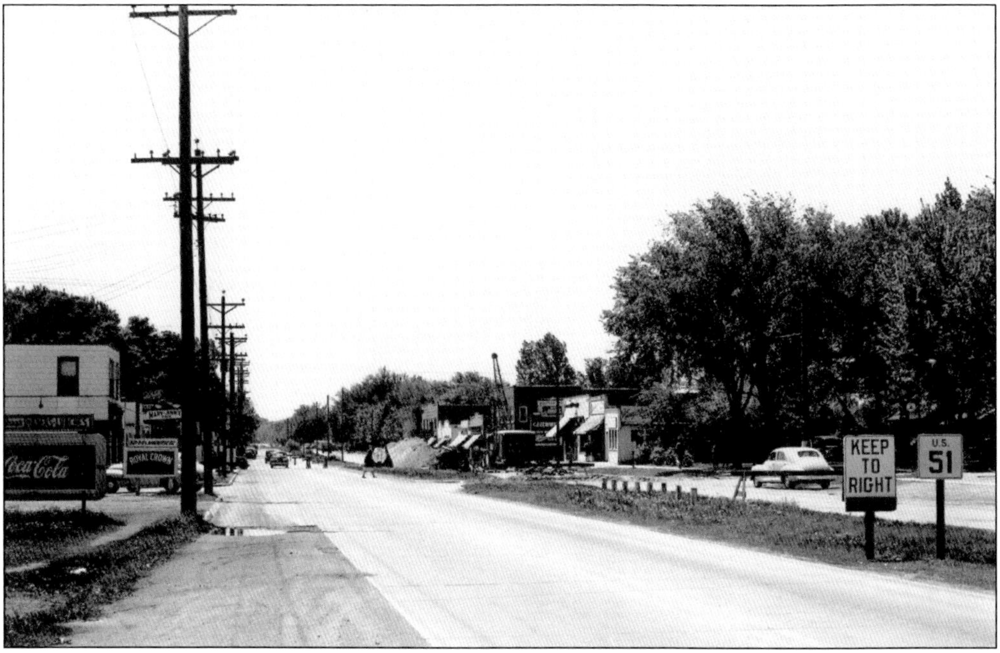

The city of Loves Park incorporated in 1947, the same year this photograph was taken. The picture shows the 5500 block of North Second Street looking south. At this time, the route was still US Route 51, as shown on the sign at right. Mary and Jimmy's Café, owned by Mary Gianquinto and Jim Licari, is at left.

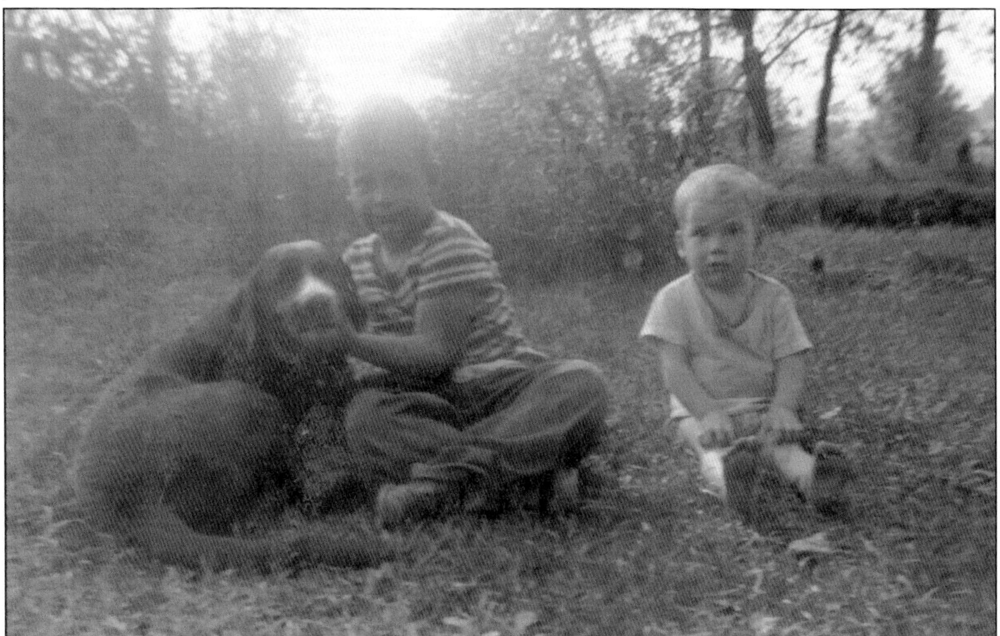

Blackie the dog, Albert Umbenhower, and David Mace (right) sit for a picture in the early 1950s. Just a few years earlier, in March 1950, Umbenhower went missing. A large search party, along with law enforcement, found him in the area of present-day Rock Cut State Park—his neighbor John H. Darnell's dog, Blackie, was by his side. (Courtesy of Sheila Mace.)

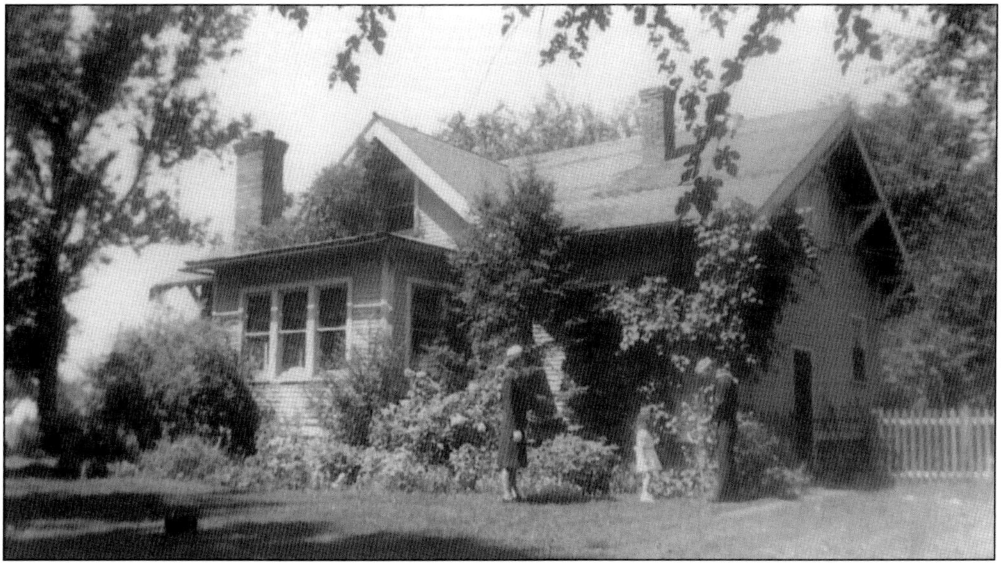

The home at 408 Sheridan Drive is shown in this 1944 photograph. Pictured here are Grace Layng Miller (left), her daughter Sharon Miller (center), and Donald Irving Layng. Sherman Levey is listed as the owner of the home at the time. The house at this address today, which is west of Nunzio's Restaurant, bears no resemblance to the one in this photograph.

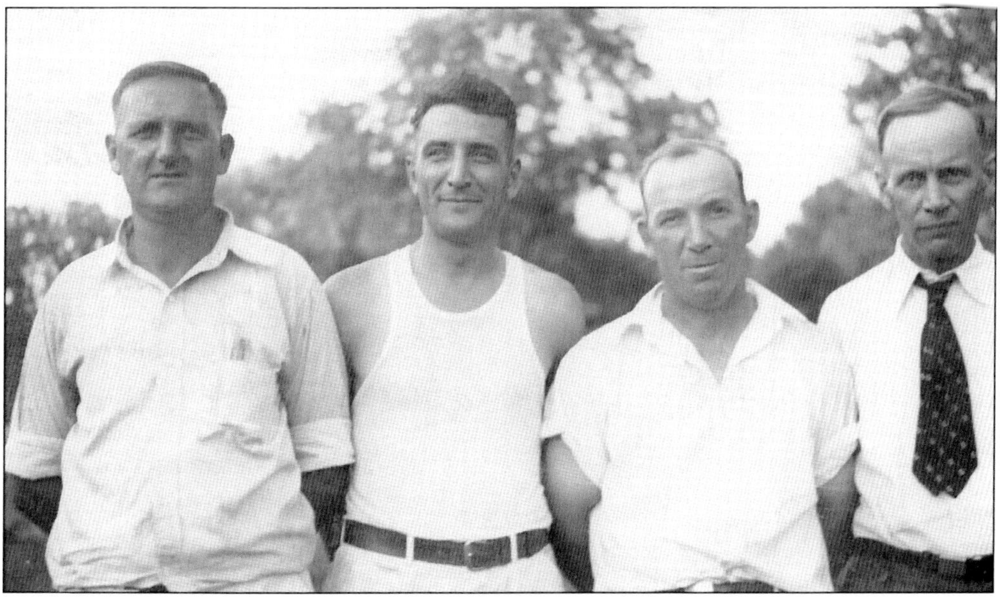

In this undated photograph, from left to right, Frank Oswald, Ralph Garman, Daniel "Dan" Timmis, and Fred Haye pose at one of the many picnics they held at various recreation areas in Loves Park. The four often got together for baseball games and other outdoor activities. (Courtesy of Mary Timmis Miller.)

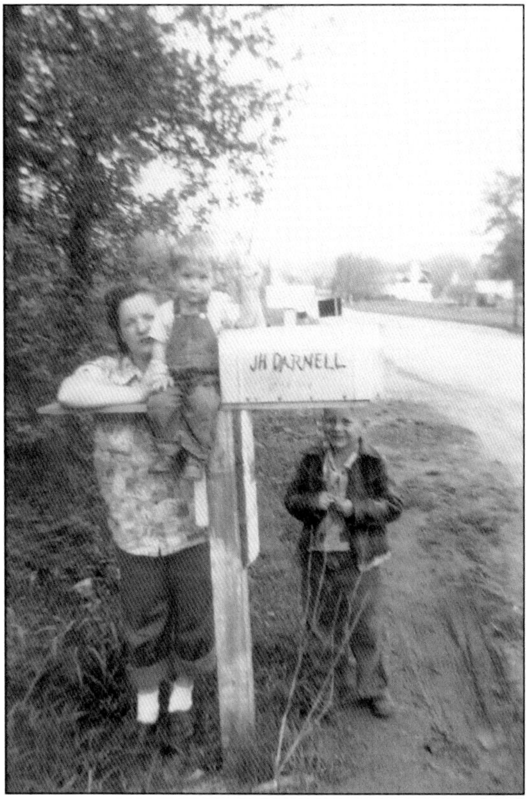

Looking west down Collins Road (now Riverside Boulevard), Rose Mace (holding her son David) and neighbor Albert Umbenhower pose for a photograph at the mailbox of John H. Darnell at 2003 Collins Road. The photograph was taken in the early 1950s, when Rose's husband, Franklin, was serving in the Korean War. (Courtesy of Sheila Mace.)

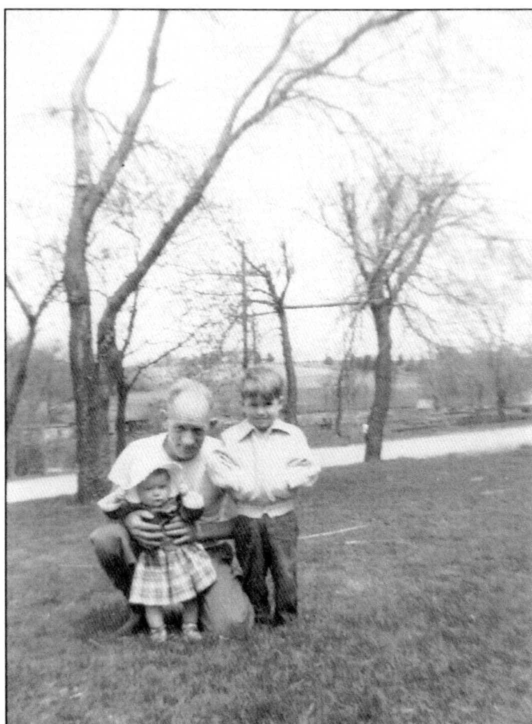

John H. Darnell poses in front of Collins Road (now Riverside Boulevard) along with his grandchildren, Sheila and David Mace, for a picture in the front yard. The photograph was taken in 1953, when the Collins Road area had not yet been developed. (Courtesy of Sheila Mace.)

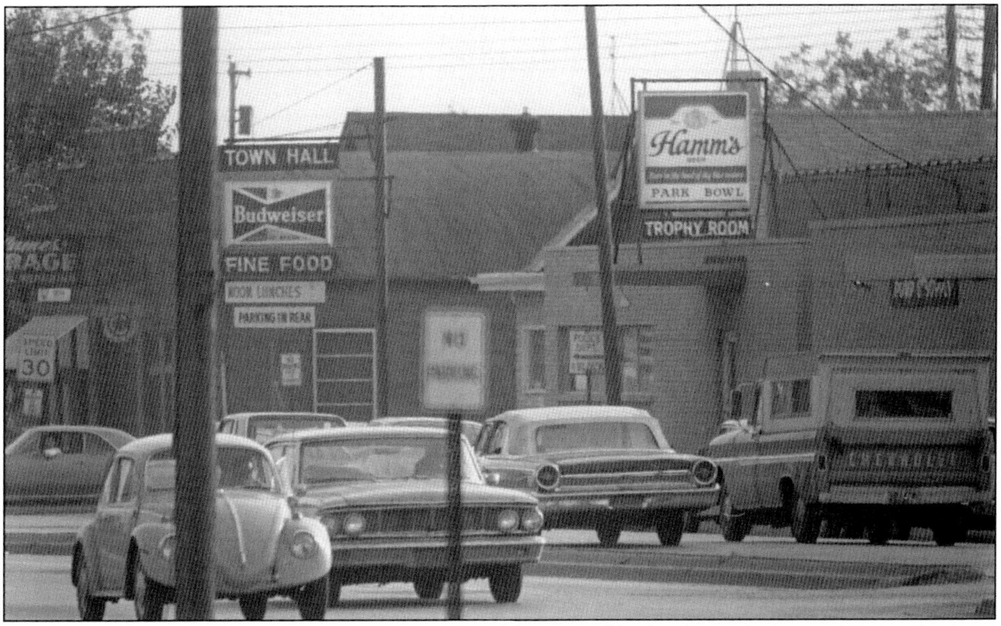

This undated photograph shows the west side of the 5600 block of North Second Street looking south. At far left is Blume's Garage, and in the center are the Town Hall Lounge and B&B Park Bowl, all of which are still open. At far right is Miner Pump, which is closed.

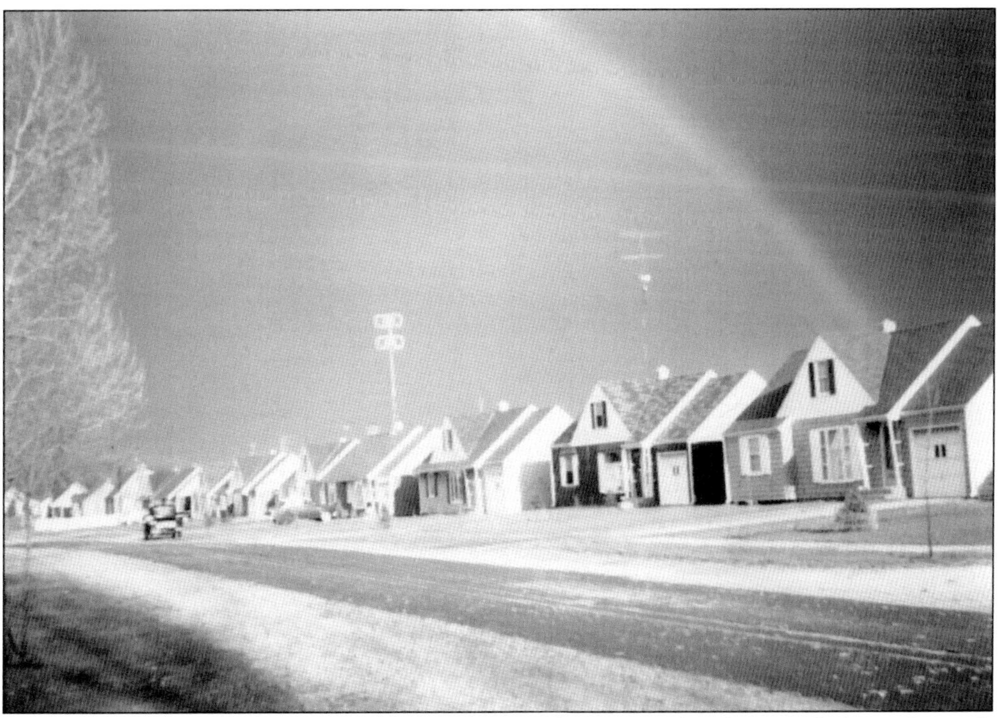

This c. 1952 photograph was taken from 222 Burrwood Avenue. The photograph shows the south side of Burrwood Avenue looking east as a rainbow arcs across the sky. Burrwood Avenue is still a residential area today, but there are many more trees now than in the 1950s.

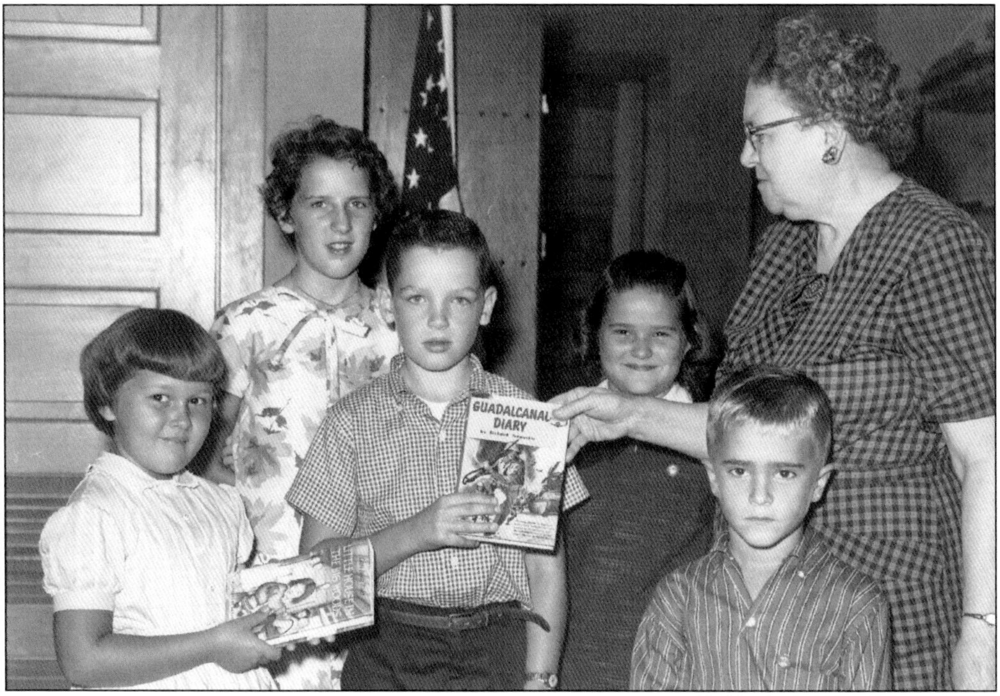

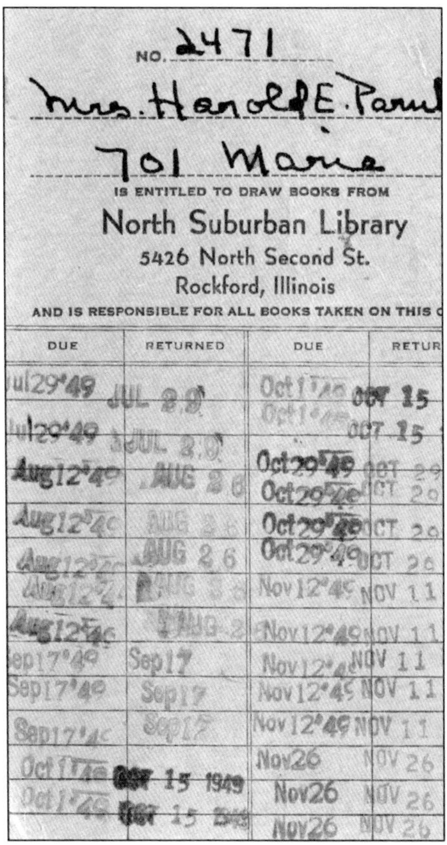

NO. 2471

Mrs. Harold E. Parn

701 Marie

IS ENTITLED TO DRAW BOOKS FROM

North Suburban Library

5426 North Second St.

Rockford, Illinois

AND IS RESPONSIBLE FOR ALL BOOKS TAKEN ON THIS C

DUE	RETURNED	DUE	RETUR
Jul29'49	JUL 29	Oct1'49	OCT 15
Jul29'49	JUL 29	Oct1'49	OCT 15
Aug12'49	AUG 26	Oct29'49	OCT 29
Aug12'49	AUG 26	Oct29'49	OCT 29
Aug12'49	AUG 26	Oct29'49	OCT 29
Aug12'49	AUG 26	Oct29'49	OCT 26
Aug12'49	AUG 26	Nov12'49	NOV 11
Aug12'49	AUG 26	Nov12'49	NOV 11
Sep17'49	Sep17	Nov12'49	NOV 11
Sep17'49	Sep17	Nov12'49	NOV 11
Sep17'49	Sep17	Nov12'49	NOV 11
Oct1'49	OCT 15 1949	Nov26	NOV 26
Oct1'49	OCT 15 1949	Nov26	NOV 26
		Nov26	NOV 26

The September 18, 1958, photograph above shows the top readers in the North Suburban Library District's summer reading program. All five of these children read 100 or more books. Head librarian Jane Pratt is presenting prizes to the top two readers—Mary Brockman, who read 154 books, and Dennis Greenlee, who read 106 books. The other three children are, from left to right, Marilyn Head (who read 104 books), Alice Koyak (who read 108 books), and John Koyak (who read 100 books). At left is Mrs. Harold E. (Daisy) Parnham's library card full of due dates from 1949.

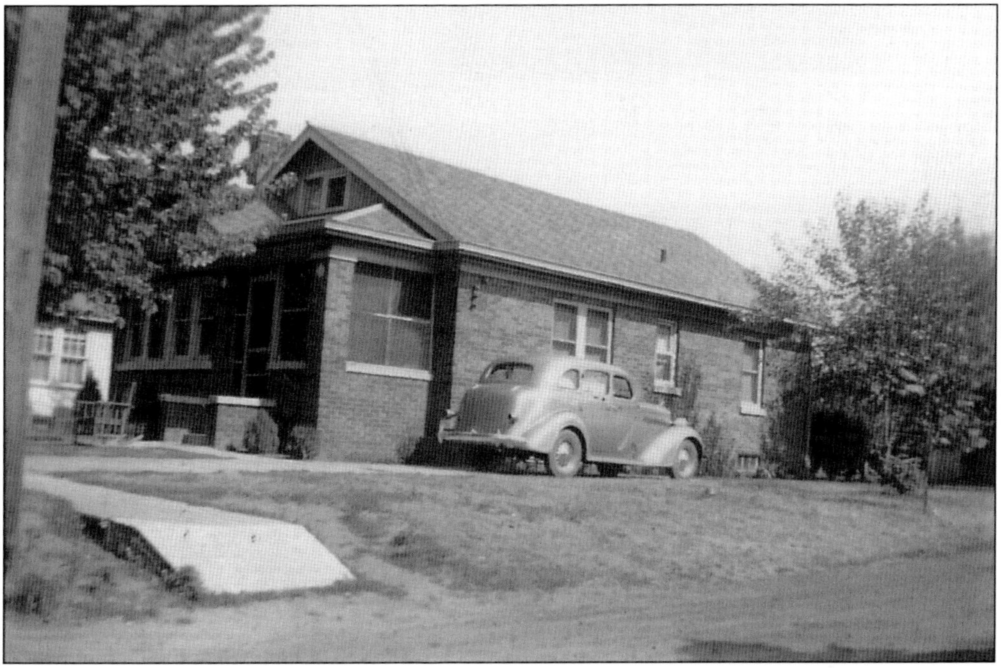

At the time this photograph was taken in 1936, the home of Uriah and Dora Hull, at 321 River Park Road, was the only brick house on the street. The image shows the family car parked alongside the residence. The home still stands today and looks much the same as it did in 1936. (Courtesy of Warren Paulson.)

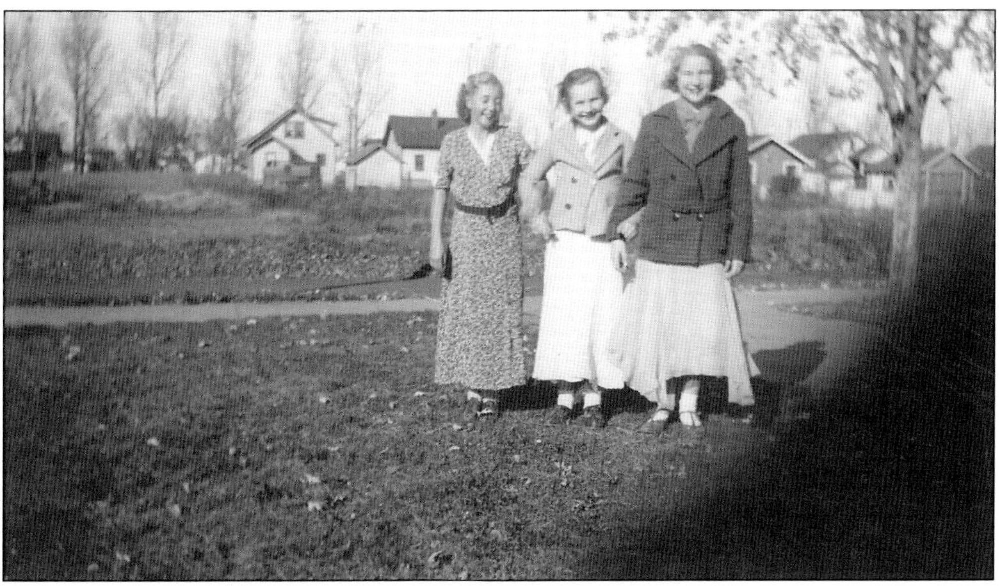

Helen Hull (left), Evalyn Smith (center), and Marion ? pose for a picture in a Loves Park neighborhood. The photograph was taken in the 1930s, and the exact location is unknown, although it is probably the backyard of either Hull's or Smith's home. (Courtesy of Warren Paulson.)

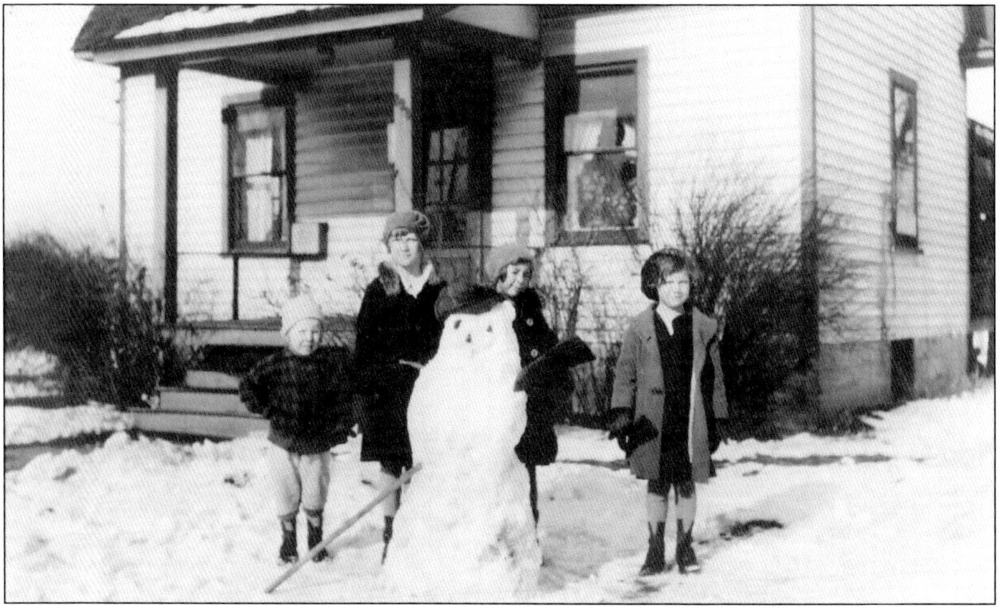

Pictured in this c. 1930 photograph are, from left to right, sisters Thelma, Grace, and Helen Hull and their friend Maxine Weyrauch. The girls are building a snowman in front of the Hull family's home at 328 Grand Boulevard; the house still stands. (Courtesy of Warren Paulson.)

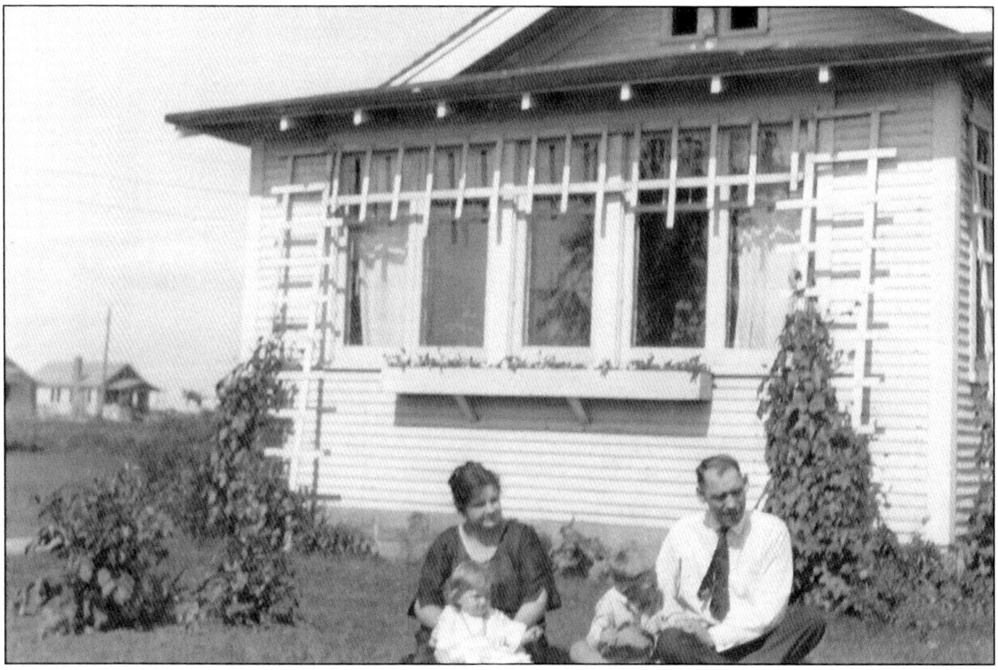

Gerdie and Isadore Olson sit for a picture with their children, Nellie Olson (left) and Norman "Norm" Olson (right), in the front yard of their home at 5313 Garden Plain Avenue. The photograph was taken in the early to mid-1920s. The house still stands. (Courtesy of Gayle Englof.)

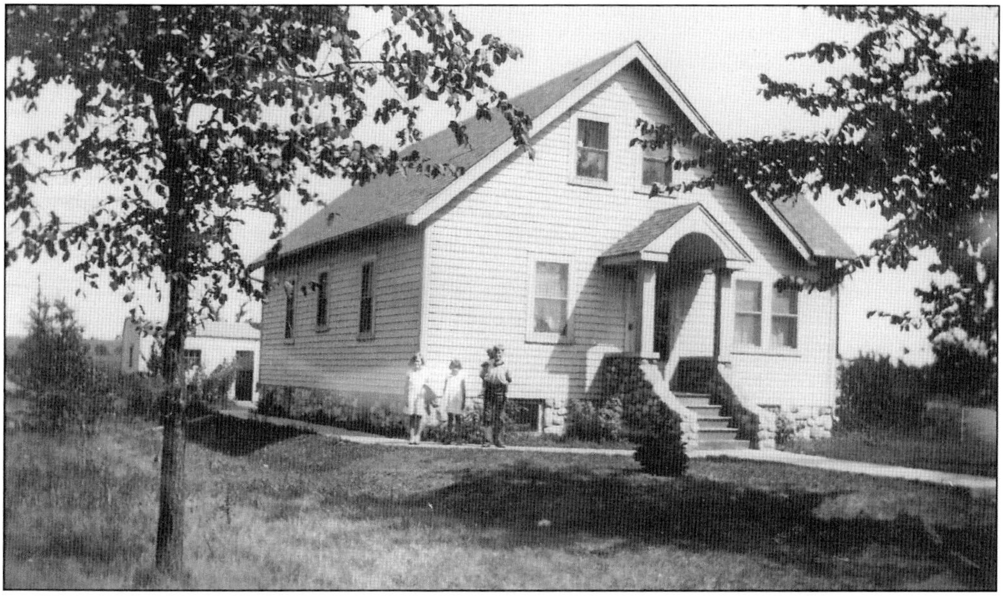

Nellie Olson (left), Edyth Gayle Morris (center), and Norman "Norm" Olson pose on the front sidewalk of the Olson's home at 5023 Illinois Street. The photograph was taken in the mid- to late 1920s, after the family moved from Garden Plain Avenue. The house still stands. (Courtesy of Gayle Englof.)

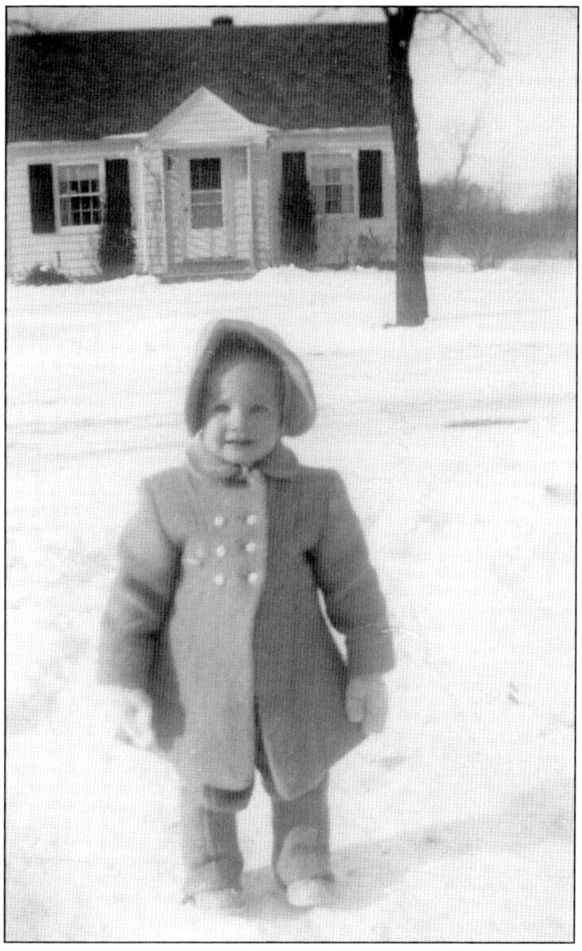

In this mid-1940s image, Connie Olson Cobb poses in the snow in the front yard of the house at 5023 Illinois Street. The home in the background is 5024 Illinois Street, directly across the street. Both houses still stand. (Courtesy of Gayle Englof.)

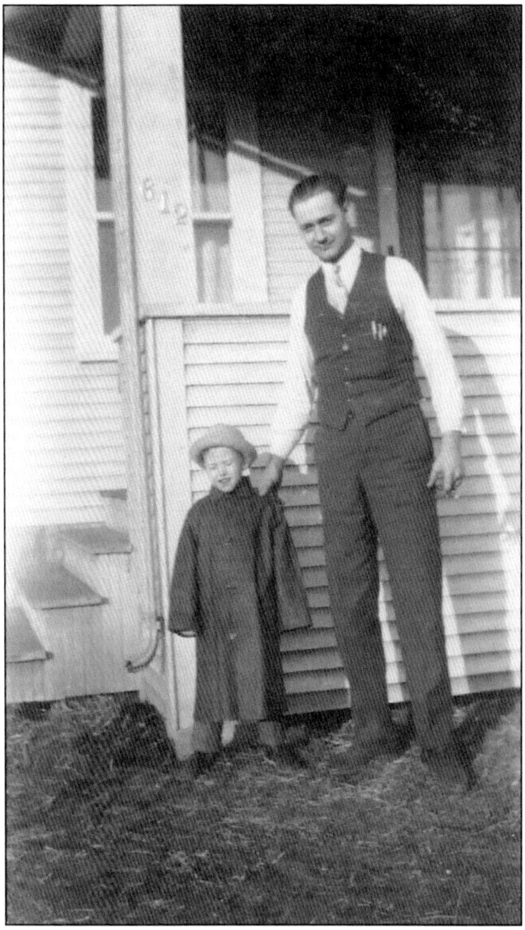

The 1926 photograph at left shows Jack Oswald and his son Charles "Charlie" Oswald in the yard near the front porch of the Oswald home at 612 River Lane. Charles is dressed in a hat and raincoat. A close look reveals the house number on the porch column. The photograph below, believed to have been taken in 1927, shows the dining room in the interior of this same house. A small, light-colored rocking horse is visible at far right. Other pieces of furniture and a large rug are also visible. (Both, courtesy of Gayle Englof.)

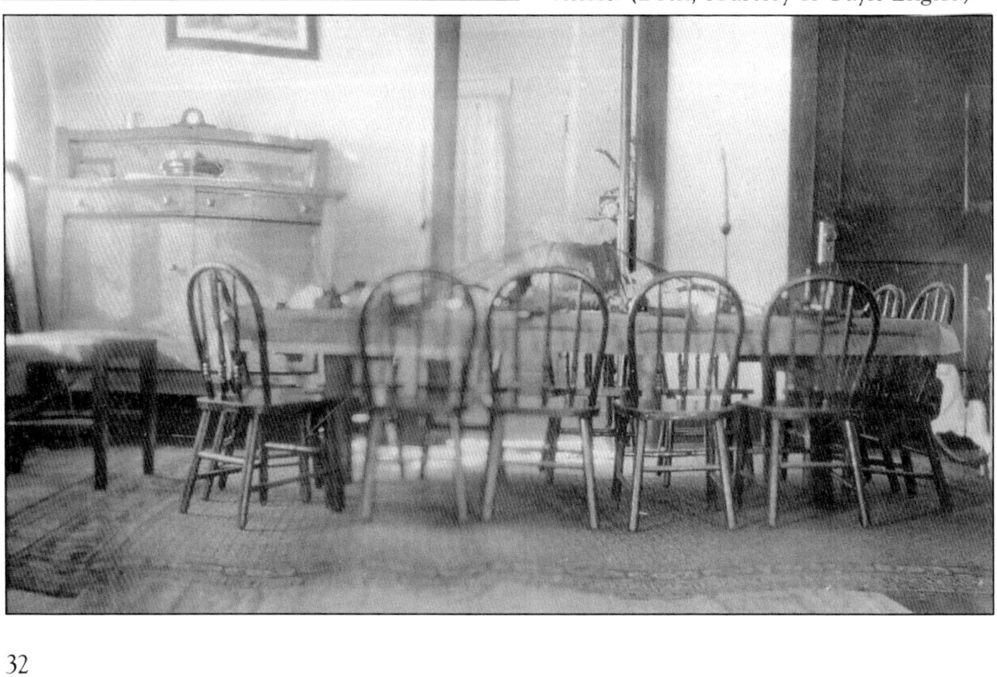

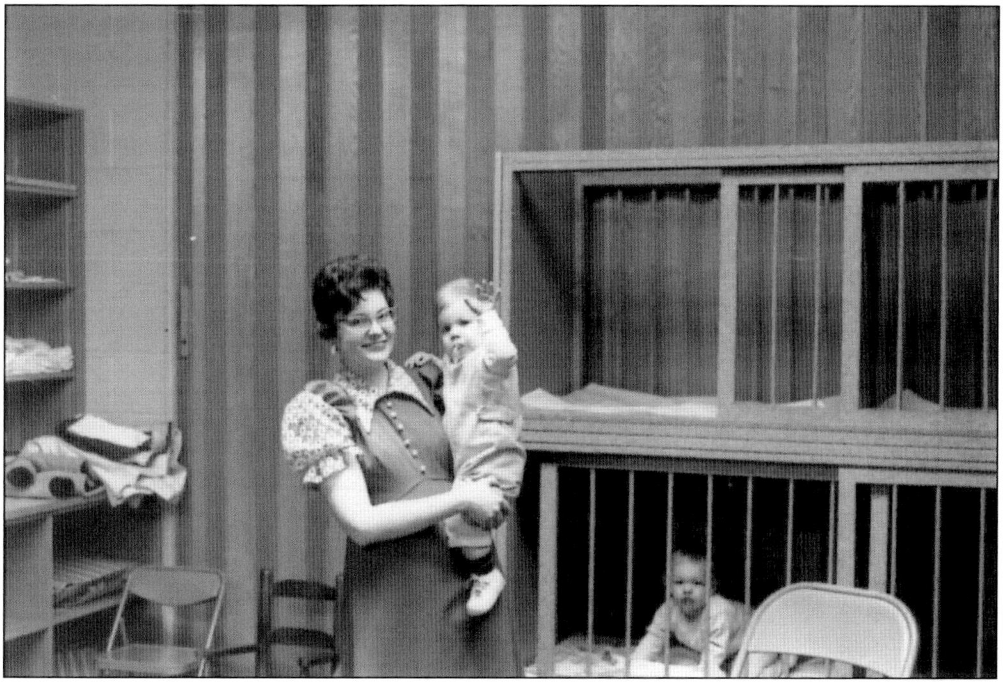

In this c. 1960 photograph, a woman watches over two children in the day care center at Bethany Presbyterian Church at 5403 North Second Street. Note the old-style playpens in the background. The woman and the children are unidentified. (Courtesy of Bethany Presbyterian Church.)

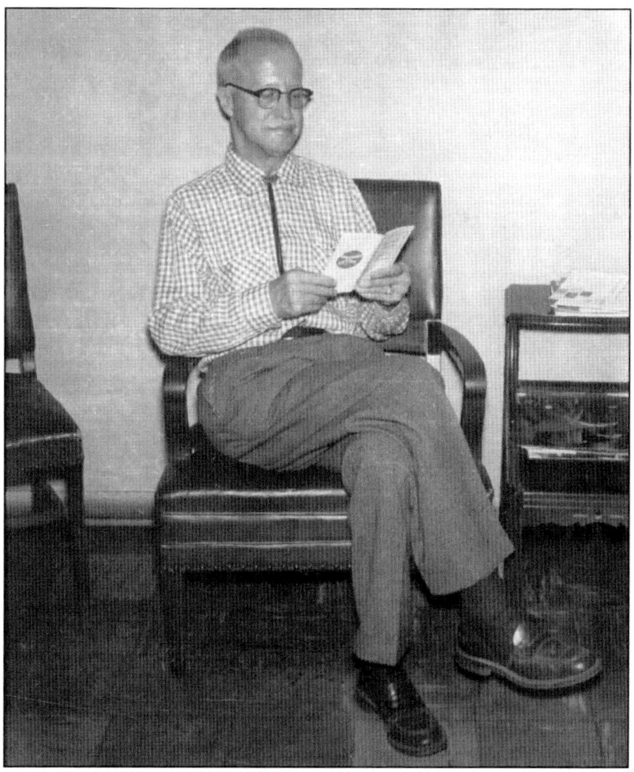

Elmer W. Johnson is pictured in this undated photograph. Johnson, a realtor, began publishing the *Loves Park News* in 1927. Johnson's brother-in-law, Lynn E. Wagoner, first printed the newspaper in a garage behind East Drive and Rose Avenue. In 1930, printing moved to Johnson's offices at the southeast corner of River Lane and North Second Street.

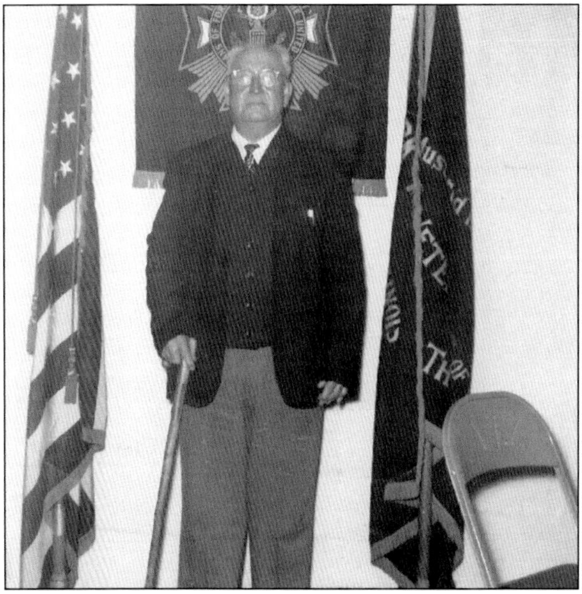

Albert M. Stephens poses on April 12, 1952 at the Loves Park Veterans of Foreign Wars Post No. 9759. Stephens served as a merchant policeman in the Loves Park area in the years before the city was incorporated in 1947. He was 73 years old when this photograph was taken. (Courtesy of Eleanor Poole.)

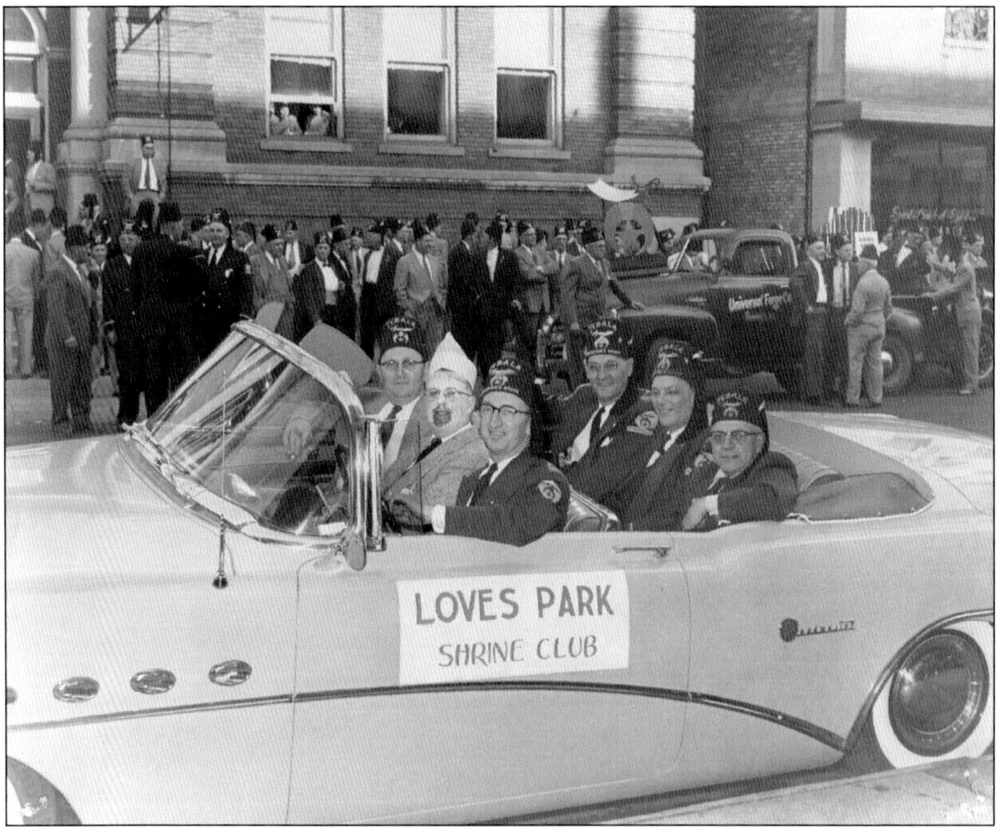

Members of the Loves Park Shrine Club are shown here driving their Buick in front of the downtown Rockford Shrine building. The middle occupant in the backseat is Edward T. Reynolds Jr., who was a Loves Park alderman from 1951 to 1955. The man on the left in the backseat is Don Laflin.

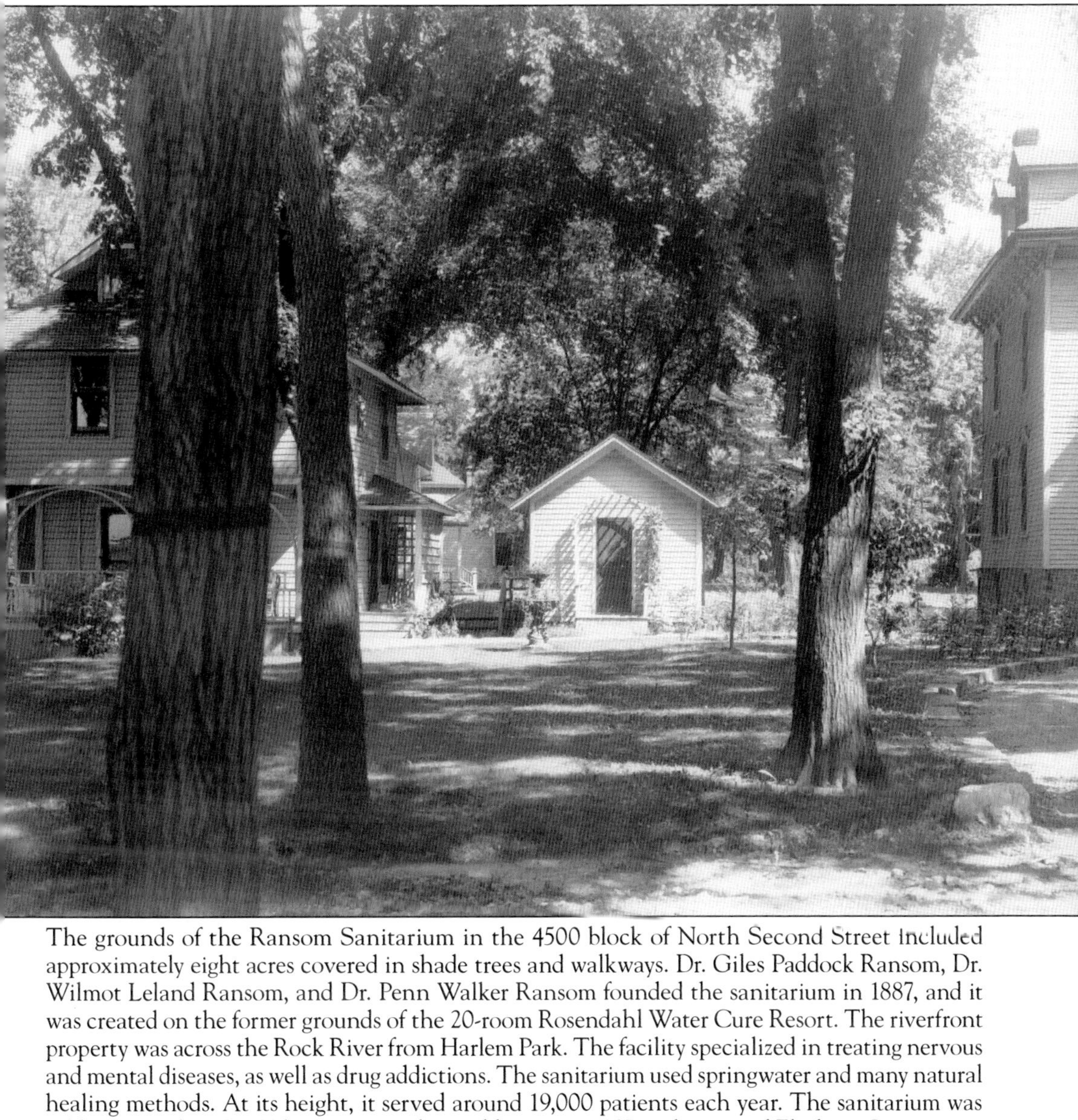

The grounds of the Ransom Sanitarium in the 4500 block of North Second Street included approximately eight acres covered in shade trees and walkways. Dr. Giles Paddock Ransom, Dr. Wilmot Leland Ransom, and Dr. Penn Walker Ransom founded the sanitarium in 1887, and it was created on the former grounds of the 20-room Rosendahl Water Cure Resort. The riverfront property was across the Rock River from Harlem Park. The facility specialized in treating nervous and mental diseases, as well as drug addictions. The sanitarium used springwater and many natural healing methods. At its height, it served around 19,000 patients each year. The sanitarium was sold to Dr. Sidney D. Wilgus in 1914, then sold again in 1937 and renamed Elmlawn Sanitarium. The facility finally closed in 1964, and the land was redeveloped. The Ransom family papers are held in the library at Northern Illinois University.

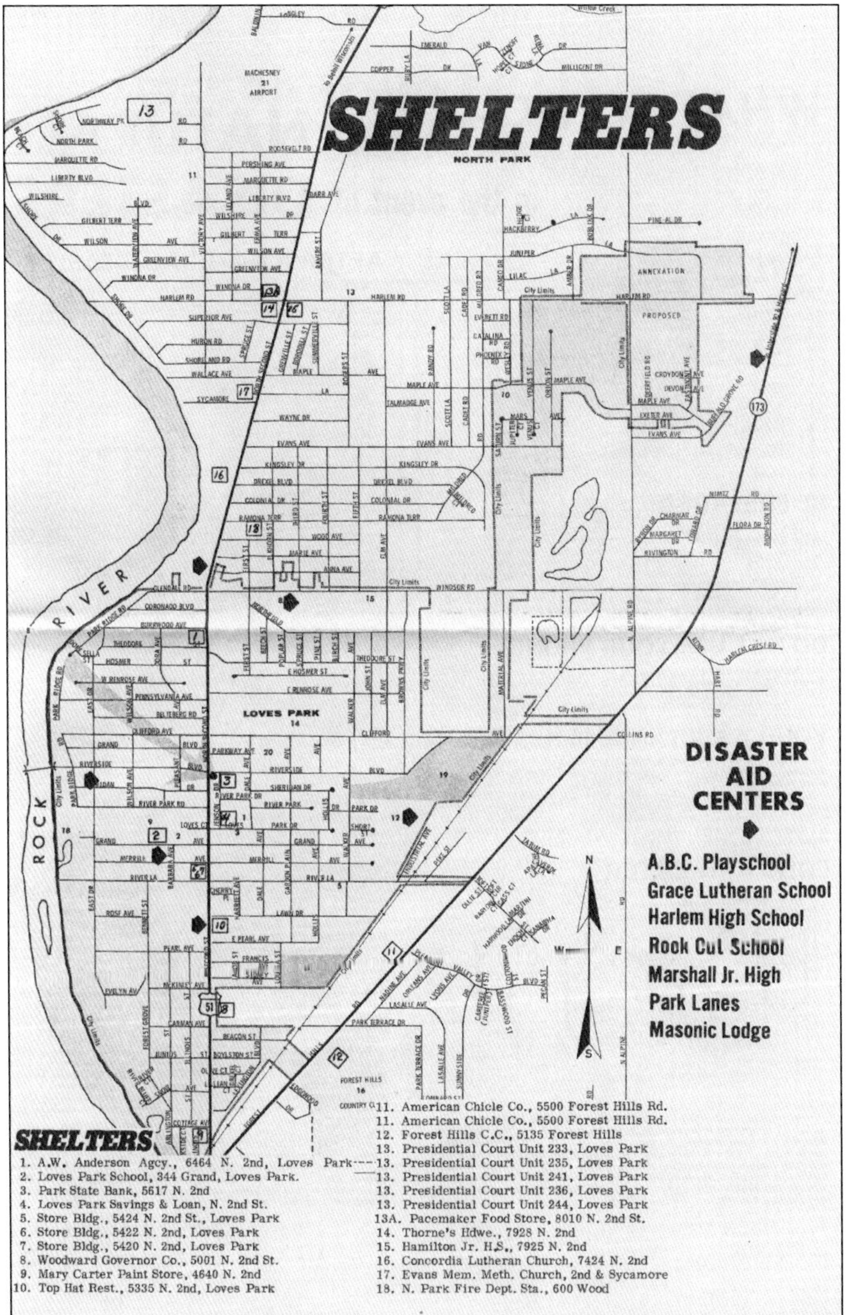

This map of bomb shelters and disaster aid areas in Loves Park was printed and distributed by the Loves Park Civil Defense organization. The exact date of publication is unknown, although it is believed to be around 1970. The eight-page spread includes detailed instructions on what to do in the event of a natural disaster and details where to go and what to do in the event of a nuclear attack. The major aid centers indicated are A.B.C. Playschool, Grace Lutheran School, Harlem High School, Rock Cut School, Marshall Junior High School, Park Lanes, and the Masonic lodge. An additional 18 shelters are listed.

Three

BUSINESSES

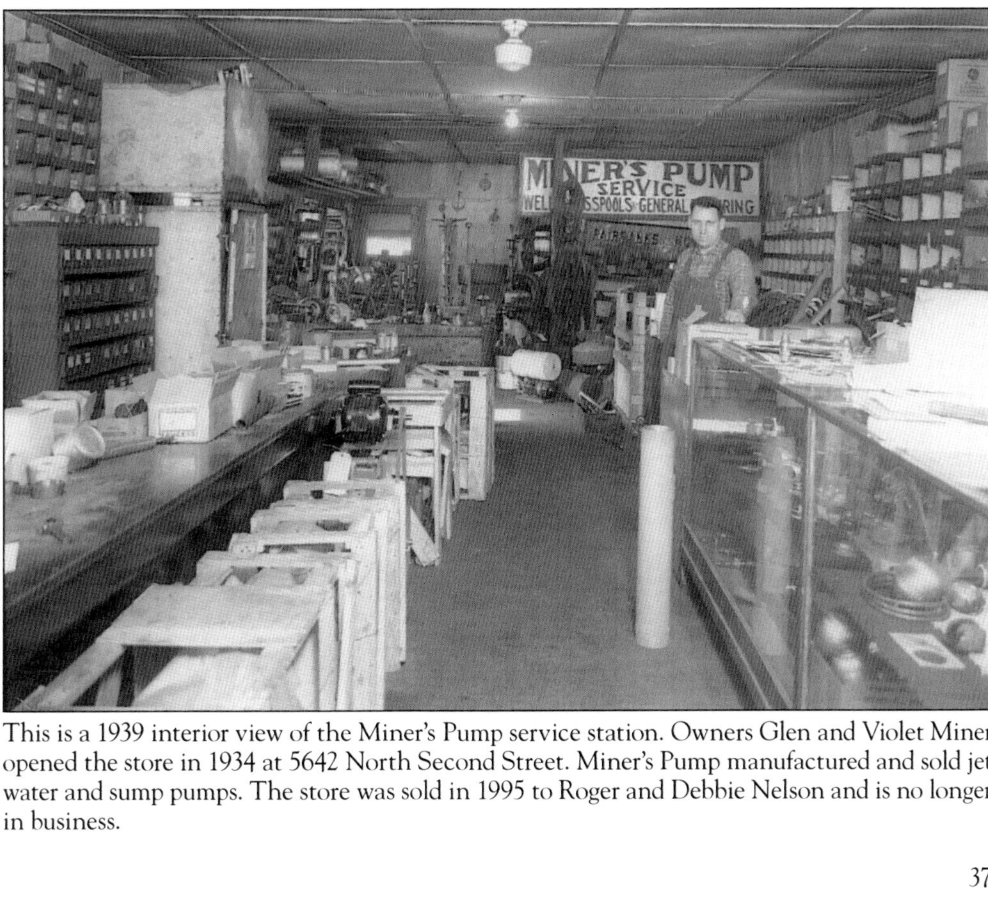

This is a 1939 interior view of the Miner's Pump service station. Owners Glen and Violet Miner opened the store in 1934 at 5642 North Second Street. Miner's Pump manufactured and sold jet water and sump pumps. The store was sold in 1995 to Roger and Debbie Nelson and is no longer in business.

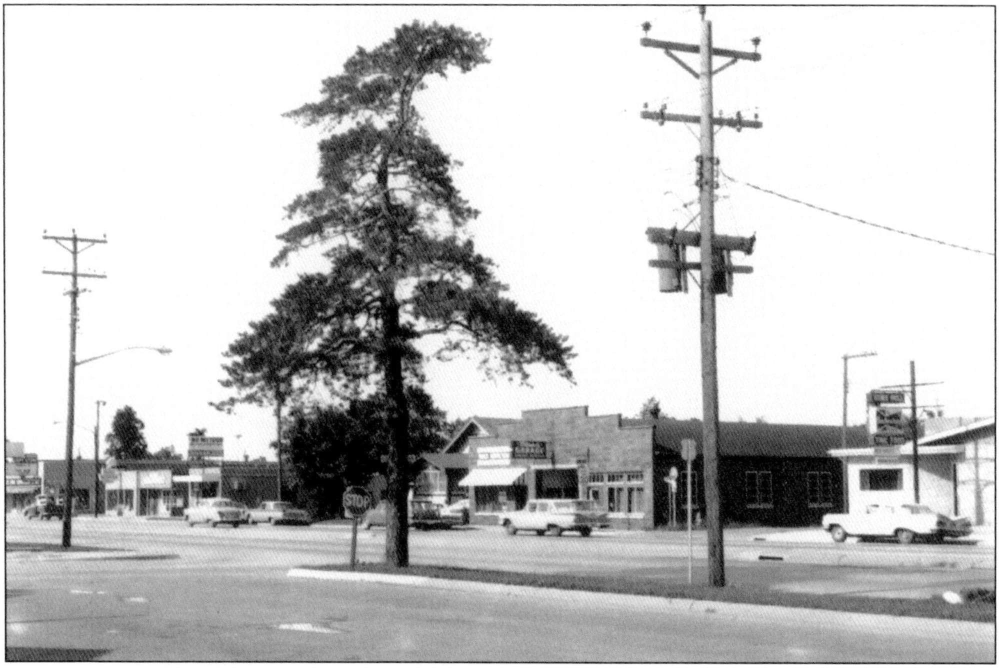

Blume's Garage, located at 5614 North Second Street near the intersection of Loves Park Drive, opened in the early 1920s. Owners also operated A&B Freight from the same location. The 1950s photograph above was taken looking west across North Second Street at the front of the garage (the building with the awning). The 1950s photograph below shows a lineup of employees; they are, from left to right, Marie Blume, Helen Klenky, unidentified, Les Alberts, unidentified, Frity Blume, unidentified, and Merv Blume. Blume's Garage is still in business in the same location; the current owner is Christine Licari.

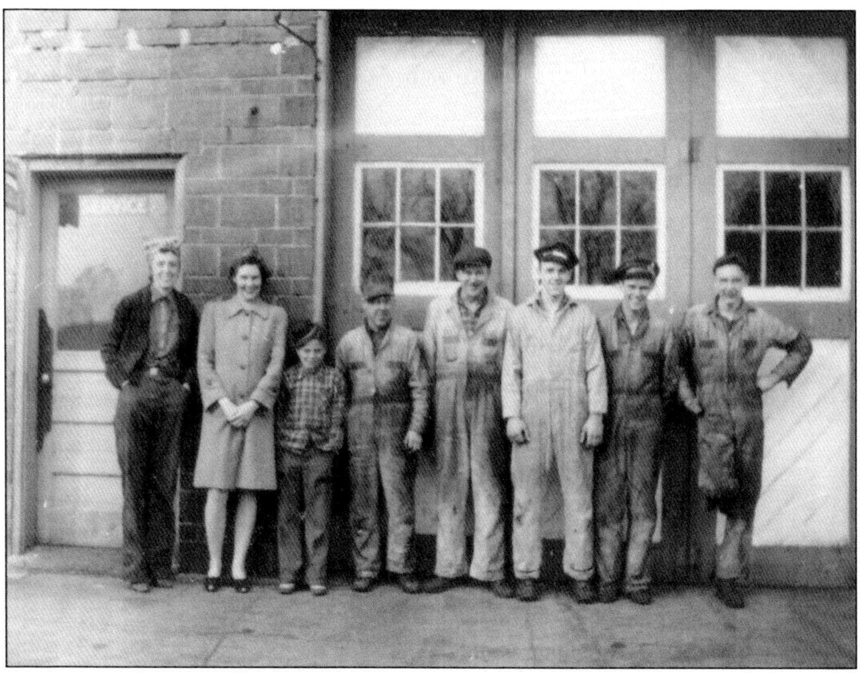

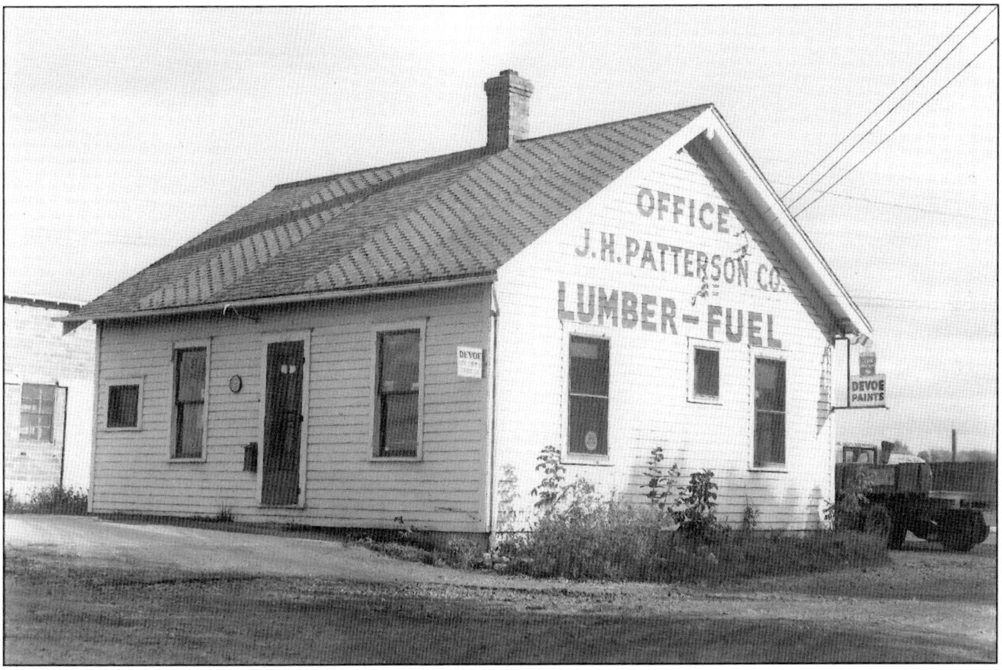

The office of J.H. Patterson Lumber, located at 721 Pearl Avenue, opened on January 21, 1921. The founder of the company was Joseph Helymun Patterson. The yard manager at the Loves Park location when it opened was R.H. Perkins. At its peak, the company had 10 lumberyards throughout northern Illinois, with locations in McHenry, Lee, Ogle, Stephenson, Boone, and Winnebago Counties. J.H. Patterson thrived until 2001, when all of the locations were either closed or sold by the fourth generation of Pattersons. The undated picture below shows a group of Patterson employees in front of the Pearl Avenue office. (Both, courtesy of Midway Village Museum, Rockford, Illinois.)

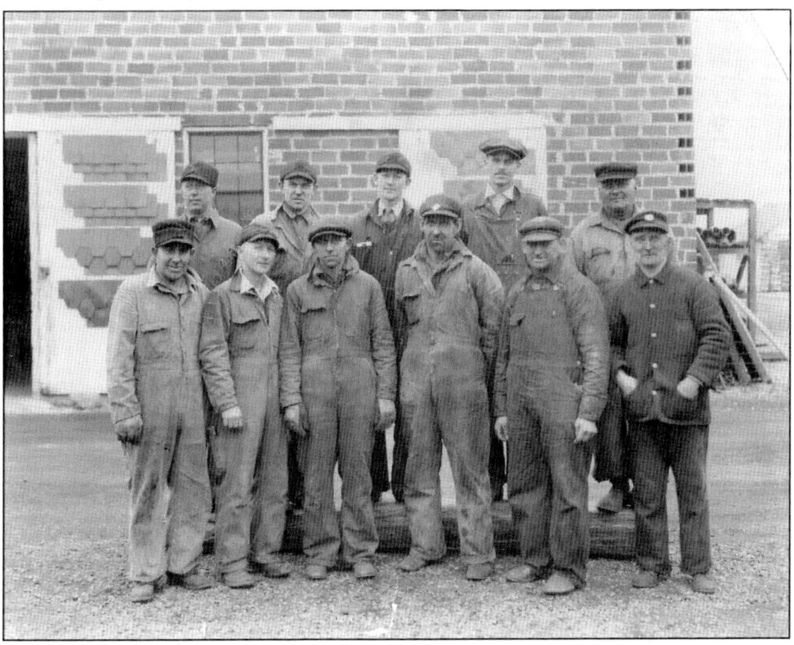

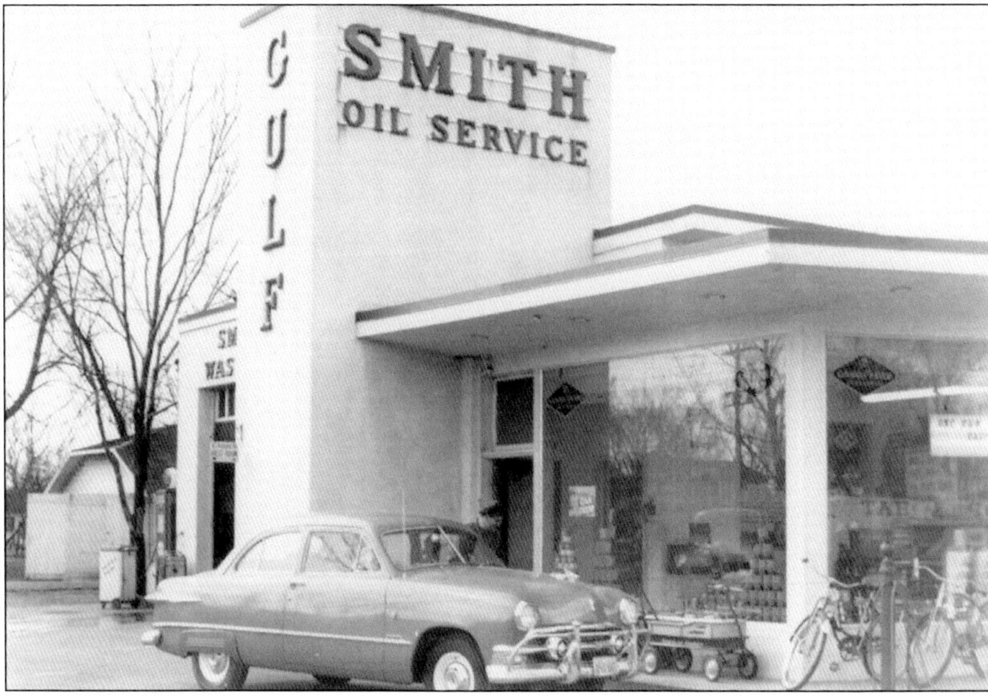

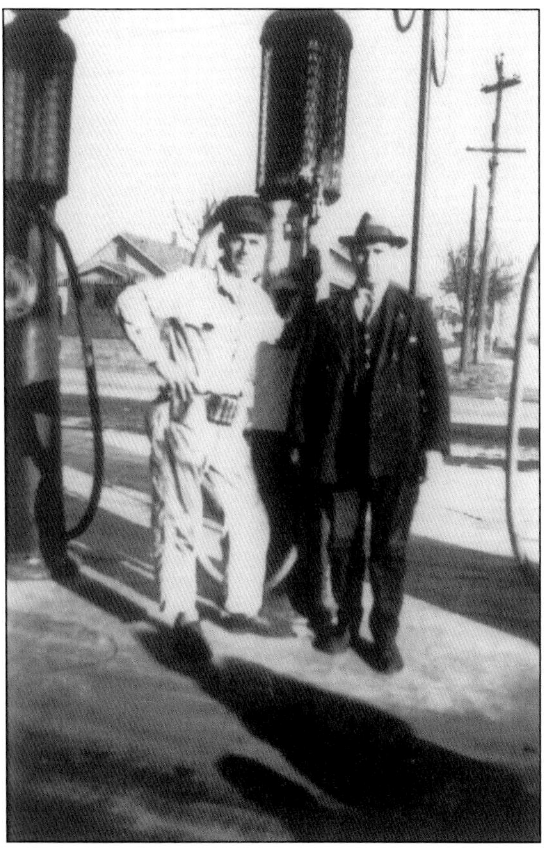

Harry Patrick owned the Smith Oil Station at 5306 North Second Street near the intersection of Pearl Avenue. The original station was built in 1924, and a new one was constructed on the same site in 1947. This photograph is undated but was taken after 1947, because it shows the updated station.

The Jones brothers—Zenor (left) and Joe—are pictured in the early 1930s in front of the Standard Oil Station that Zenor managed. The station was located at 6401 North Second Street near the intersection of Clifford Avenue. Note the old gas pumps behind the brothers.

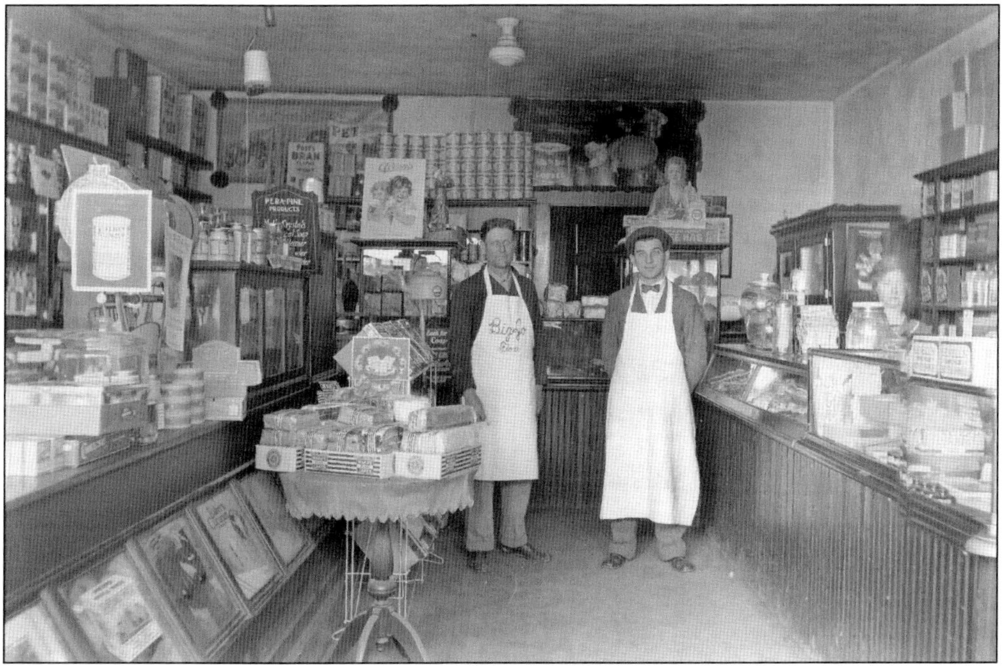

Bredsteen's Pioneer Grocery was located at 5504 North Second Street near the intersection of River Lane. The store, owned by Alfred "Al" Bredsteen, sold canned and bulk foods. Bredsteen's was also the first store in Loves Park to sell fresh meat and milk. The interior view above shows, from left to right, Alfred Bredsteen, William H. Rogers, and Alfred's wife, Agnes, who is behind the counter. In 1917, the store purchased the 1925 Dodge delivery truck pictured below with Alfred behind the wheel. The Bredsteen store closed in 1950 after having been open since 1912.

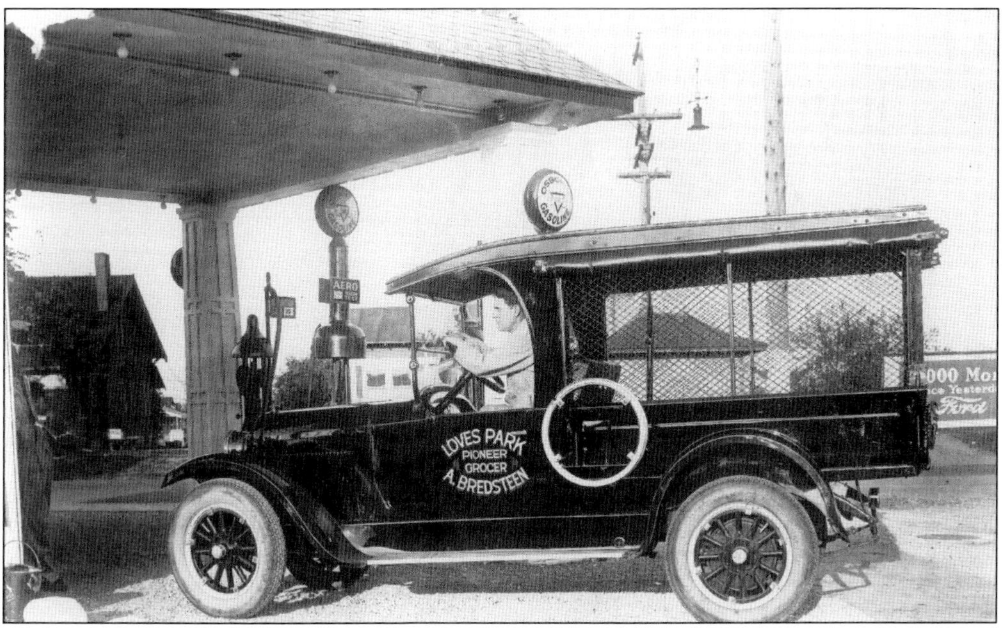

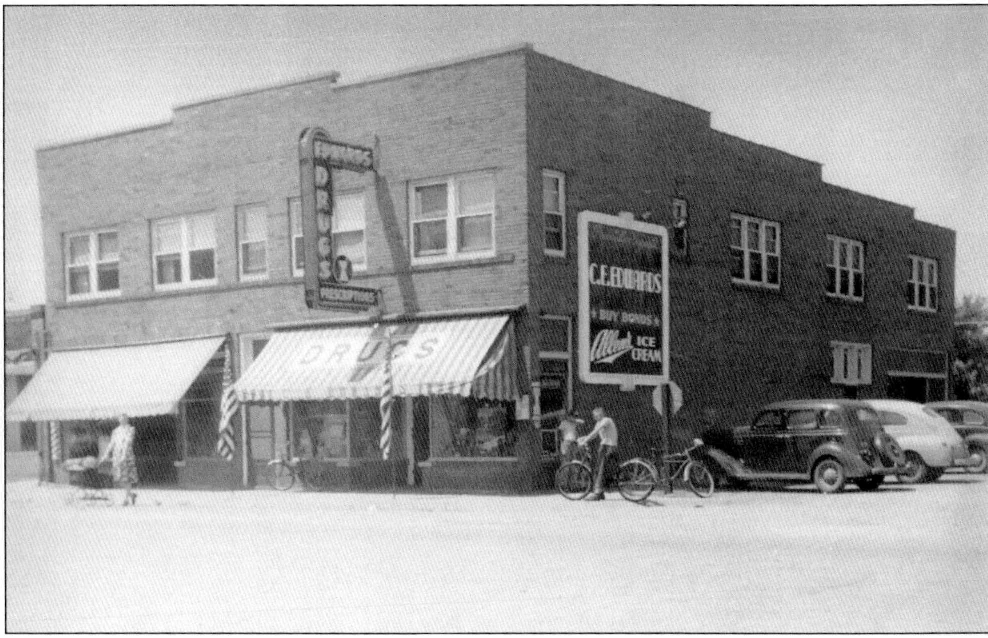

Charles E. "Speed" Edwards was a pharmacist at this drugstore located at 5452 North Second Street at the intersection of River Lane. It advertised "dependable drugs" and "veterinary remedies." The second floor of the building contained apartment units that were rented out. Edwards served as city clerk from 1953 to 1965. (Courtesy of Midway Village Museum, Rockford, Illinois.)

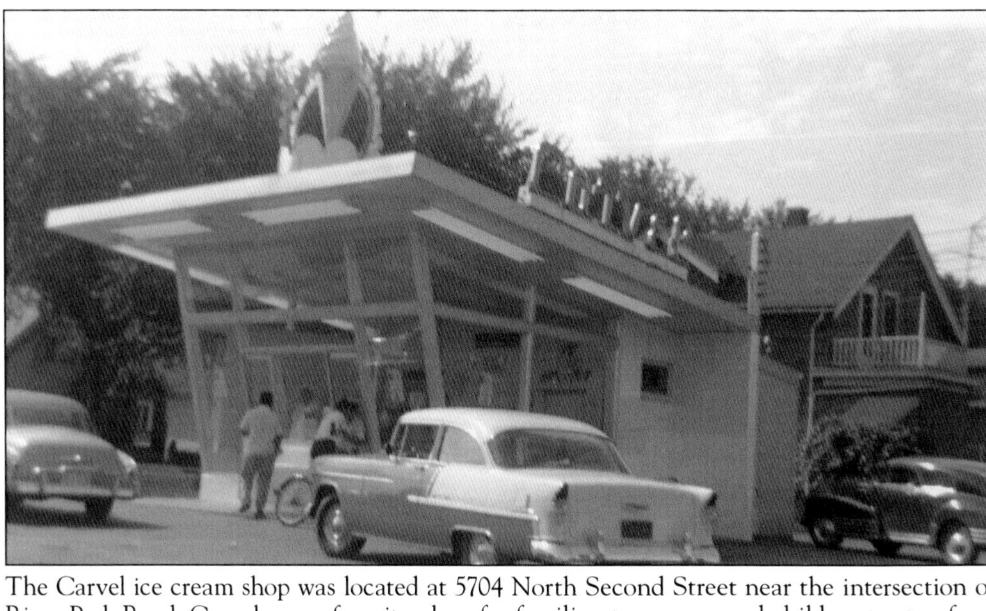

The Carvel ice cream shop was located at 5704 North Second Street near the intersection of River Park Road. Carvel was a favorite place for families, teenagers, and children to stop for a scoop of ice cream and was easily recognized by the large ice cream cone on top of the building. This photograph was taken in 1955.

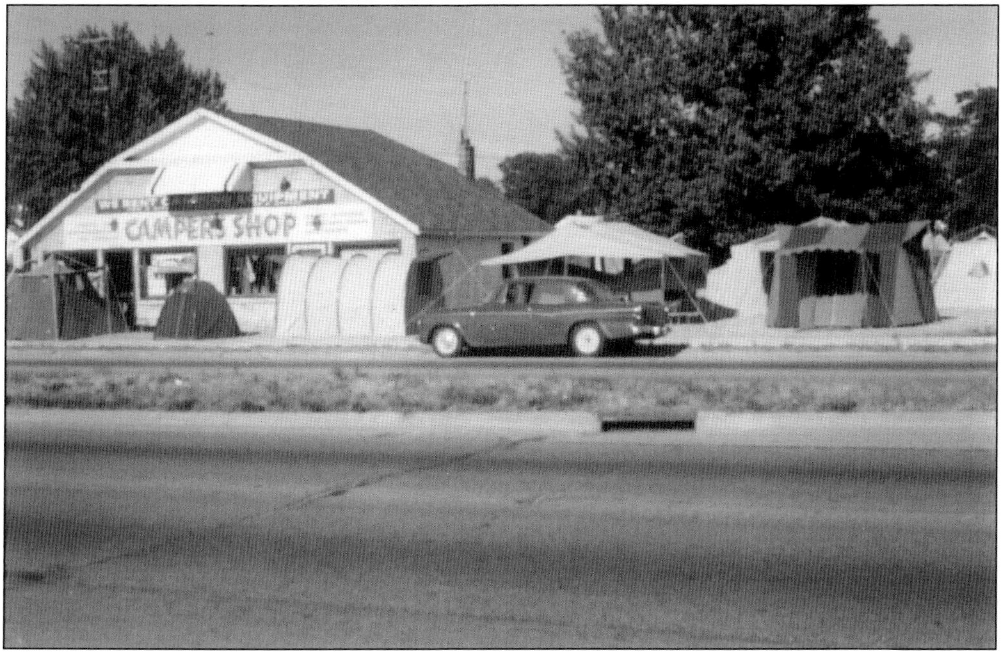

The Camper's Shop, owned by Hawley Beebe, was located at 4825 North Second Street near the intersection of Olive Court. It was advertised as having the area's most complete line of camp trailers, camping equipment, and tents. It also rented all types of camping equipment. This photograph was taken in July 1965.

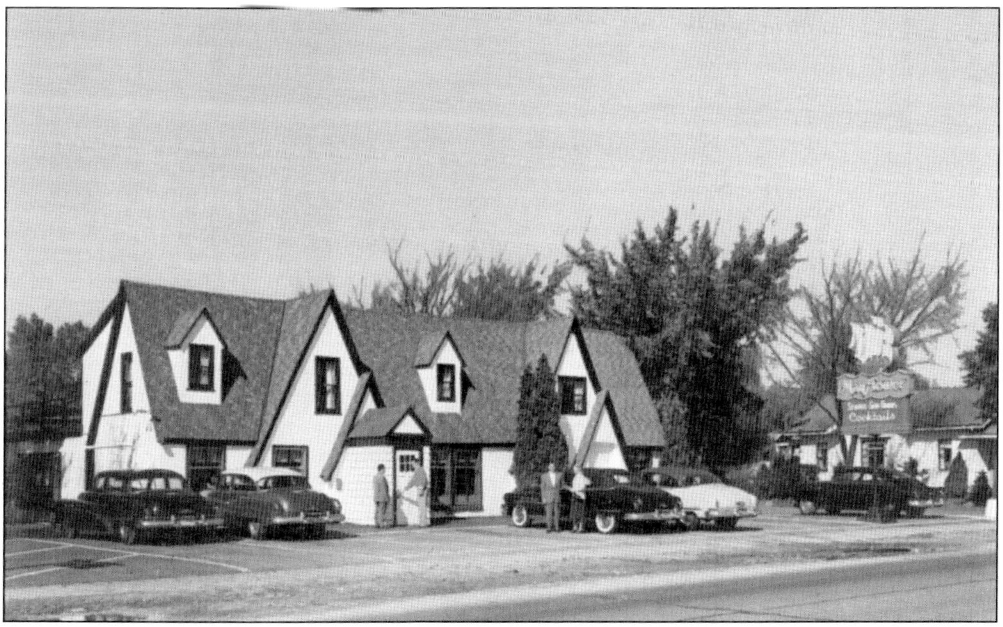

Before the Mayflower Restaurant opened at 5040 North Second Street, a gas station operated in this location. The restaurant advertised everything from sandwiches to complete dinners. This vintage postcard is undated. The building, which now houses the Hope and Anchor Pub, retains its unique exterior appearance. (Courtesy of Brian Landis.)

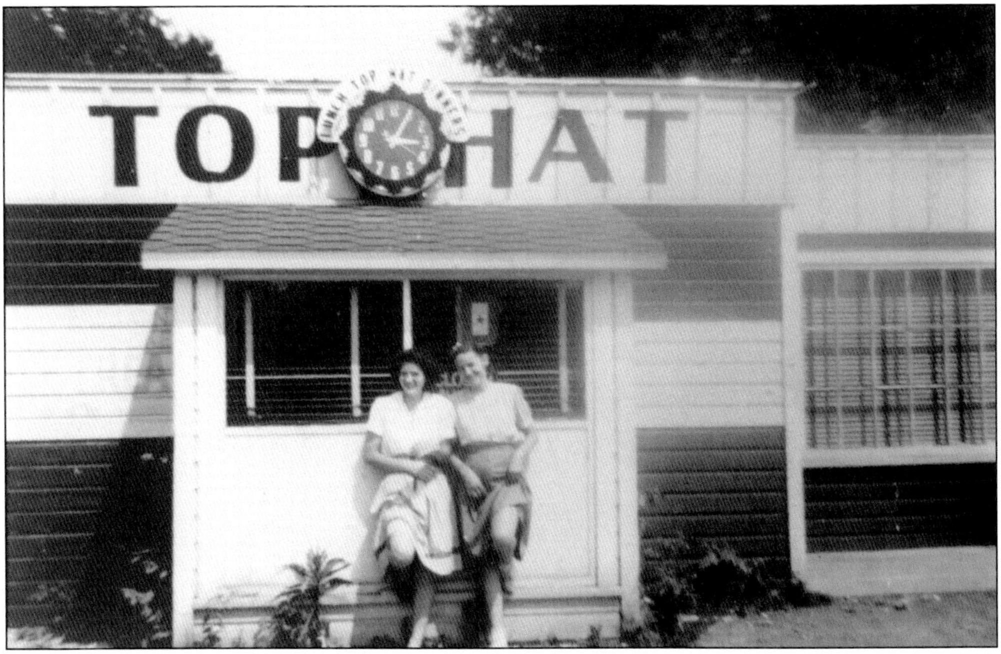

Owners A.C. Elliott and Merle Bergsten opened the first Loves Park Top Hat Restaurant at 5215 North Second Street on July 12, 1941. The first building, pictured above, had clapboard siding and one counter that could seat 14 people. The two girls in the photograph above are Marion ? (left) and Lucy ?. The diner served everything from burgers to sundaes. The Top Hat has changed owners and gone through numerous transformations over the years. The location at 5335 North Second Street closed and was torn down in 2003. The Delehanty Funeral Home at 401 River Road is pictured below. When it was originally founded in 1949 by Thomas and Lorraine Delehanty, it was located on the Weldon farm at the corner of North Second Street and Merrill Avenue. In 1955, the funeral home moved to its current location, where it has undergone two renovations—one in 1970 and one in 1984. (Below, courtesy of Nicole C. Lindsay.)

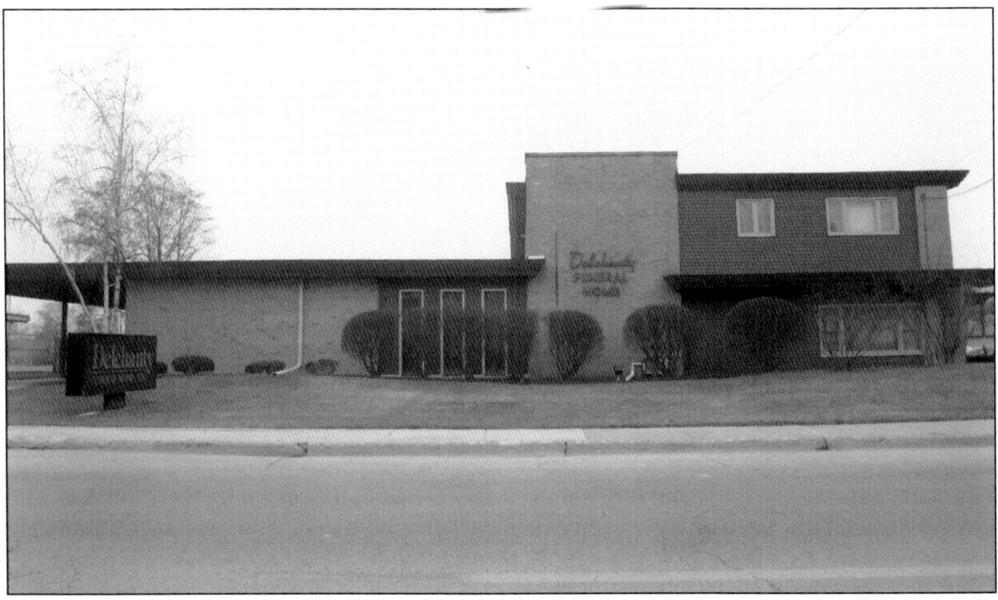

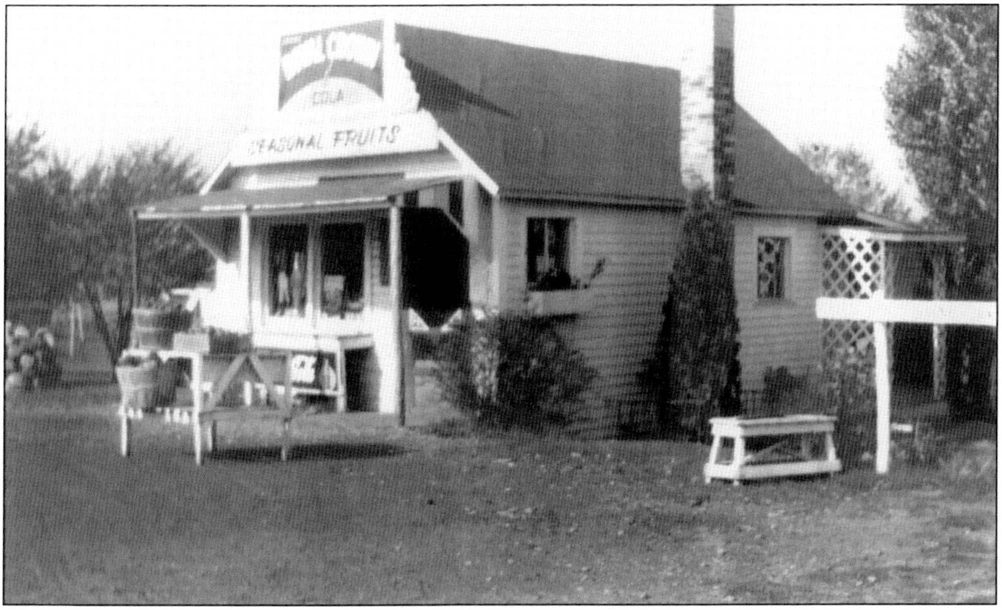

Stone's Seasonal Fruits, located at 7104 Forest Hills Road, is pictured here in 1943. Glen H. Stone started with a small fruit stand in 1936, and the business eventually grew to include a grocery store and restaurant. Glen and his wife, Olive, lived next door at 7108 Forest Hills Road. Glen's son, Clifford L. "Bud" Stone, took over in 1971, and the store closed in 1973.

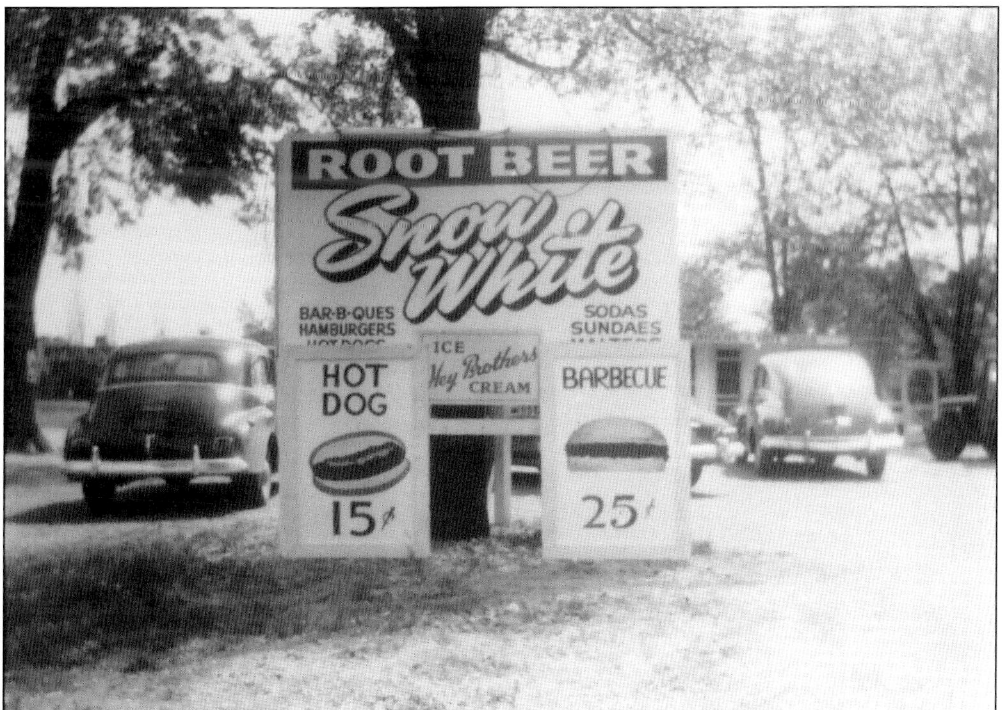

This c. 1948 image shows the outdoor menu at the Snow White Root Beer Stand located at 4722 North Second Street. The stand was owned by Charles R. Manderville. Manderville's daughter, Jeanne Manson, would often sleep in the back of the store while her mother, Lucille, cooked.

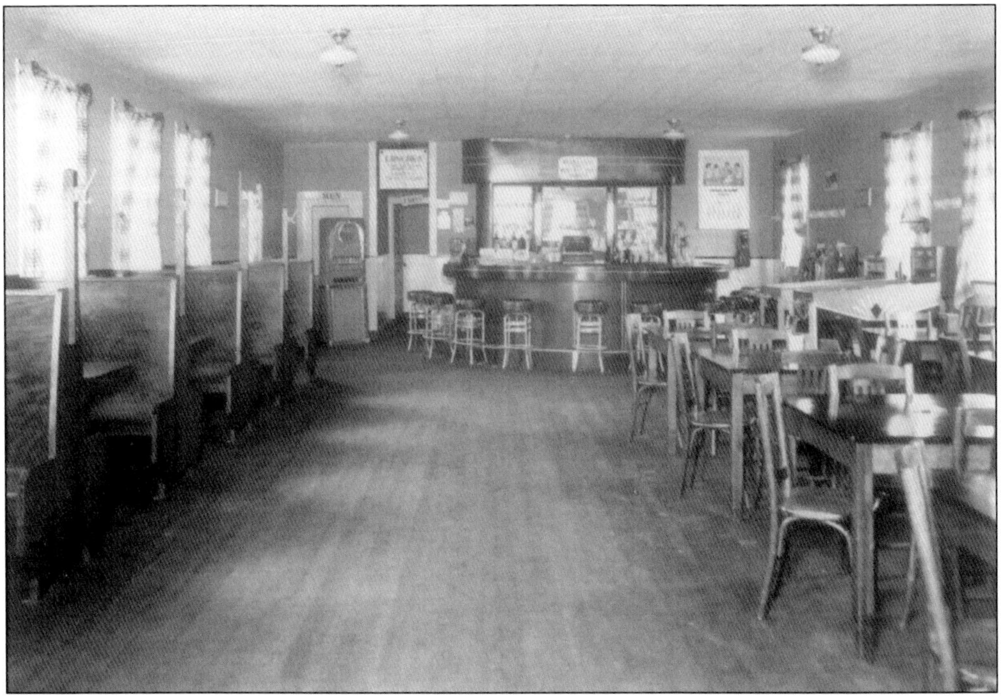

This is a c. 1938 interior view of the Town Hall Tavern at 5624 North Second Street, which was owned by Adolph Oyen and James A. Clarke. Notice the old cigarette machine in the back left corner by the men's room. The Town Hall Lounge, as it is now called, is still in business today.

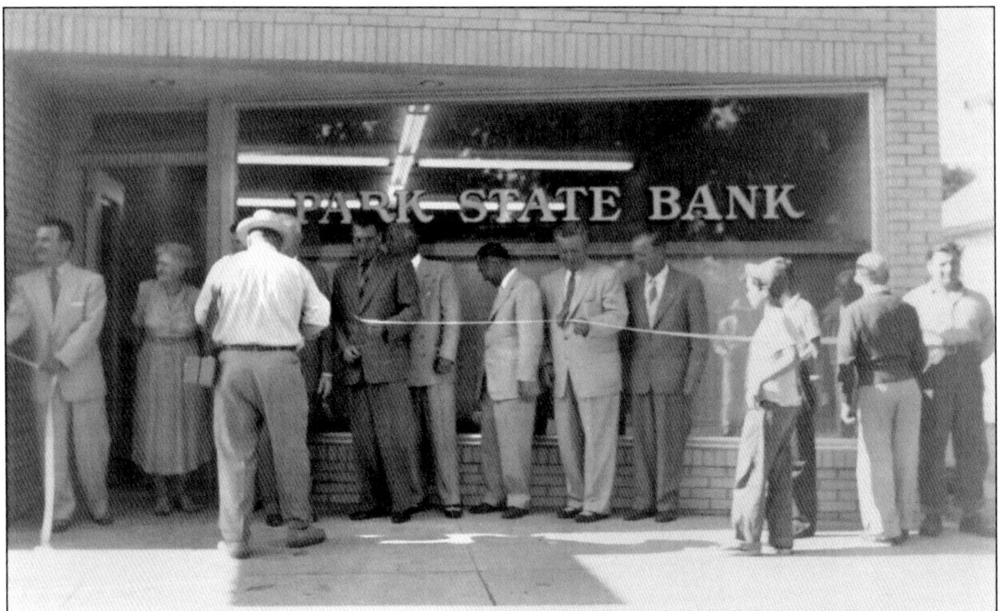

Local citizens and dignitaries are gathered on July 3, 1953, for the official ribbon-cutting at the new Park State Bank at 417 Grand Avenue. The location was only temporary, but was considered a success. Deposits were said to have reached almost $1 million after six months of operation.

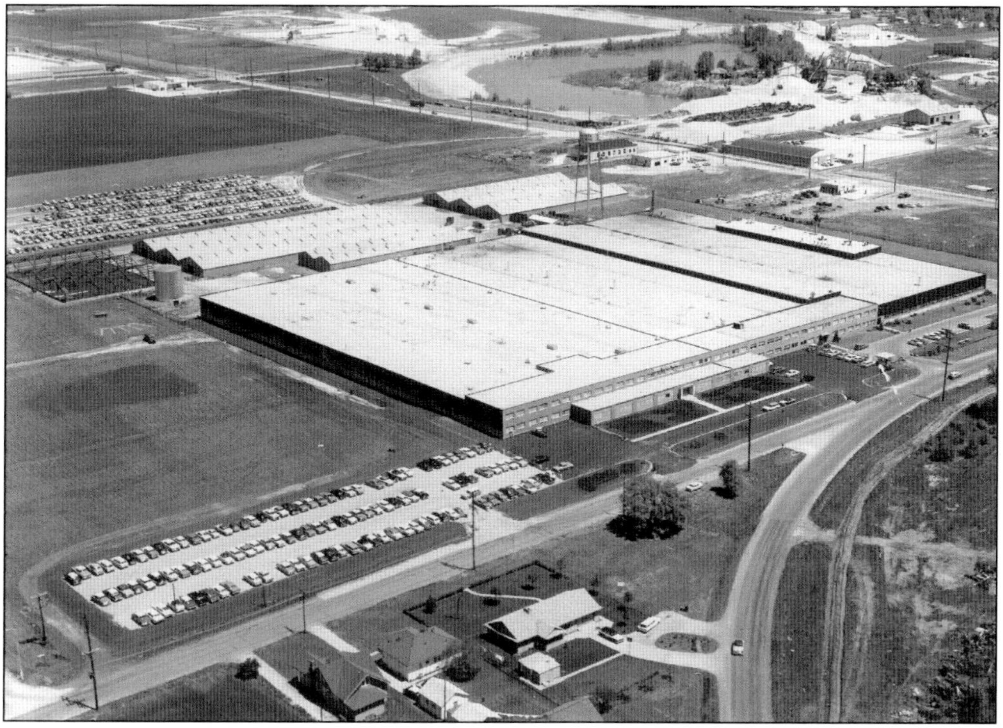

In this undated aerial photograph of the Barber-Colman facility at 1354 Clifford Avenue, Material Avenue is visible at the top of the photograph, as well as the curve where Clifford Avenue and Riverside Boulevard meet. The Loves Park Barber-Coleman facility opened in July 1954 and made various types of machinery. Numerous area residents worked there at one point or another, including Darryl F. Lindberg, the current mayor of Loves Park.

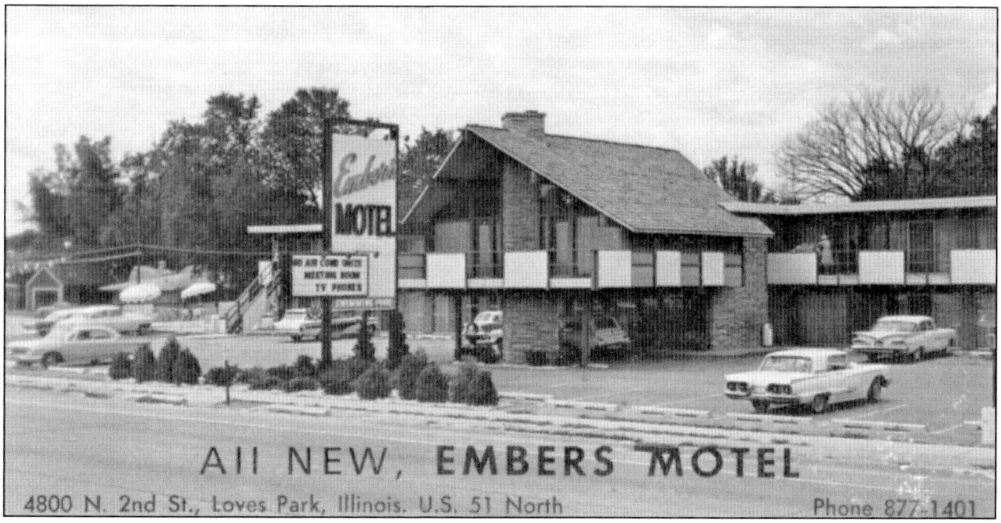

This vintage postcard advertises the all-new Embers Motel at 4800 North Second Street. The motel boasted "deluxe accommodations" with 60 air-conditioned rooms, free television, a restaurant, swimming pool, meeting rooms, and nearby golf courses. The lodging is still open and is now called the Clayton House Motel; it has the same address and phone number. (Courtesy of Nicole C. Lindsay.)

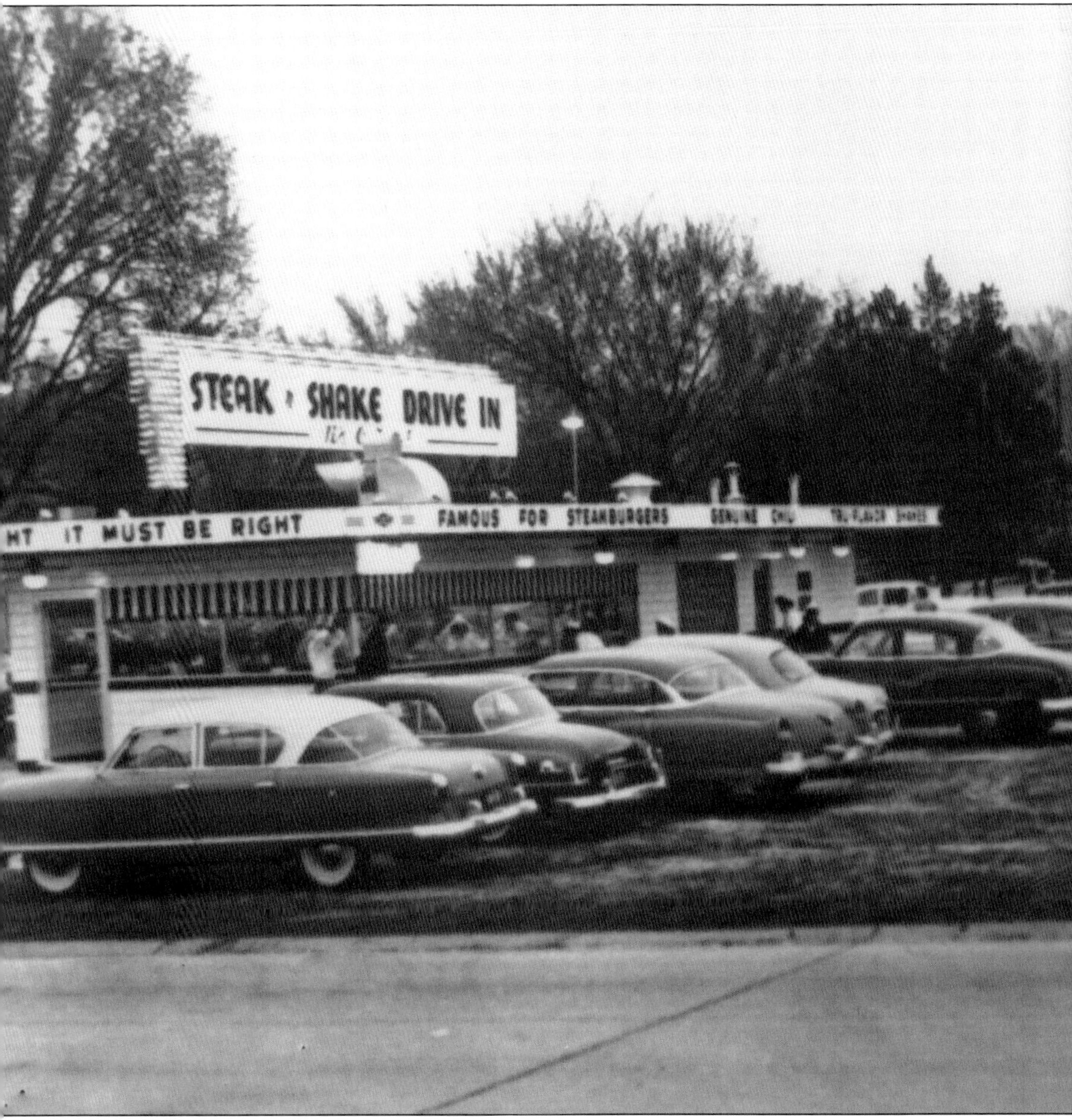

The Steak and Shake Drive In is pictured here on opening day—April 29, 1954. It was located at 4615 North Second Street and was popular with area residents immediately after opening. The street in the background of the photograph is Forest Hills Road, and the restaurant was one of the

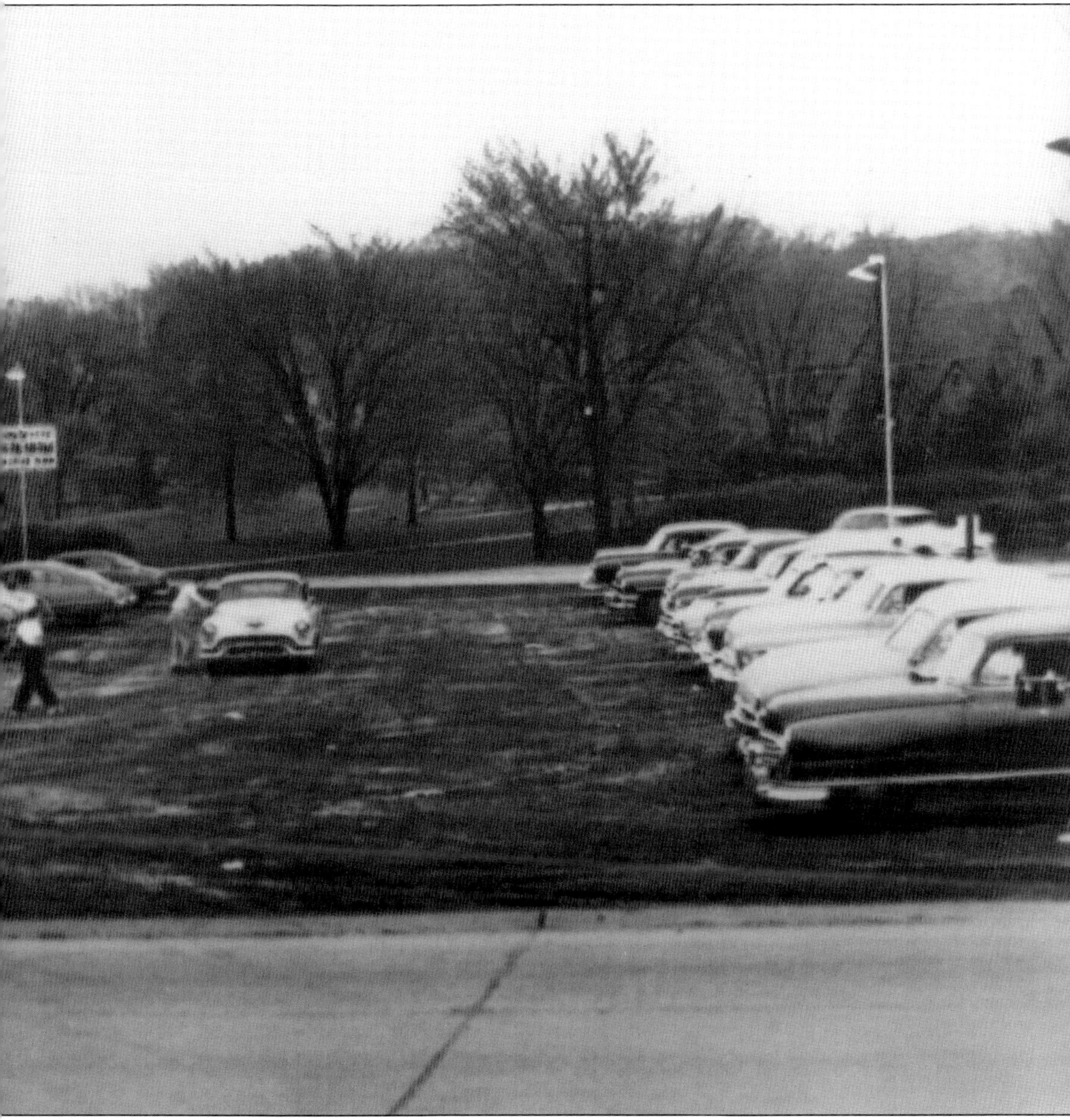

first businesses seen by those entering the city from the south. This piece of land, in the vicinity of Snow's Crossing (see page 13), is where the Loves Park welcome sign is currently located.

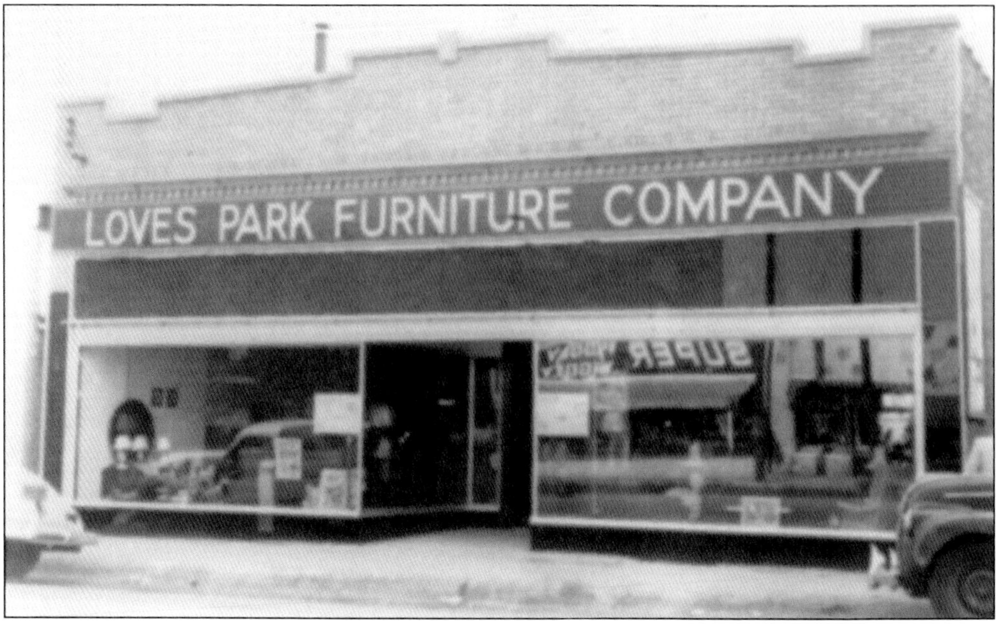

Loves Park Furniture Company is pictured at its 5440 North Second Street location in the 1950s. The Piggly Wiggly was directly across the street, and the reflection of the Piggly Wiggly sign is partially visible in the furniture store's windows. Loves Park Furniture Company was operated by Lawrence S. Perrett and sold furniture, television sets, bedding, and flooring.

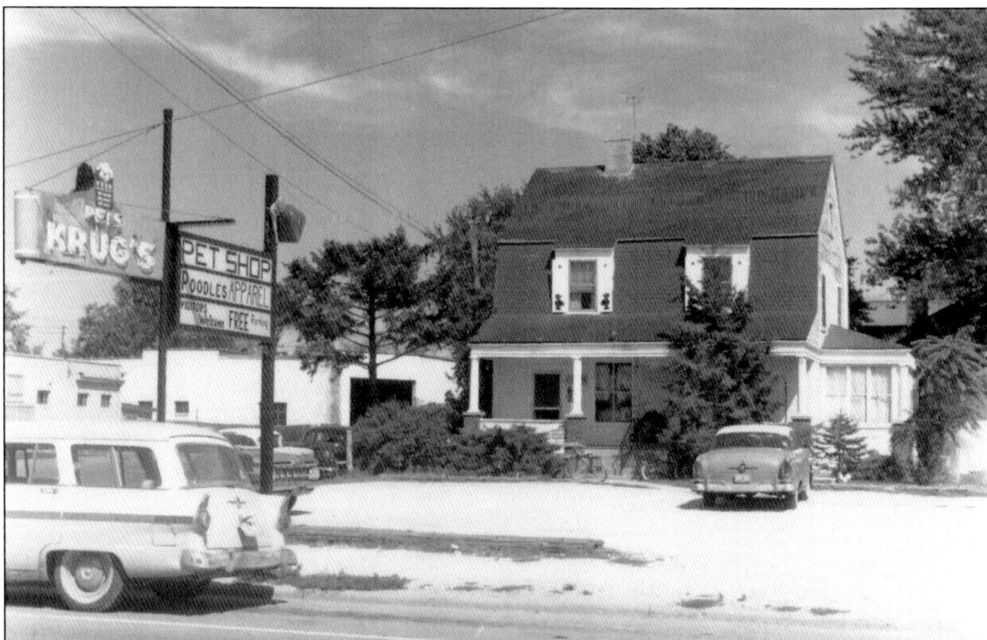

This 1960 image shows Krug's Pet Shop at 5425 North Second Street. Note that the sign advertises free parking. Krug's Pet Shop remained in business for approximately 30 years; after it closed, the building was home to Ride 'N Stride. The building still stands and looks much the same as it did in 1960. It now houses Corey's Motorworks.

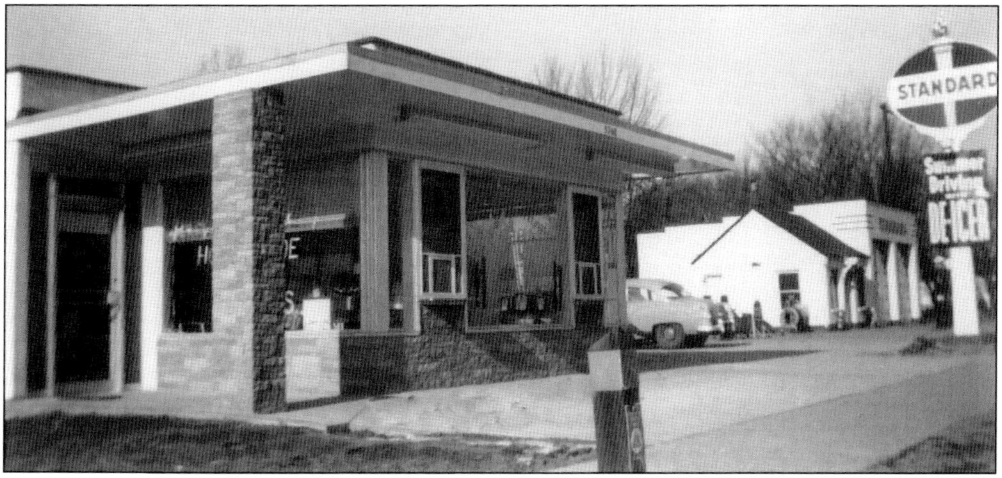

The Parkette Drive In, owned by Robert D. Holdridge, was located at 5708 North Second Street—the former site of Gill's Dairy Dreem. The address is posted on the top of the building in the front. This photograph, taken in 1956, shows Hull's Standard gas station just to the north.

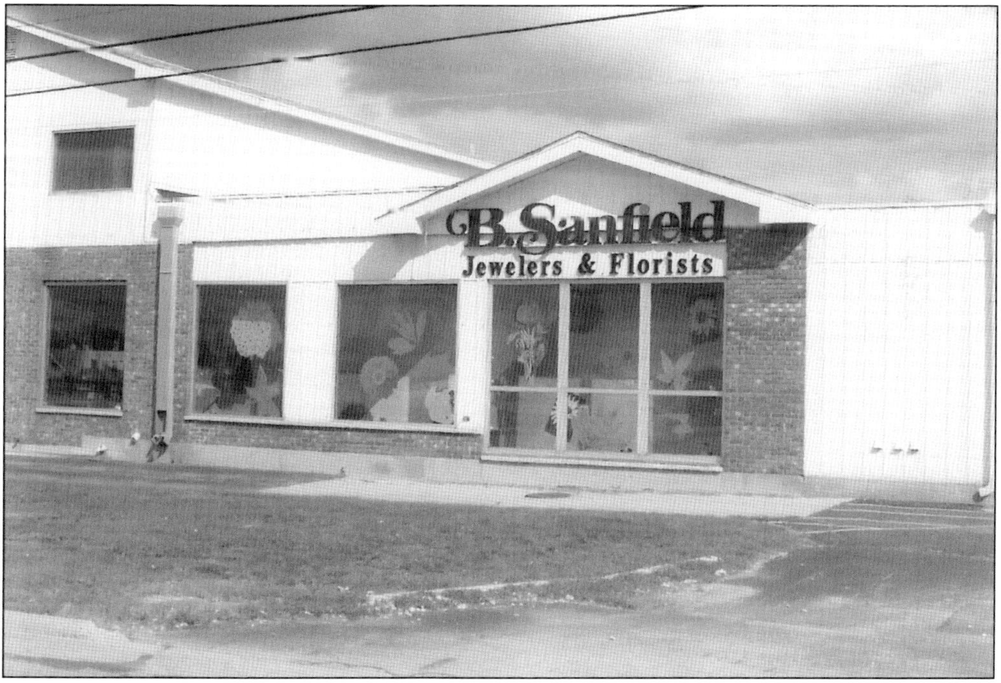

B. Sanfield Jewelers and Florists, owned by Lee Hartsfield, opened in 1971 at 6505 North Alpine Road. The store was known for its friendly atmosphere and fine jewelry and gifts. After 38 years in business, B. Sanfield closed in 2009 and sold the land to Walgreens, which tore down the building and constructed a new store. (Courtesy of City of Loves Park.)

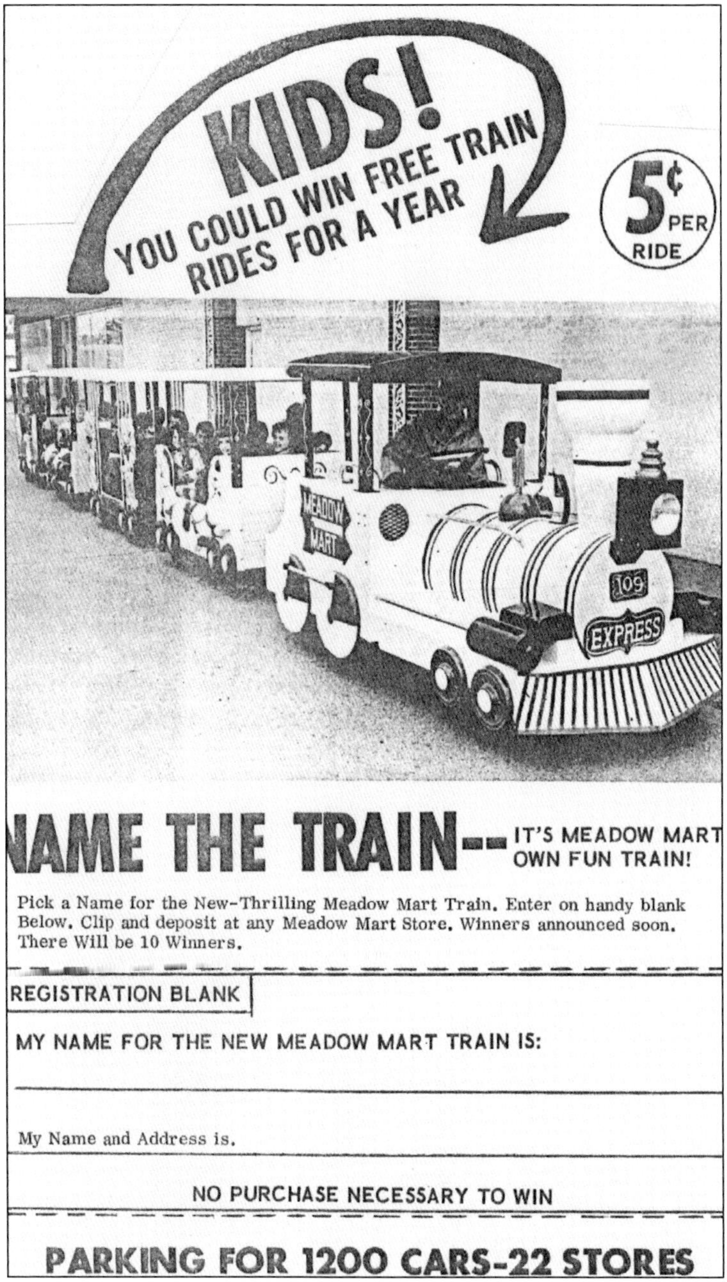

The Meadow Mart Shopping Center, located in the 6300 block of North Second Street, held a grand opening on August 23, 1956. The shopping center boasted 22 stores and parking for 1,200 cars. This undated flyer advertises train rides around the shopping center for just 5¢, as well as a contest to name the new train. Ten winners were chosen, and children could win free train rides for a year. The Meadow Mart Shopping Center is still open, and while countless stores have come and gone throughout the years, the shopping center remains the oldest of its kind in the Rockford area. Meadow Mart has also experienced several fires over the years. The first occurred on January 4, 1959, the second was on May 26, 1973, and the most recent was on June 11, 2012. (Courtesy of Brian Landis.)

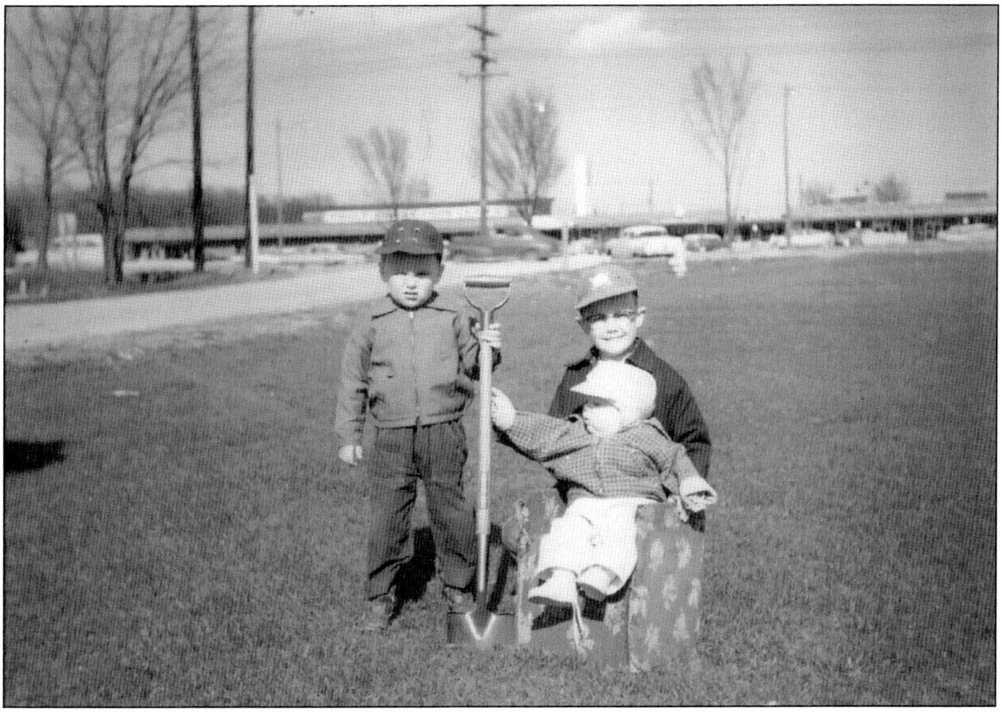

Arthur W. "Art" Anderson opened his first insurance office, A.W. Anderson, in 1955 at 6499 North Second Street (in the Meadow Mart Shopping Center, which had an address on Windsor Road at the time) with only two employees. The original office is pictured below as it looked in 1955. That location is now Doc's Diner. Anderson's business was a success, and in 1959, he broke ground on a new office at 6464 North Second Street. In the image above, Anderson's sons—Steven (left), Gary (front), and Jeffrey—are shown at the ground breaking of the new office building. All three of Anderson's sons now work at AW Anderson Agency. (Both, courtesy of Steven Anderson.)

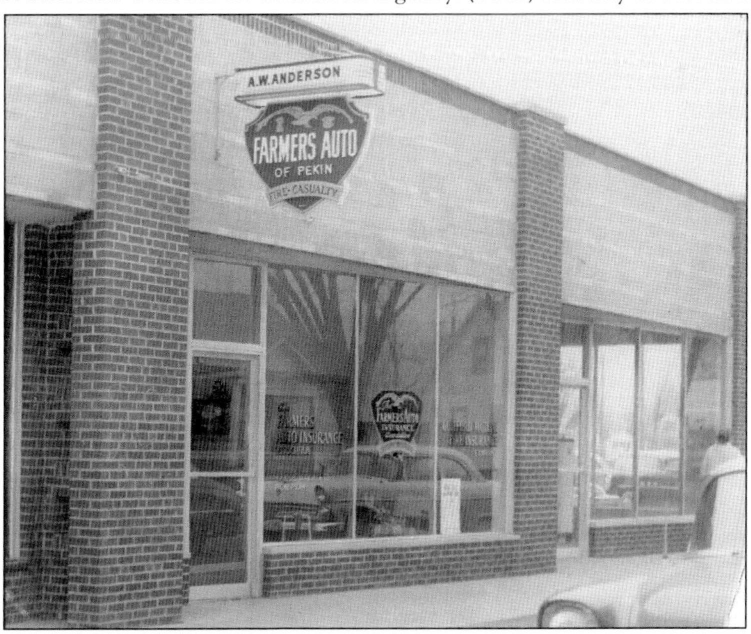

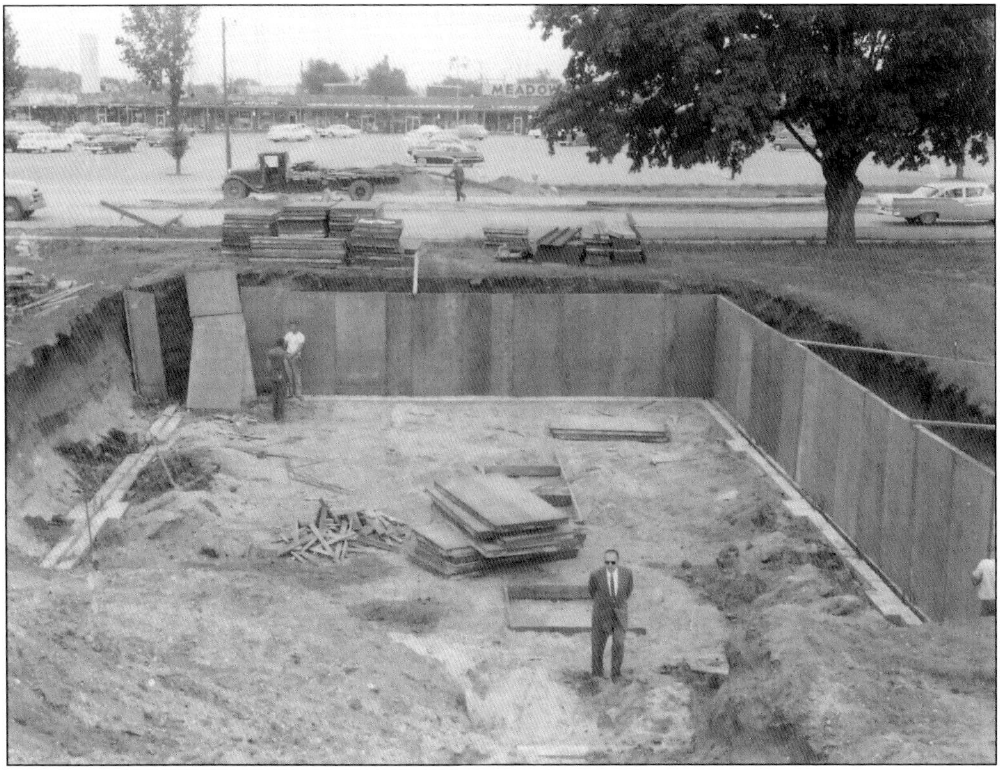

The 1959 image above shows the construction site of the new A.W. Anderson building at 6464 North Second Street, with the Meadow Mart Shopping Center in the background. A postcard from the time period notes the agency offers "all lines of general insurance." In the image below, the completed building is shown as it looked in the 1960s. Arthur W. "Art" Anderson was not only a successful businessman—he also gave back to the community of Loves Park in countless ways. The gymnasium at Harlem High School is named after him, and the local history room at North Suburban Library District also bears his name and that of his wife, Betty. The park where the Field of Honor Memorial stands is the Arthur W. Anderson Peace Park. (Both, courtesy of Steven Anderson.)

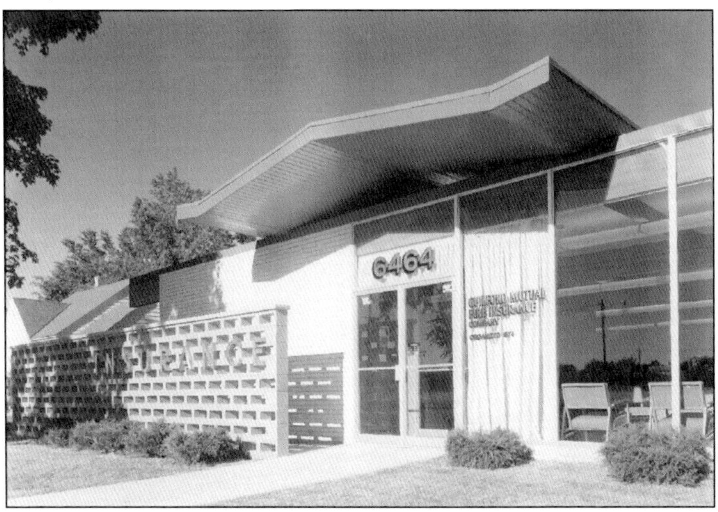

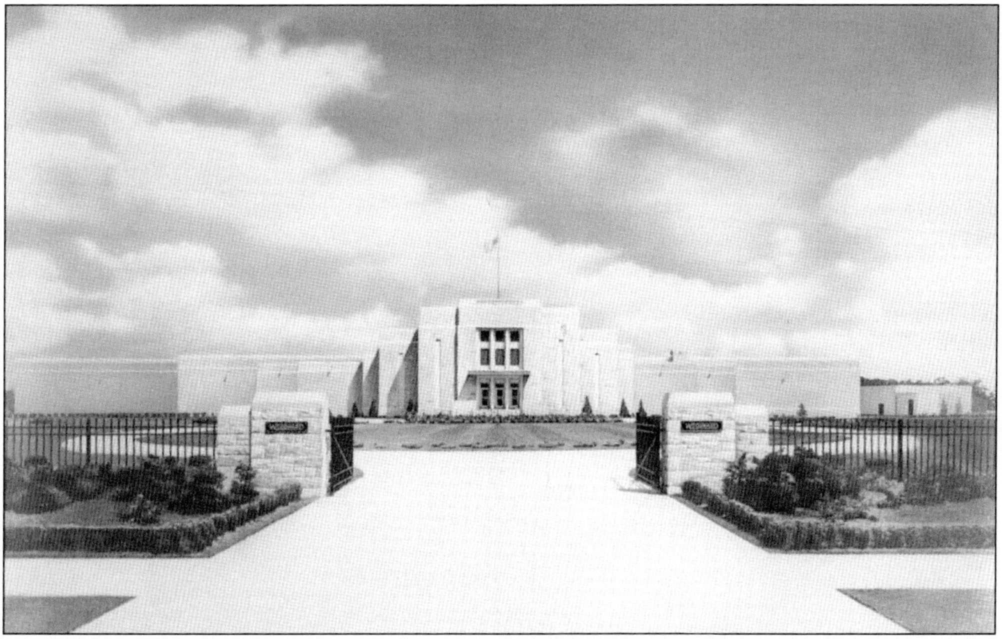

This vintage postcard shows Woodward Governor Company (now called Woodward, Inc.) in its early days. The company opened its Loves Park location at 5001 North Second Street in 1941. The postcard describes the building as a "modern, air-conditioned plant" that manufactures "hydraulic, water wheel, diesel, and aircraft governors." Below is a photograph of the first bonus party, which was held at the North Second Street location on October 9, 1941. Woodward Governor Company was founded in Rockford, Illinois, by Amos W. Woodward in 1870. His first patent—no. 103,813—was granted on May 31, 1870, for an "Improvement in Water-Governor." At the time, Woodward was working for N.C. Thompson Company in Rockford. (Above, courtesy of Nicole C. Lindsay; below, courtesy of Woodward, Inc.)

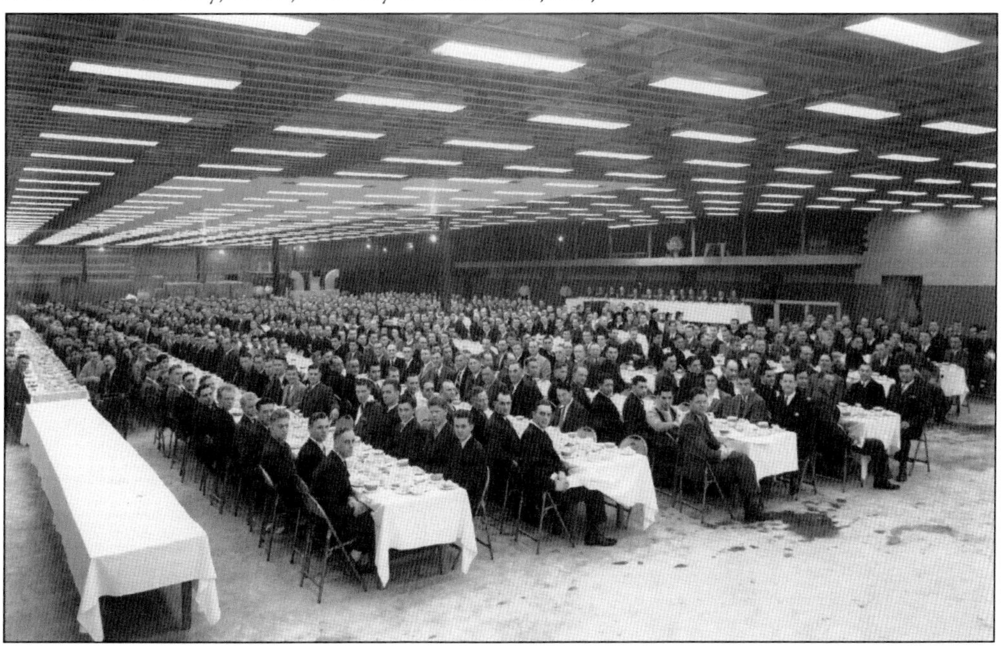

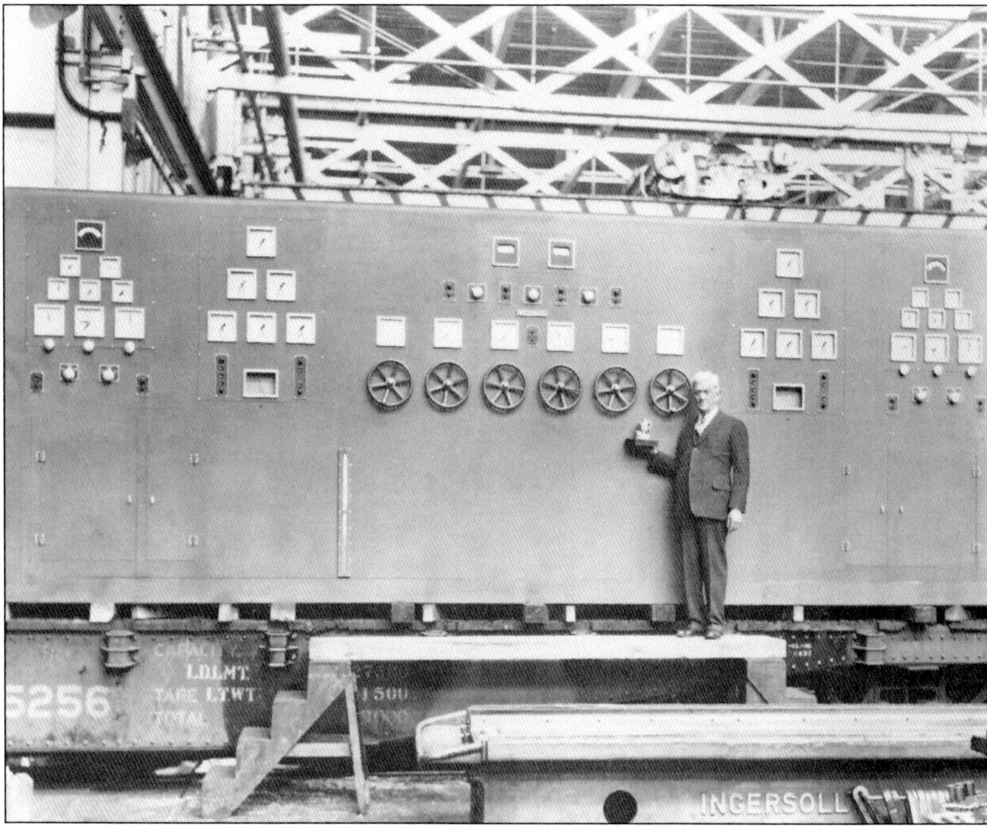

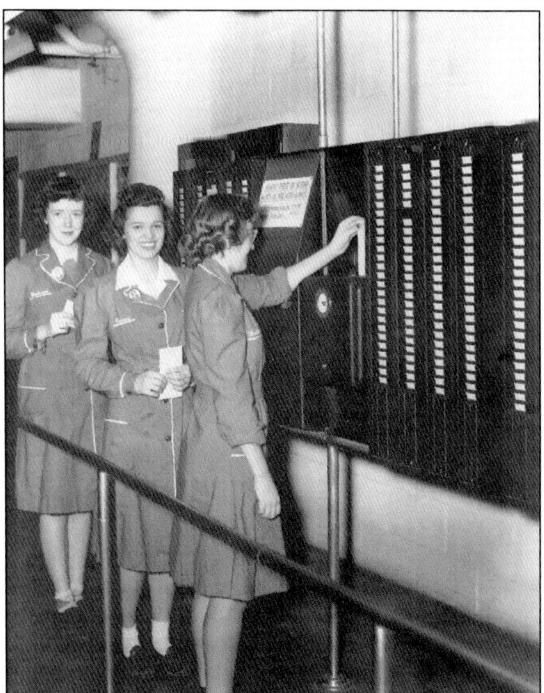

The 1937 photograph above shows Elmer Woodward, son of Amos Woodward. He is comparing the smallest and the largest Woodward governors. He holds the airplane propeller governor in his hand, and he is standing in front of the Bonneville Dam cabinet actuator. The photograph at left shows three unidentified Rockford College students punching their time cards in the fall of 1942. Rockford College students enrolled in a wartime work-study program at Woodward. With the men away at war, many women worked at Woodward in their absence. The sign next to the time clock reads: "Every piece of scrap hurts us and aids the Axis." (Both, courtesy of Woodward, Inc.)

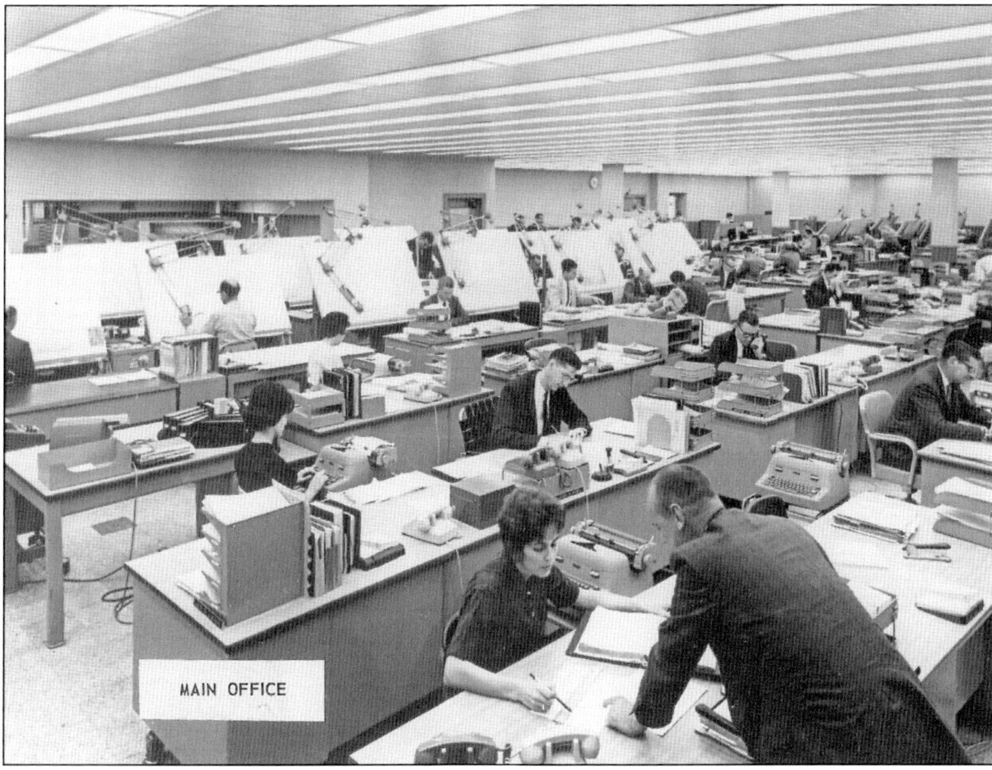

The main office at the Loves Park location of Woodward Governor Company is pictured above on November 18, 1964. Note the telephones, typewriters, and drawing-board lights. None of the office staff members are identified. The photograph below shows three unidentified individuals standing outside near the bell during one of Woodward's three Centennial Open Houses. This one was held on June 7, 1970. The actual centennial was celebrated on May 31, 1970, which was exactly 100 from the day Amos W. Woodward received his first patent. The festivities included a presentation of gifts from Woodward's three overseas plants, three open houses, and the making of a motion picture called *A Will and a Way*. (Both, courtesy of Woodward, Inc.)

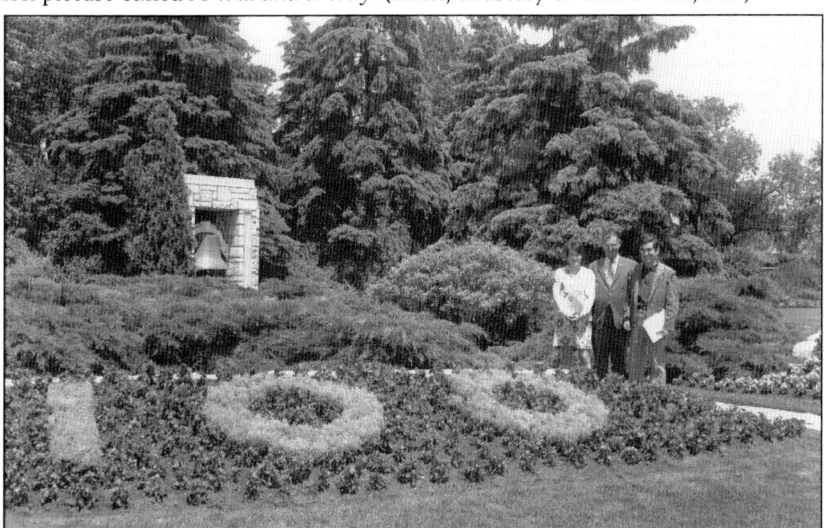

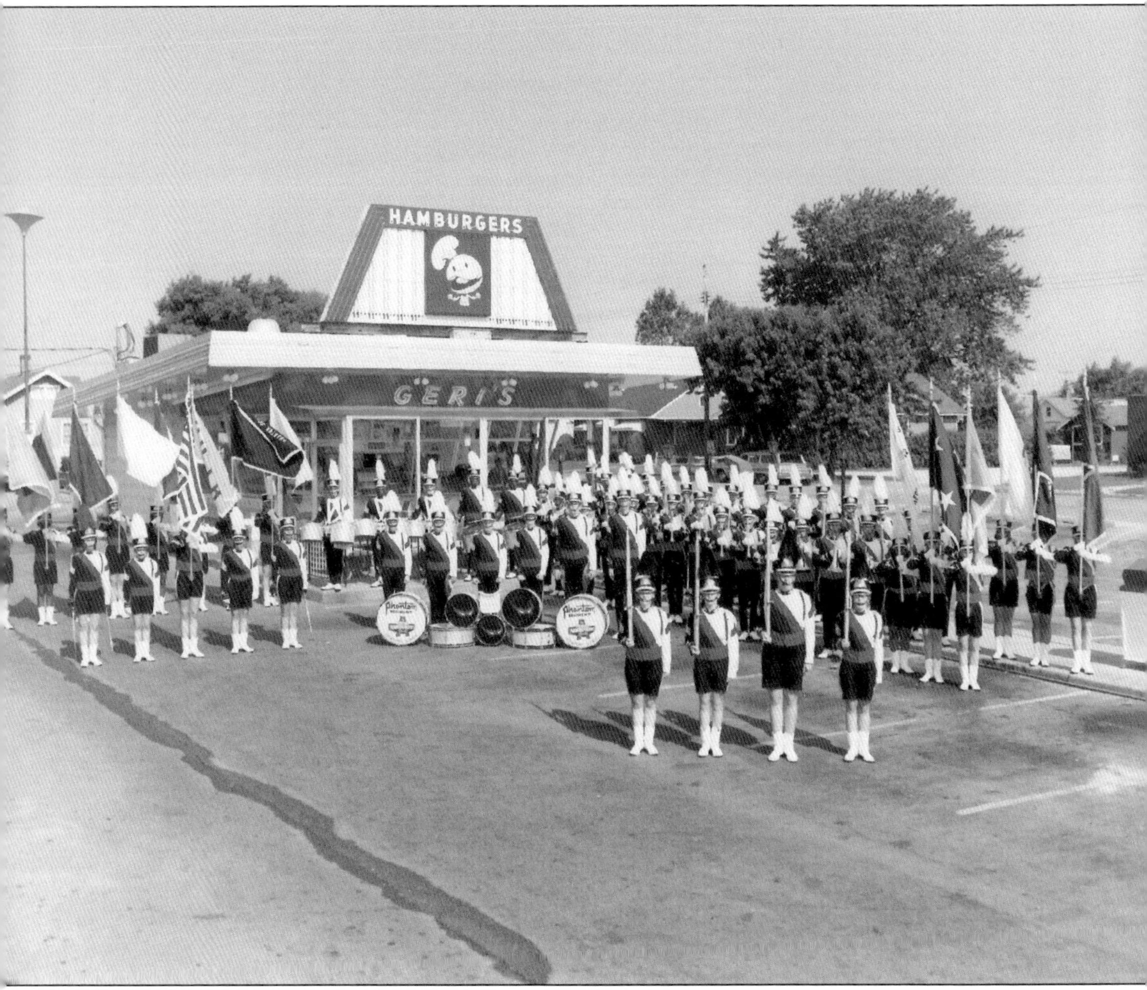

In this c. 1969 image, the Phantom Regiment poses in front of Geri's Hamburgers at 5518 North Second Street in Loves Park. The street in the background is Merrill Avenue. Geri's was a popular hamburger chain with locations in southern Wisconsin and northern Illinois. It started in 1962 and was modeled after the early McDonald's restaurants. The interior colors of most Geri's were red, white, and blue. The early drive-through style had very little in the way of seating, but later restaurants had interior seating and a more extensive menu. Geri's Corporation closed in 1981, but some Geri's remained open and operated independently. The last Geri's Hamburgers was located in Beloit, Wisconsin, and finally closed in 1999. The Phantom Regiment is a famous drum and bugle corps based in Rockford, Illinois. It was formed in 1956 and has performed all over the United States and internationally. (Courtesy of Midway Village Museum, Rockford, Illinois.)

Four

TRANSPORTATION

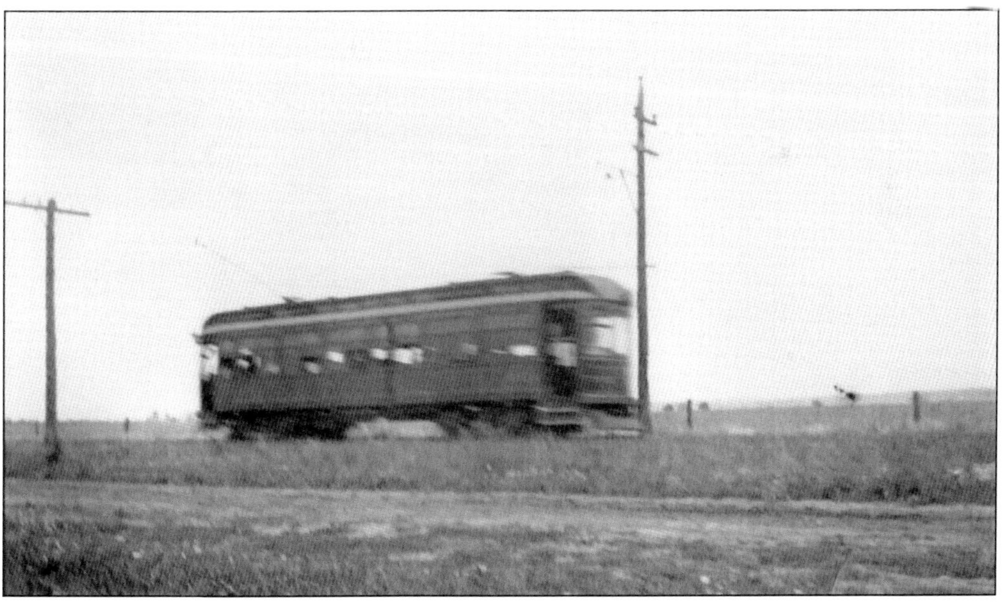

The Interurban rail line provided transportation for commuters between Rockford, Illinois, and Janesville, Wisconsin. There were stops in Rockford, Loves Park, Roscoe/Rockton, Beloit, and Janesville. The line ran from 1900 until the 1930s. This undated photograph shows an Interurban car in motion on the tracks near North Second Street in Loves Park.

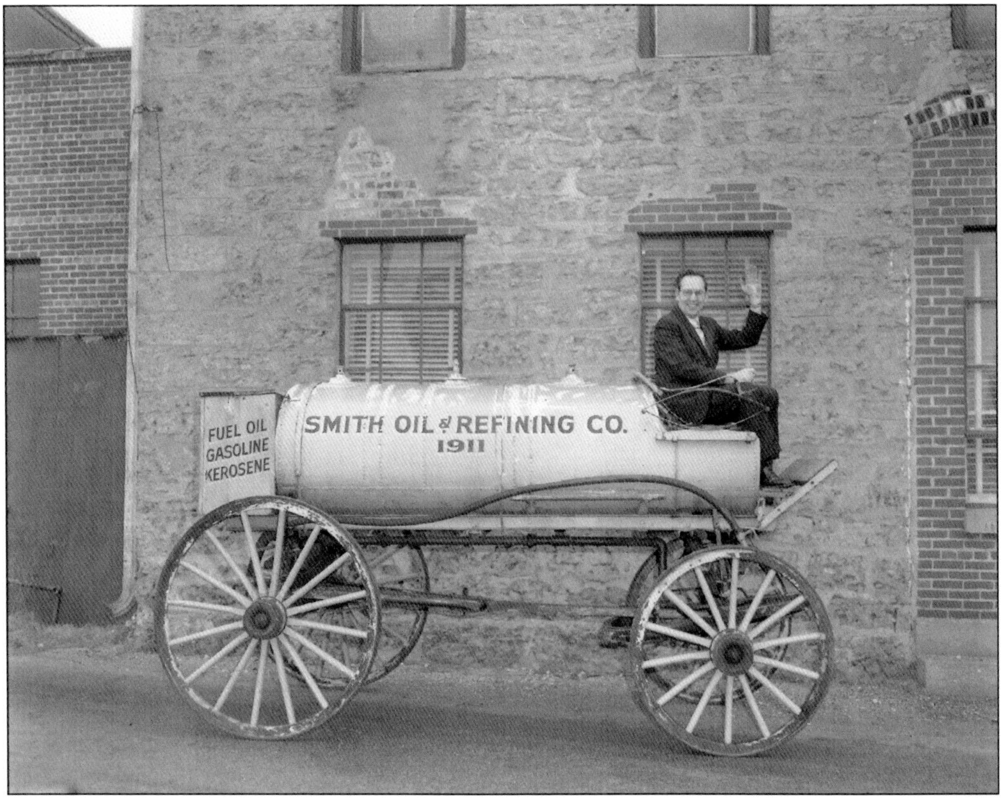

The man is unidentified, and the date of the photograph unknown, but what this is is a Smith Oil & Refining Company delivery wagon in Loves Park. The exact address is also not known. Smith Oil & Refining Company was founded in Rockford in 1911 by C.G. Smith. (Courtesy of Midway Village Museum, Rockford, Illinois.)

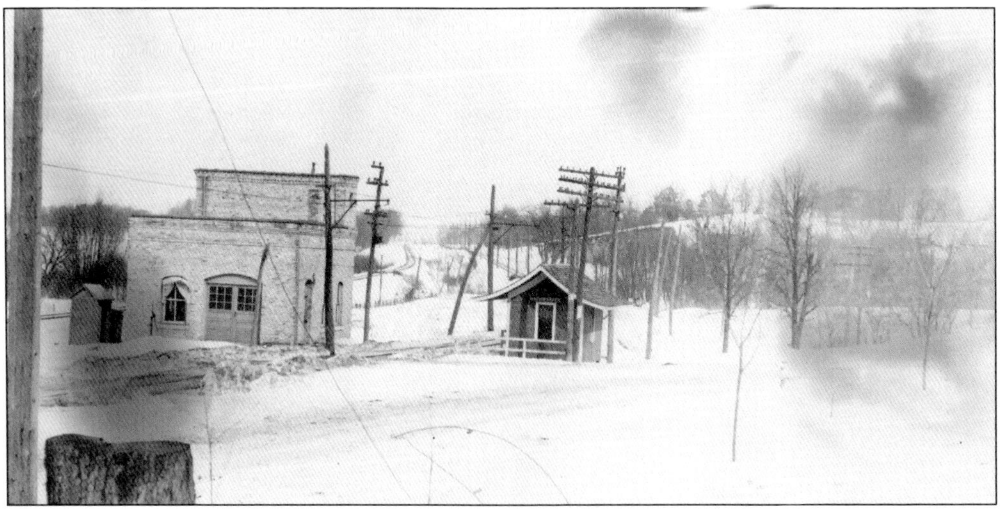
The area known as Blueberry Hill is just north of what is now the North Second Street cloverleaf and the Auburn Street Bridge. The two railways visible in this photograph belong to the Interurban and the Chicago & North Western. The brick building at left is an Interurban substation. The photograph is believed to have been taken between 1910 and 1919.

The top photograph shows the original home of Nathum C. Bement (see page 16), owner of Rock Valley Tractor Company; the middle photograph shows the Rock Valley Tractor Company factory at 418 Grand Avenue; and the bottom photograph shows the finished-tractor assembly area of the factory. The man in the undated bottom image is unidentified.

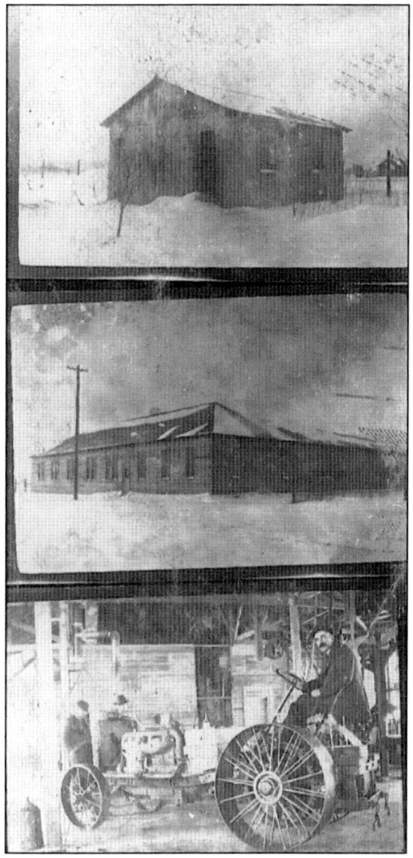

This undated photograph shows a Loves Park Fire Department truck. Roy E. York was appointed by mayor Homer E. Burton to be the city's first fire/police chief in 1947, and on September 29, 1947, the department officially became responsible for fires within the city limits. The city's own fire department was officially created on September 6, 1949.

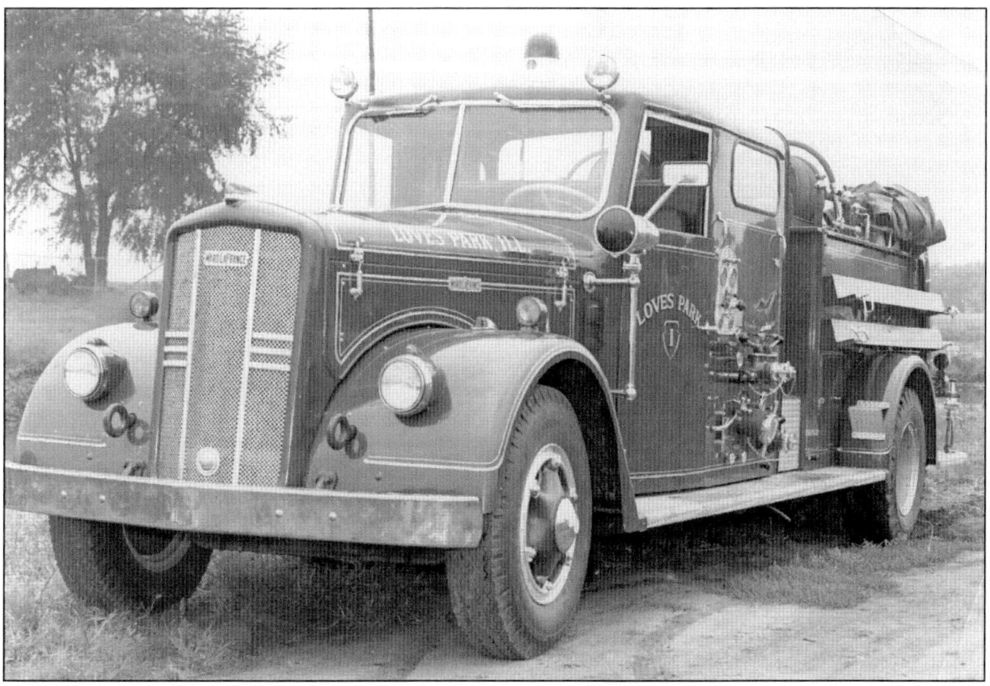

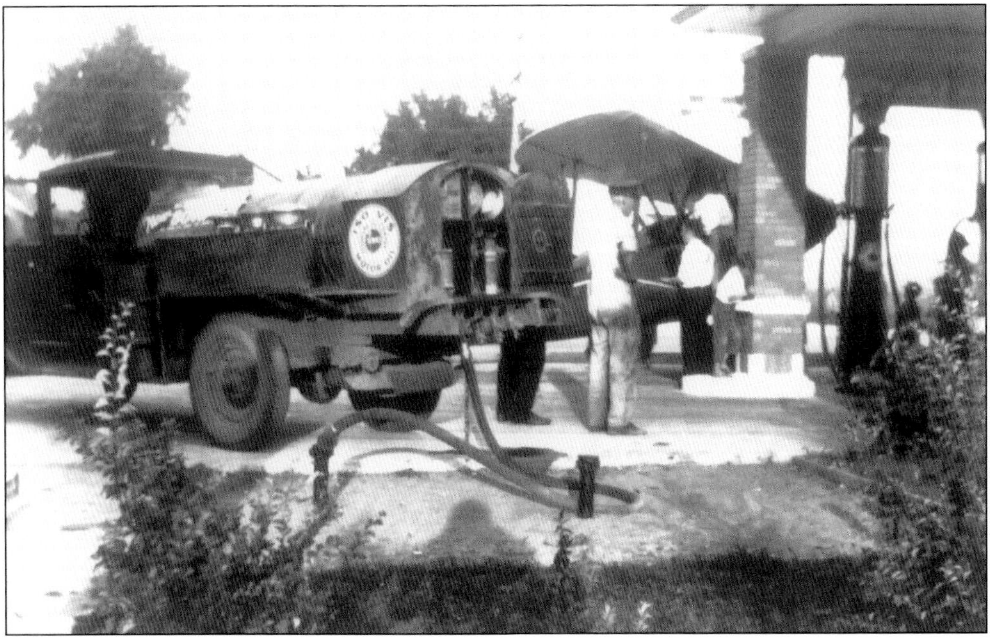

This airplane ran out of fuel at a convenient location. It was able to land in a field near the intersection of North Second Street and Riverside Boulevard and gas up at the Standard Oil Station at 6104 North Second Street, which was just across the road. The photograph is from around 1930, when Zenor Jones managed the station. Standing at the rear and wearing a hat, the driver of the oil truck is identified as "Cowboy" Alden.

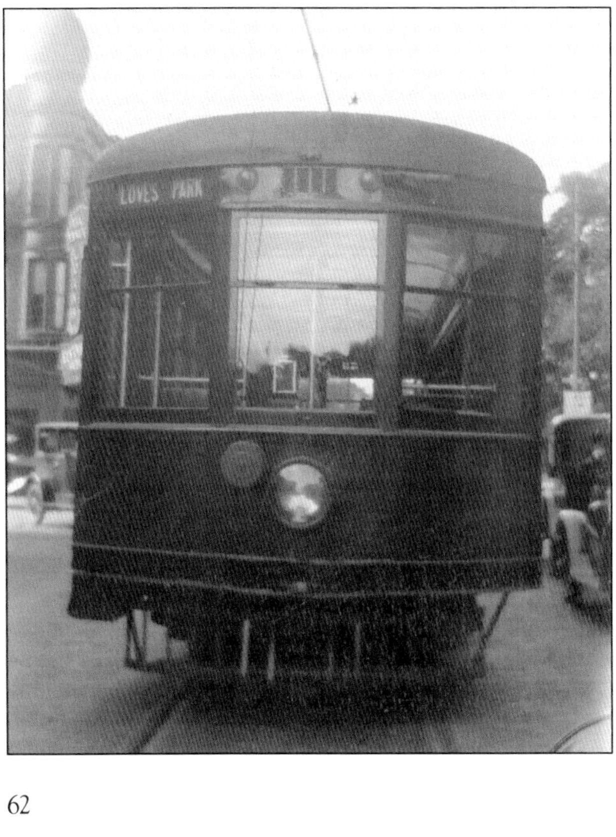

This 1934 photograph shows a streetcar in downtown Rockford at the corner of State Street and Church Street. It is not known whether the streetcar was arriving or departing for Loves Park, but it is clearly the Loves Park car (as indicated by the sign in the top corner of the front window). (Courtesy of Brian Landis.)

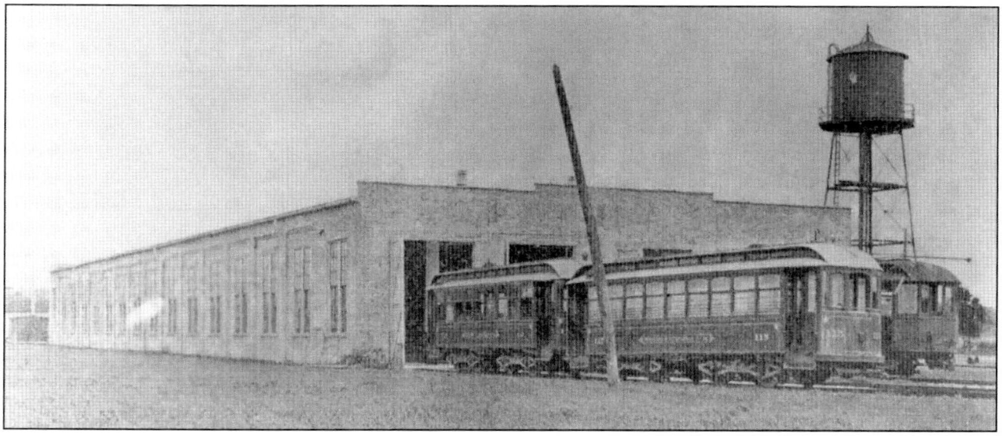

The Interurban north repair shop, which was located on the grounds of what is now Woodward, Inc. at 5001 North Second Street, is shown in this undated photograph. Train No. 113 is visible on the track at left. There was also another Interurban repair shop located in Rockford at the intersection of First Avenue and Kishwaukee Street.

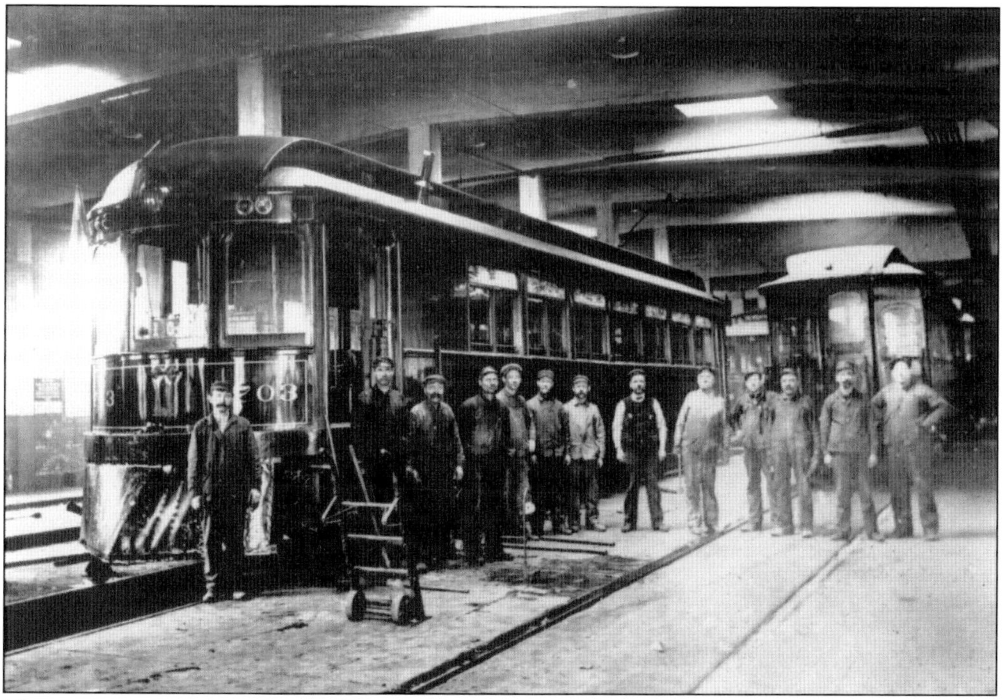

There is some speculation as to where this photograph was taken, but it is believed to be an interior view of the work crew at the Interurban north repair shop, which was at 5001 North Second Street. The photograph shows railcar No. 703 and was taken between 1911 and 1930.

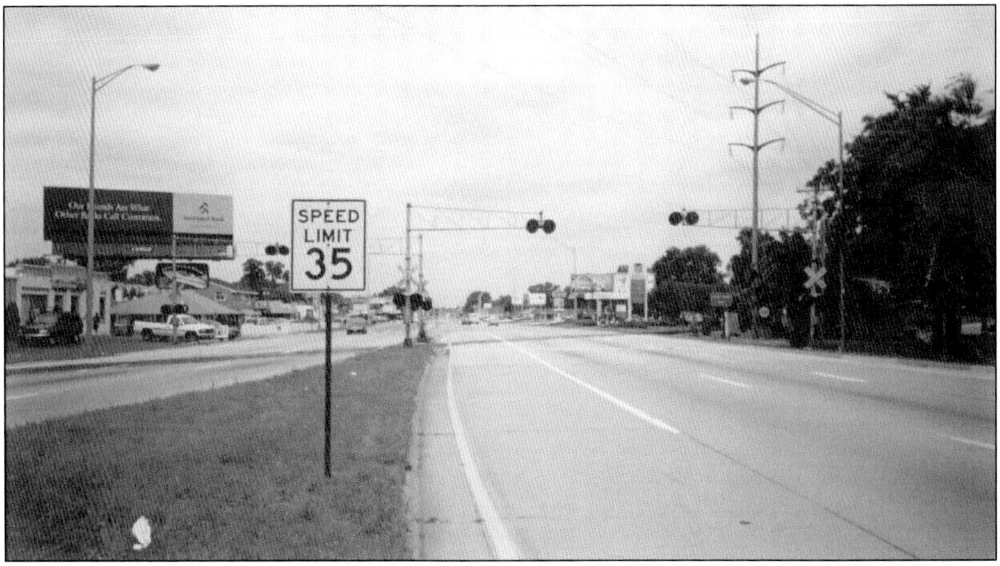

Compare this modern photograph of the area formerly known as Snow's Crossing to the photograph taken between 1915 and 1920 (see page 13). One set of railway tracks is still visible at far right, but the area, looking north on North Second Street, is now paved and completely developed. (Courtesy of Brian Landis.)

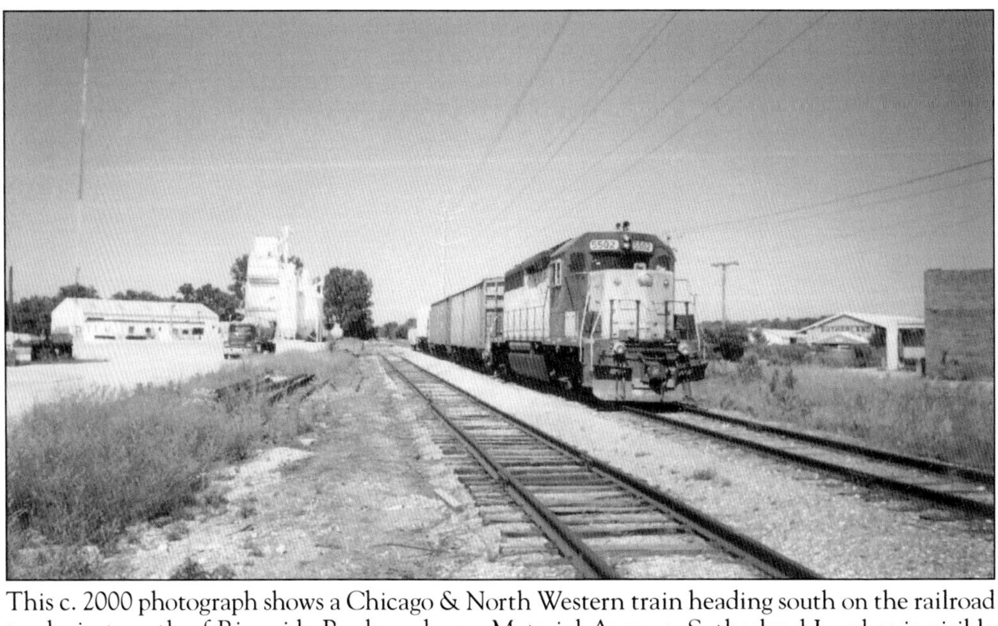

This c. 2000 photograph shows a Chicago & North Western train heading south on the railroad tracks just north of Riverside Boulevard near Material Avenue. Sutherland Lumber is visible at right, and Meyer Ready Mix is on the left. Both businesses are now closed. (Courtesy of Brian Landis.)

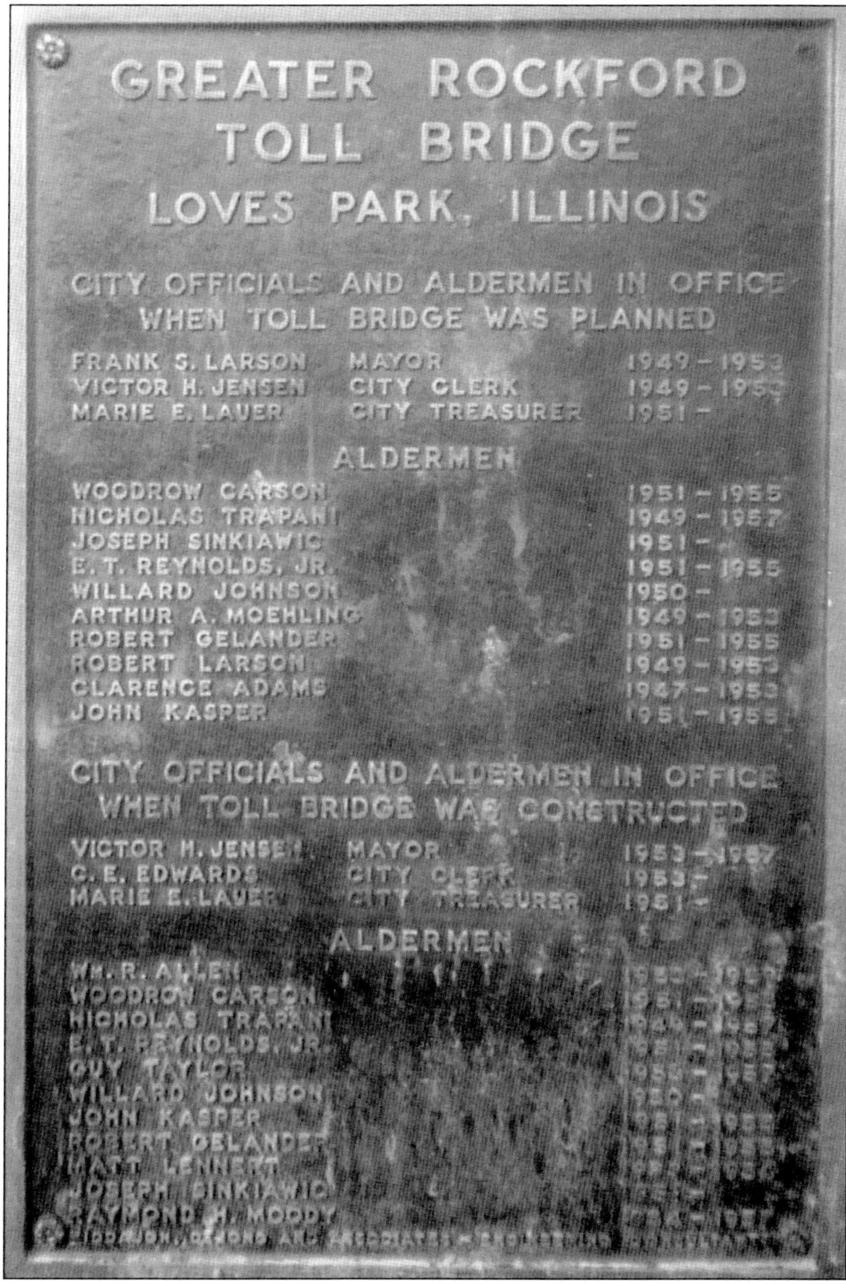

This plaque adorned the Loves Park (Riverside) Toll Bridge. Work on the bridge began in mid-June 1953. The construction contract for $636,771 was awarded to Shappert Engineering of Belvidere, Illinois. The plan was to collect tolls through 1994 in order to pay for the bonds. Construction went rather smoothly, and the bridge opened on August 9, 1954. The first driver to pay a toll was Mabel (Mrs. Earl L.) Kaney, of 620 Merrill Avenue, who drove across at 6:00 a.m. on Wednesday, August 11, 1954. Tolls were priced as follows: 5¢ for pedestrians, 10¢ for passenger cars, 15¢ for light and medium trucks, and 25¢ for heavy trailer trucks and buses. The city celebrated the opening of the bridge with an event that included fireworks, a motorcade, and an official ribbon-cutting. Although there were many skeptics, the bridge turned out to be a great success.

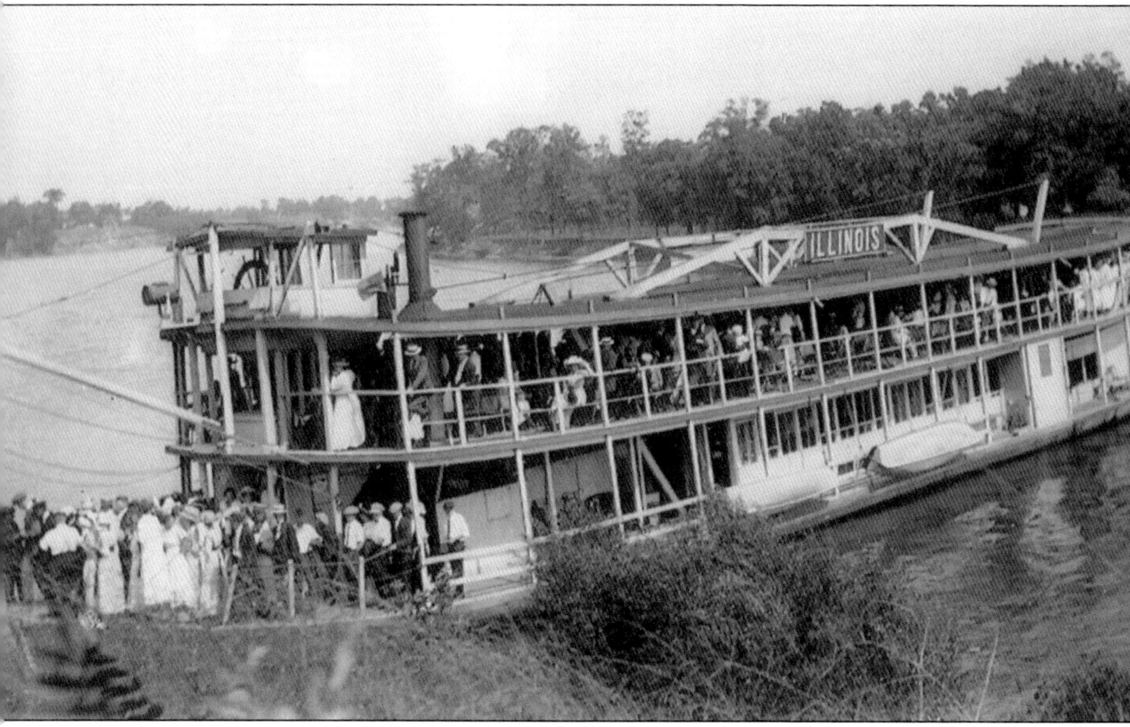

The steamship *Illinois*, shown in this c. 1912 photograph, was built around 1900 and cruised the Rock River, stopping at various points in and around Rockford and Loves Park. The ship was 125 feet long and 26 feet at the beam. Passengers could stroll along either of the ship's two open-air decks, and popular music was played so passengers could dance as well. The ship often picked up people at the Mulberry Street dock in downtown Rockford and took them to Harlem Park, a popular amusement park across the river from Loves Park. Sometimes, it stopped at the area now known as Martin Park in Loves Park. It was said that the ship could hold as many as 1,000 people. The *Illinois* was destroyed by a fire on March 1, 1924.

Five

EDUCATION

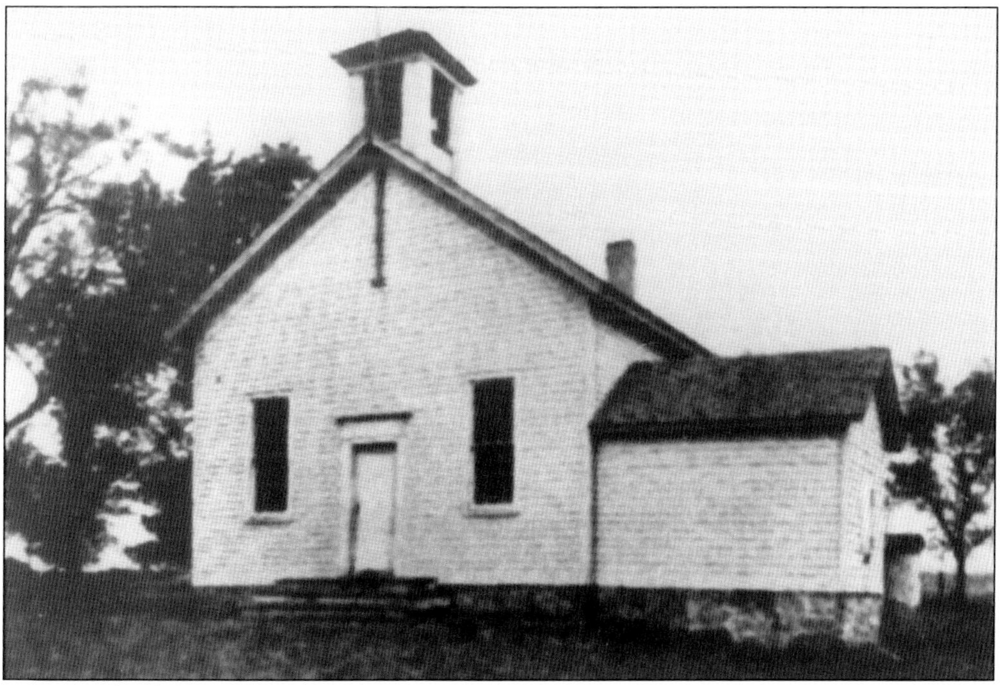

Lovejoy School, known as District 49, was a one-room schoolhouse built in Harlem Township. It was named after Andrew James Lovejoy III, who was born in the township on December 5, 1845. Lovejoy died in 1919. Lovejoy School was abandoned when the Harlem Consolidated School District was founded in April 1910.

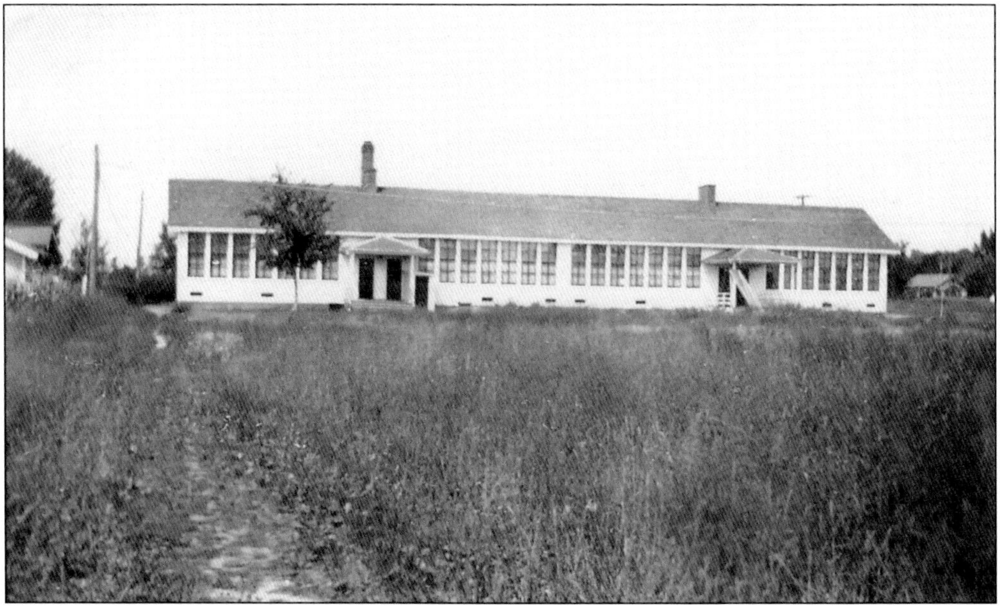

The Loves Park Grade School annex on River Park Road is shown above. Not only was the River Park Road location used as a school, but in 1924, Grace Lutheran Church held services there while the congregation's church was being constructed at 343 Grand Avenue. Below is a photograph of a first-grade class in front of the River Park Road school. The teacher is Miss Bordwell, and the only identified student is Margaret Timmis, who is farthest to the right in the first row. The original grade school was located at 344 Grand Avenue. On March 6, 1926, a new brick Loves Park Grade School was opened at that location. (Above, courtesy of Gayle Englof; below, courtesy of Mary Timmis Miller.)

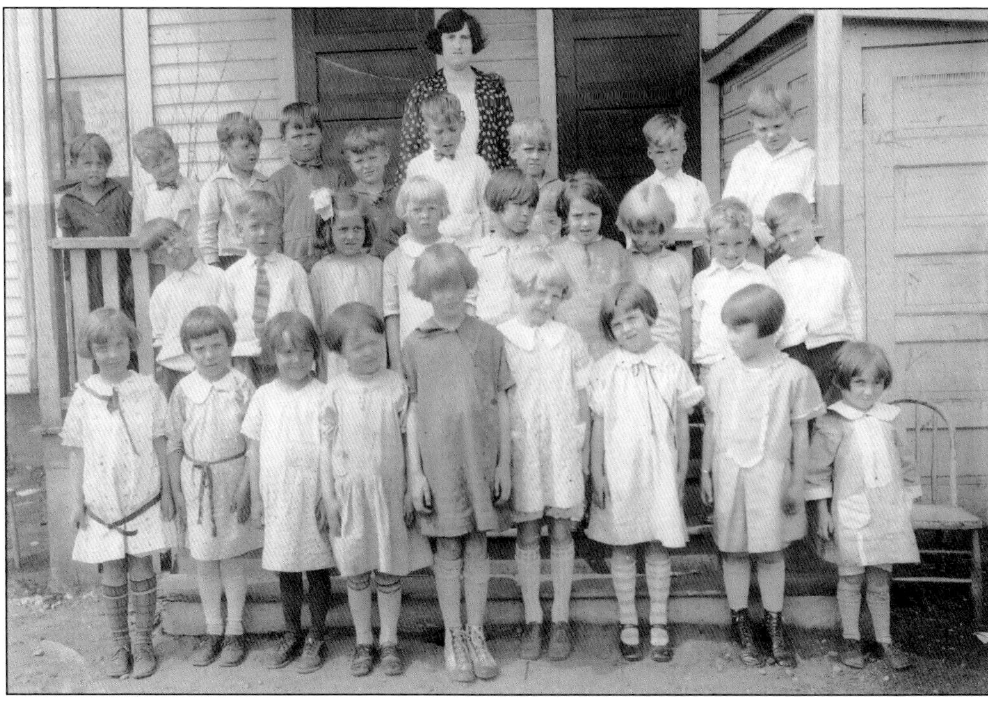

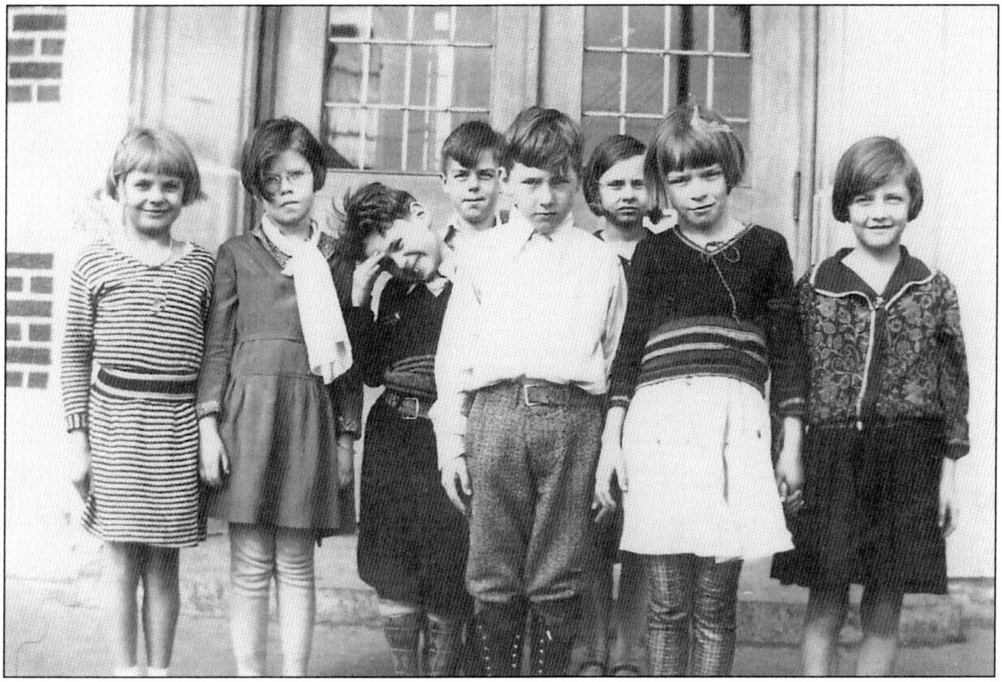

A group of schoolchildren is pictured above in front of the Loves Park Grade School in the late 1920s. They are, from left to right, Delores Olson, unidentified, Robert Hartman (head tilted), unidentified, unidentified, Carol Brendt, Mary Timmis, and Nellie Olson. Below, a group of students poses for a picture during a music festival called "Pirates and Principals." None of the individuals are identified, and the exact date is illegible, but it was the month of May sometime in the 1930s; the school often held plays and music festivals in May and celebrated May Day with outdoor activities. (Both, courtesy of Gayle Englof.)

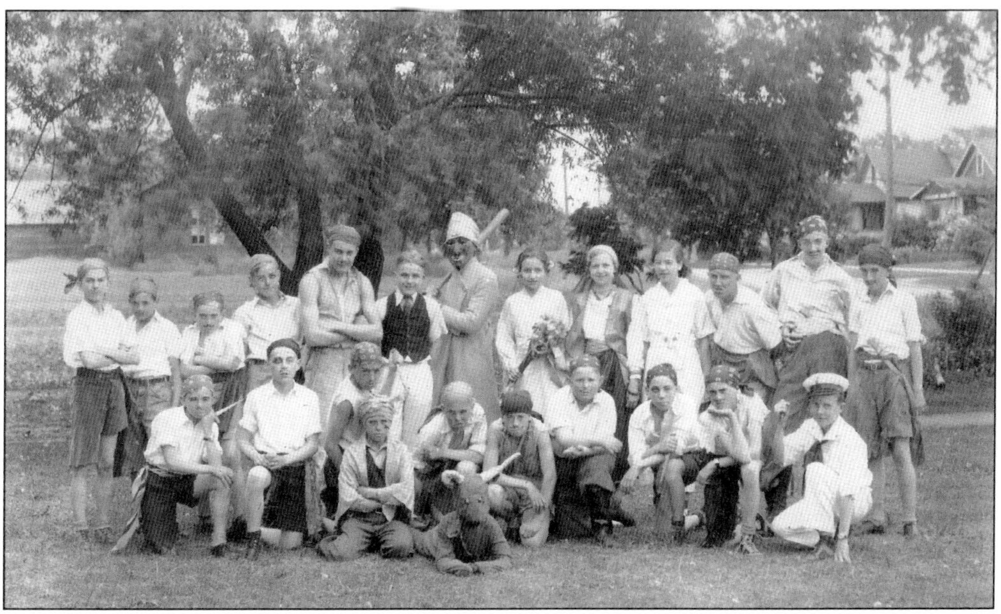

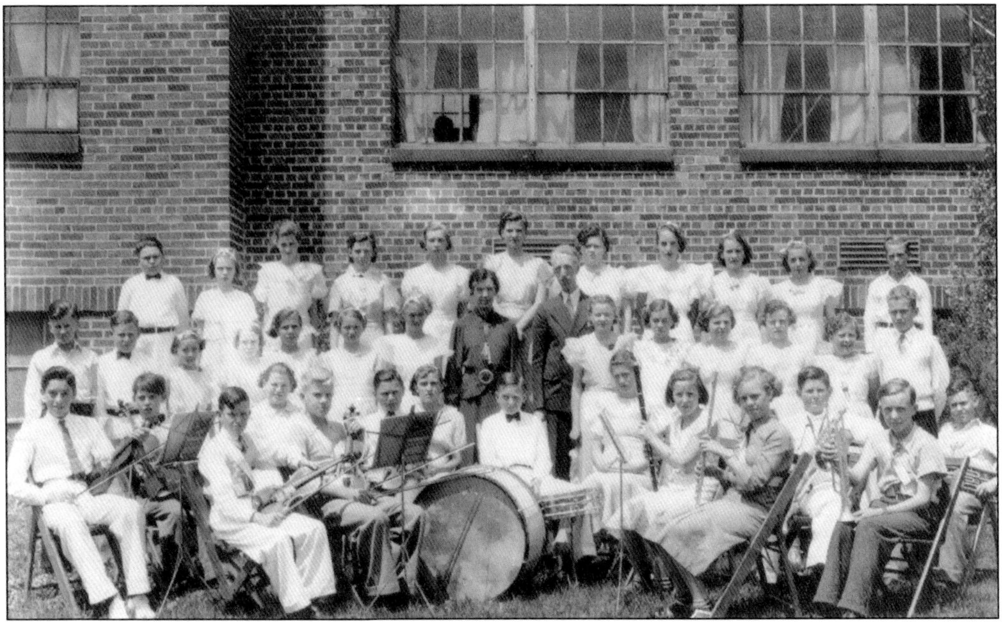

In the 1936 image above, the Loves Park School Orchestra and Glee Club pose for a picture in front of the school at 344 Grand Avenue. The only identified student is Ray Johnson, who is third from right in the first row. Below, the eighth-grade class poses for a graduation picture in front of the same school on May 20, 1937. Principal Russel Hovey is the man wearing a suit at far left in the photograph. Hovey later became superintendent of the Harlem School District and also ran for city clerk, but he was defeated by Charles E. "Speed" Edwards. The only students identified in the image below are Mary Timmis, who is fifth from left in the second row, and Helen Hull, who is ninth from left in the second row. (Above courtesy of Gayle Englof; below, courtesy of Mary Timmis Miller.)

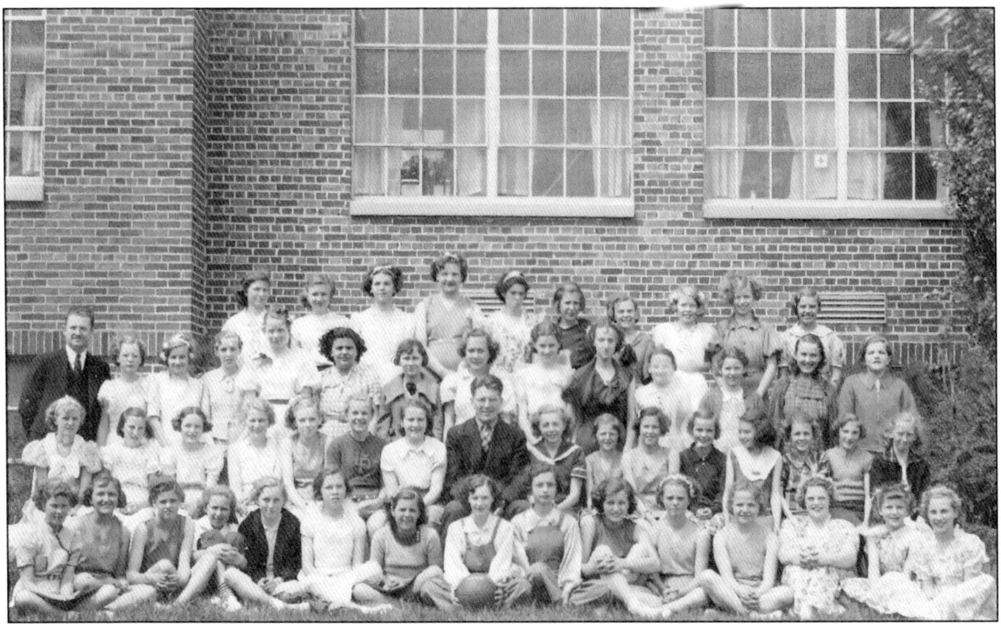

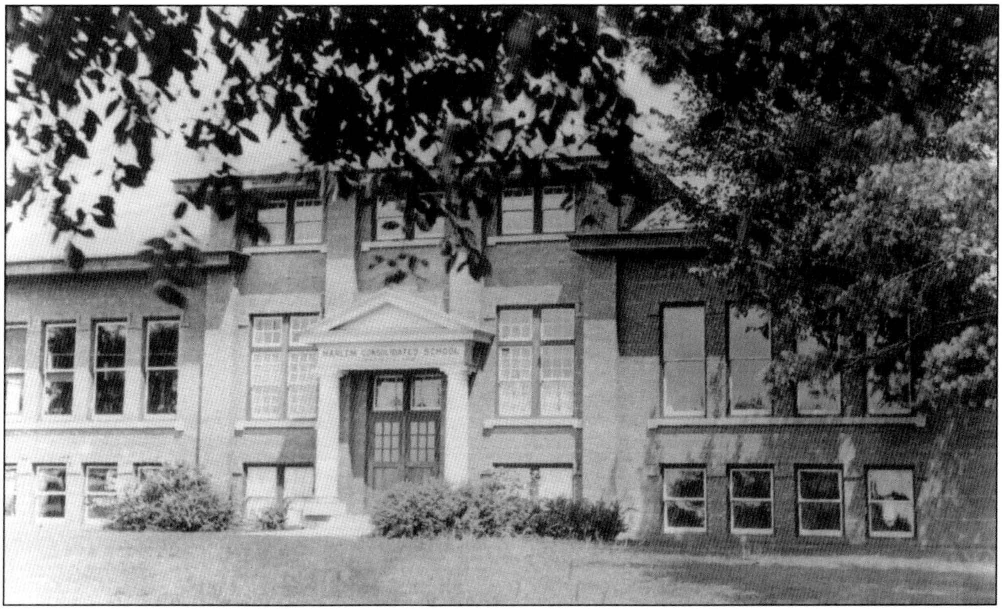

The c. 1915 image above shows a front exterior view of the Harlem Consolidated School, which was located at the intersection of Harlem Road and North Second Street—the original site of the Free Soil School. The Harlem Consolidated School building was completed on March 6, 1911, and dedicated on April 26, 1916. It consolidated four districts—Lovejoy (District 49), Bruner (District 52), Free Soil (District 56), and Union (District 61). The floor plan of the school (below) shows how it was designed. It was built to include "high ceilings with plenty of light." The basement contained restrooms, a home economics room, and laboratories. The main floor had four classrooms, a central hall, cloakrooms, a principal's office, and teachers' lockers. The attic was used as a gymnasium.

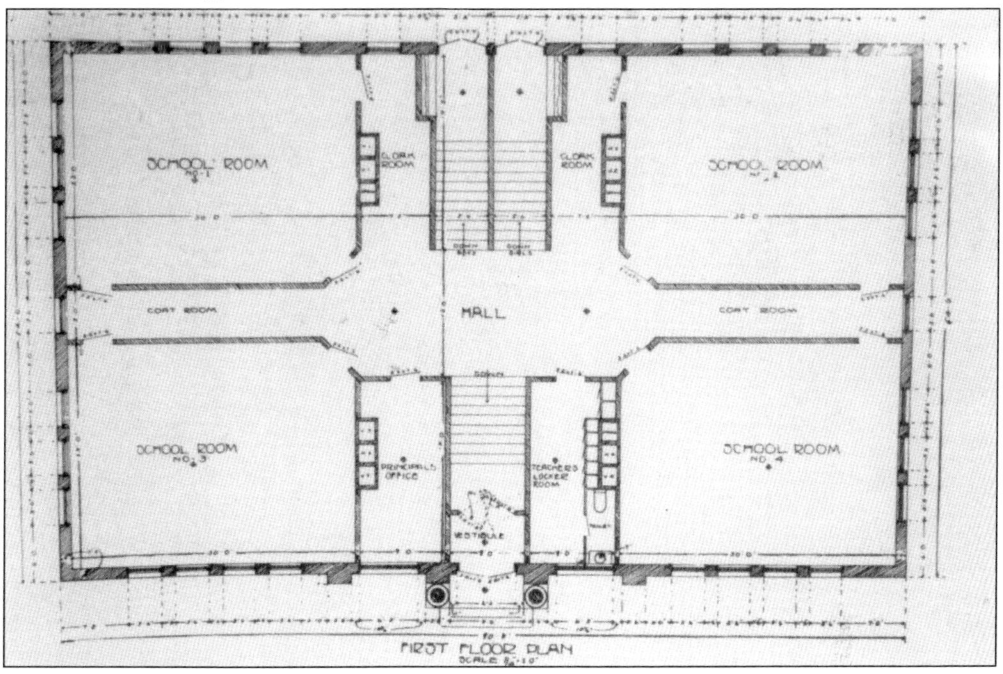

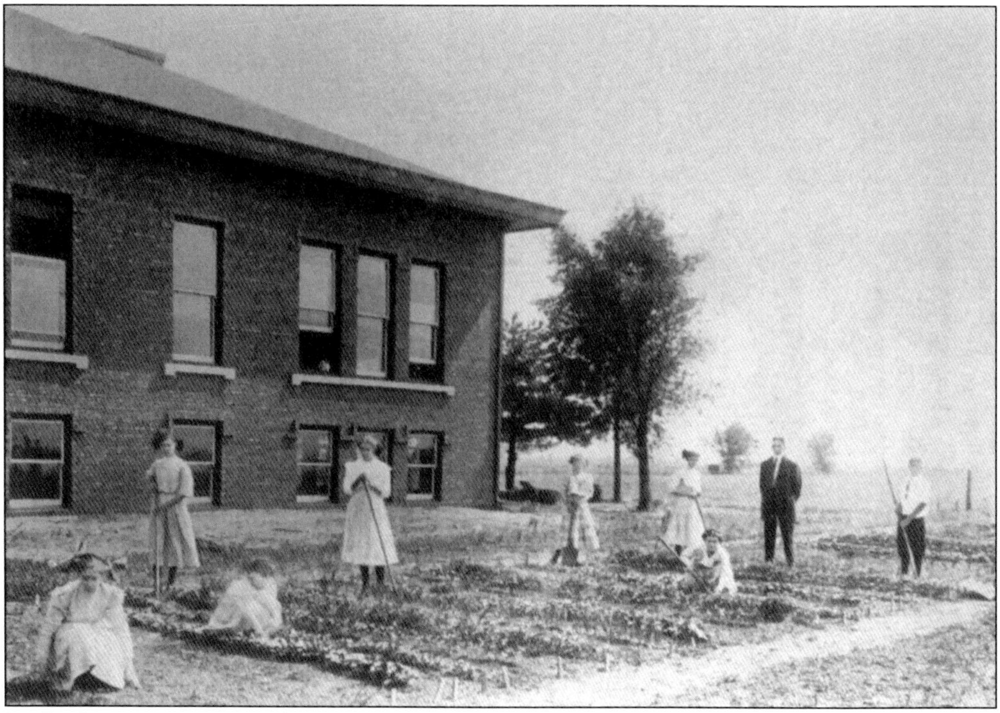

In the June 1911 picture above, a teacher oversees students working in the garden at Harlem Consolidated School. The garden was used as an outdoor, hands-on classroom for the agricultural classes. In the 1913 image below, the Harlem Consolidated School Band poses in front of the school. The band members are unidentified. In this era, the band held a monthly supper and concert event for the community; residents could come and have dinner while listening to the band perform various pieces. The first HCS band was organized during the summer of 1911.

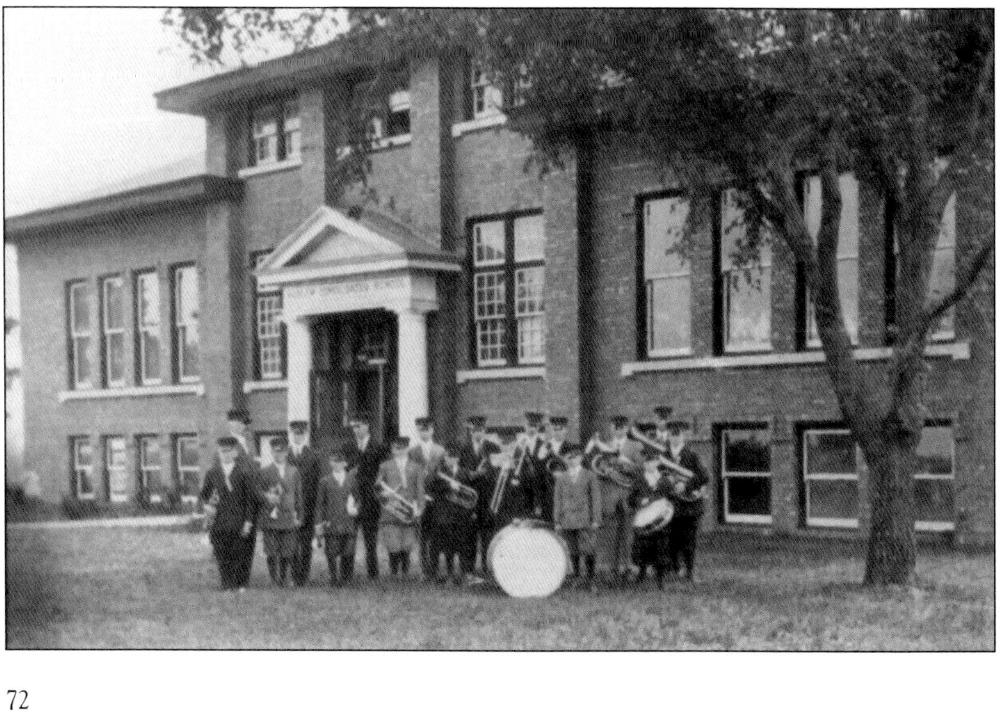

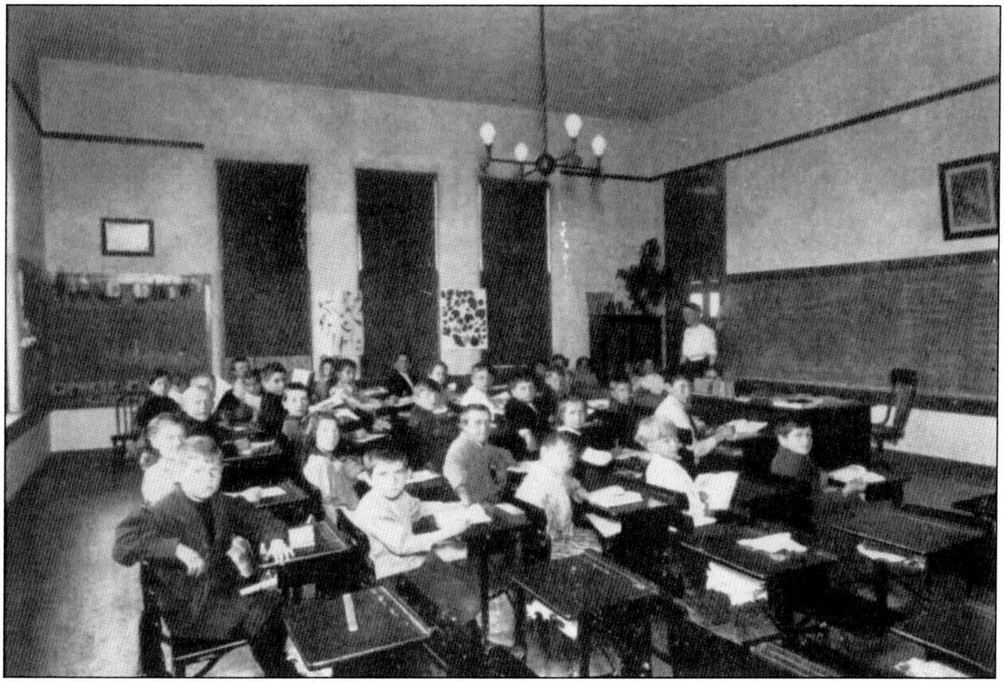

The primary room of the Harlem Consolidated School is shown in the undated image above. At the back of the room is the teacher, Bessie Wier, who was one of two teachers at the school when it was dedicated in 1916. The principal at that time was C.C. Burns, and the other teacher was B. Fruit. Wier was a graduate of Central Illinois State in Normal, Illinois. Note the gasoline lights that were used in the building. The students are unidentified. The photograph below shows a race being held on the grounds of the school in 1923. None of the racers or spectators are identified.

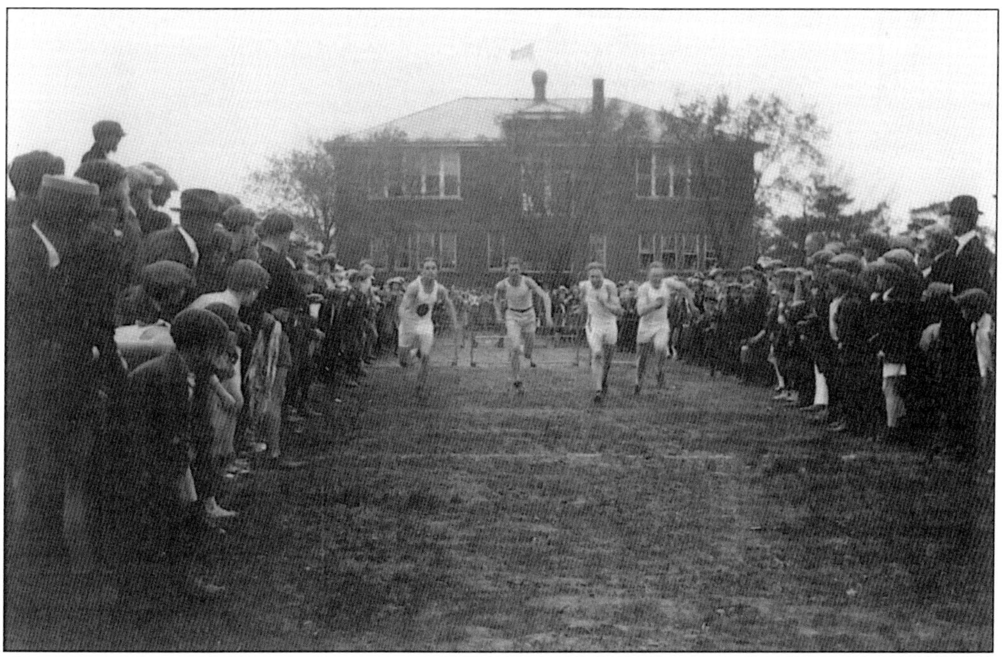

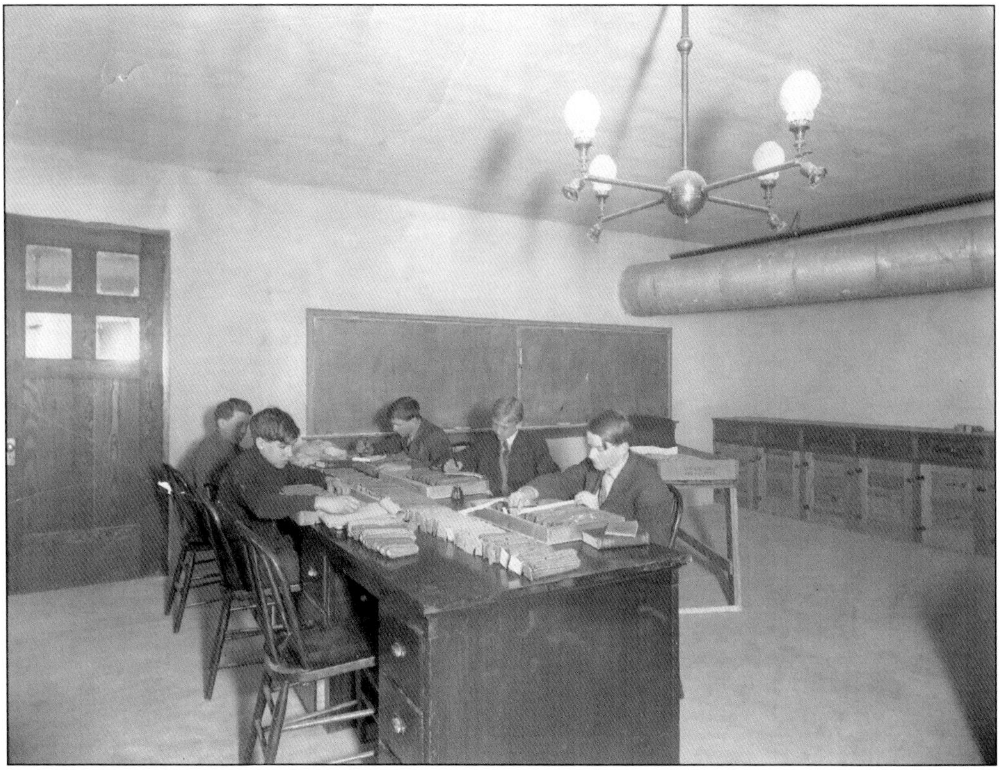

The c. 1913 photograph above shows a group of five students testing and judging corn in the Agriculture Lab at Harlem Consolidated School. The students are, clockwise from left, Glenn Wehmeyer, William "Bill" Mullone, Wilbur Shephard, Irving Pearson, and unidentified. The 1912 photograph below shows the school's chemical lab; the students are unidentified. The lab had recently added a Babcock milk tester so the students could conduct tests using various cows. The school noted that the previous summer, approximately $300 worth of equipment was added to the chemical lab, which would allow for more tests to be done.

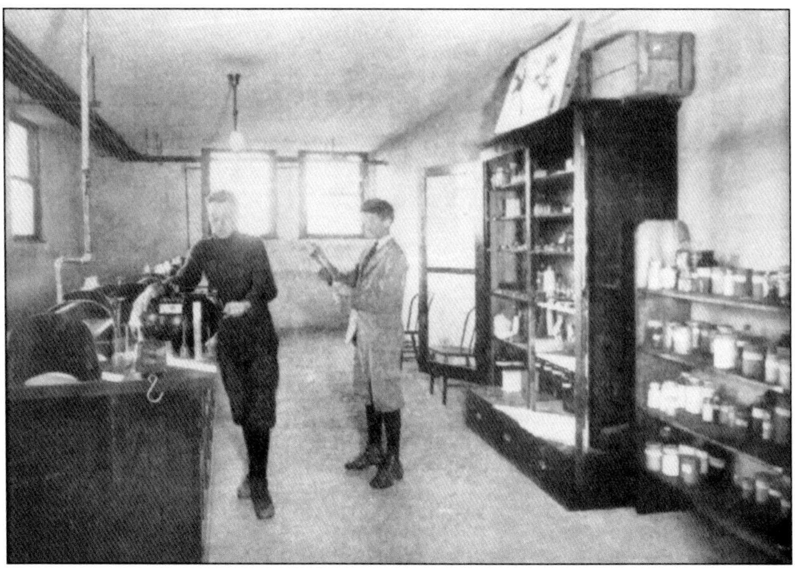

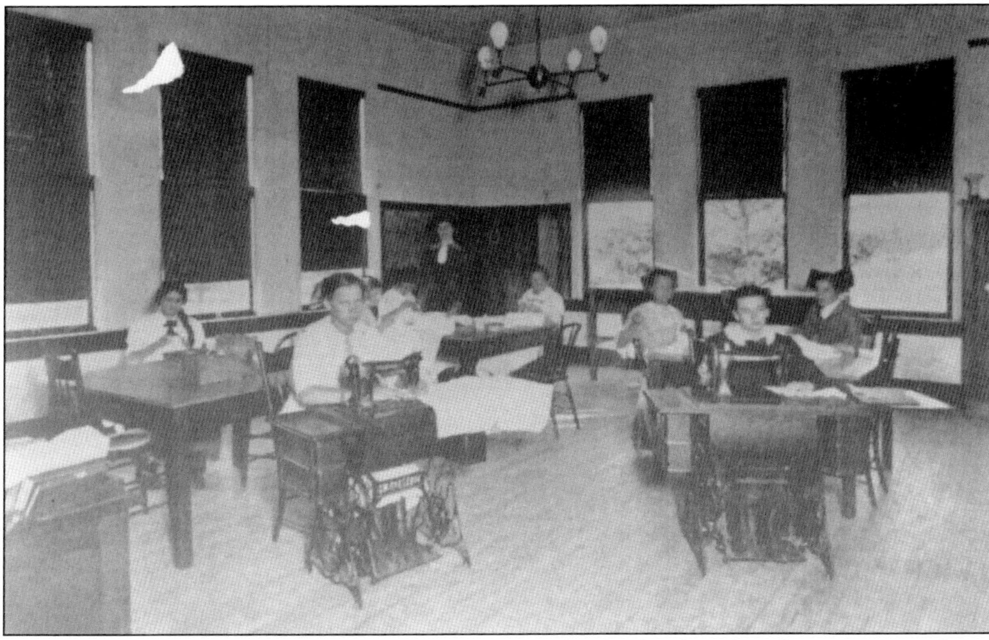

Students in a domestic science class at Harlem Consolidated School work at their sewing machines and tables in the undated photograph above. Neither the teacher nor any of the students is identified. In the c. 1912 image below, clothing sewn by the domestic science class is displayed around the classroom. The students are unidentified. Domestic science classes included instruction in both cooking and sewing. Other classes that were part of the four-year high school curriculum in the early 1900s included agrology (a type of soil science dealing with growing crops), biology, chemistry, mechanical drawing, manual training (physical education), and physics.

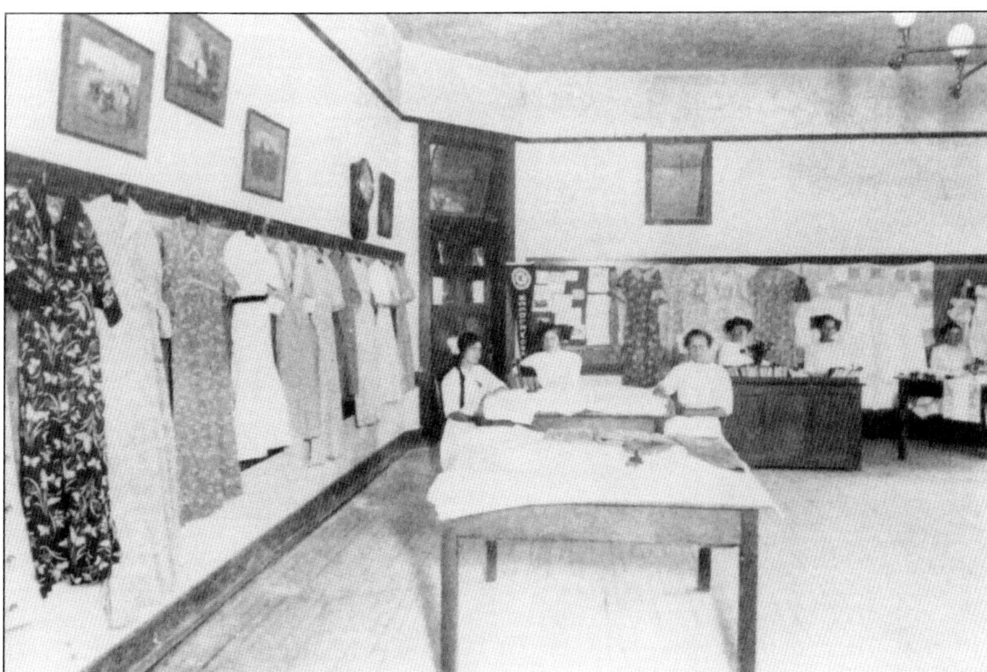

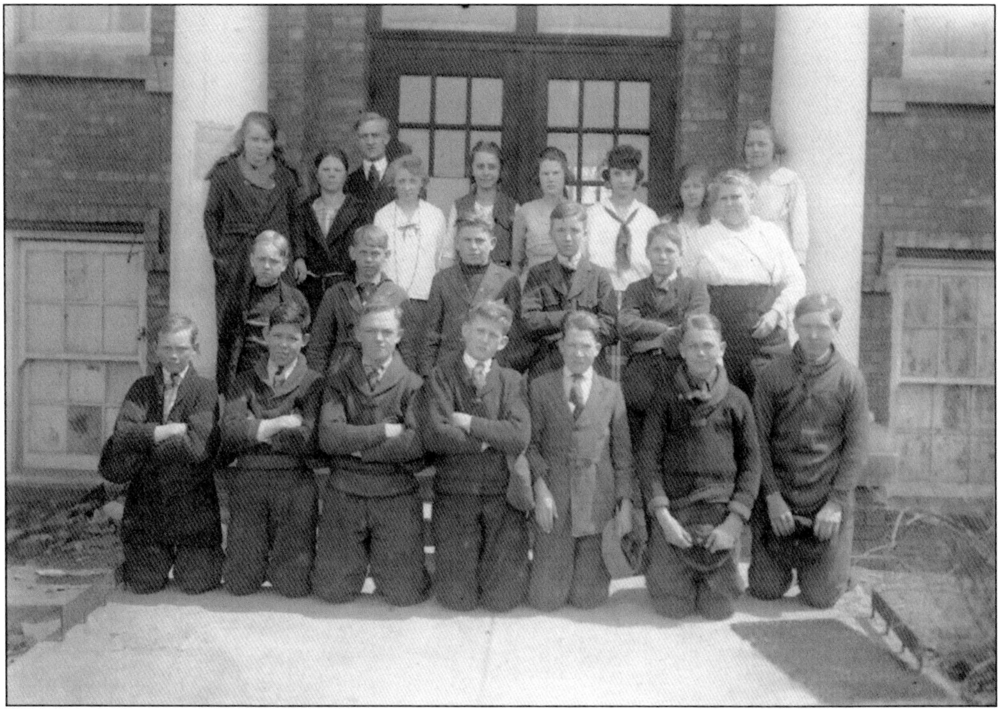

In the 1920 image above, the eighth-grade class at Harlem Consolidated School poses on the front steps. The only individuals identified are William "Bill" Burkman (far left in the first row), Loyal Anderson (third from left in the first row), Fred Collins (third from right in the first row), and Robert E. Burden (far right in the first row). As of 2012, Burkman was 105 years old and still living in the area. The 1911 picture below shows principal C.C. Burns practicing with the boys' basketball team in the attic of the school. The boys are unidentified. The girls' basketball team also practiced in the attic and was supervised by female teachers.

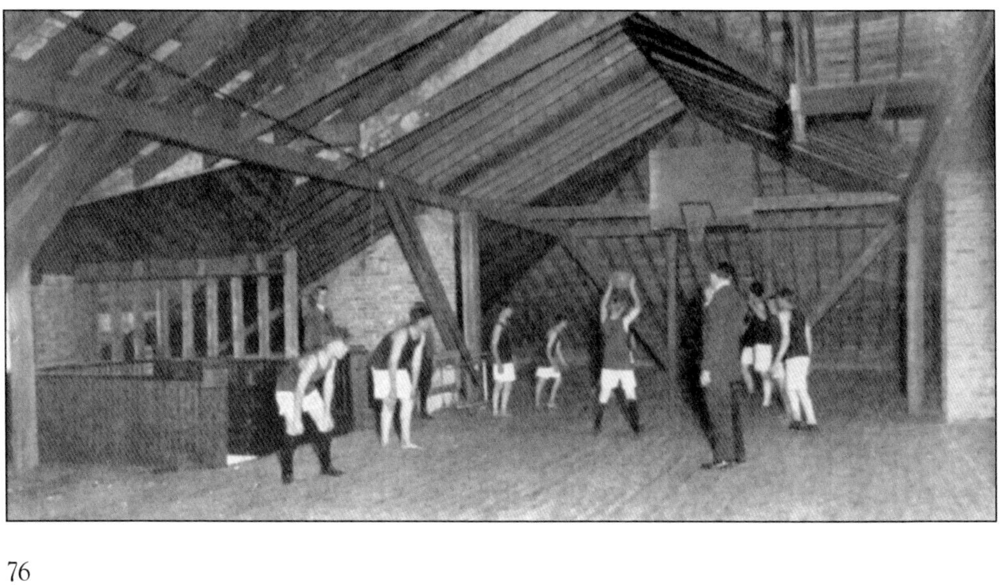

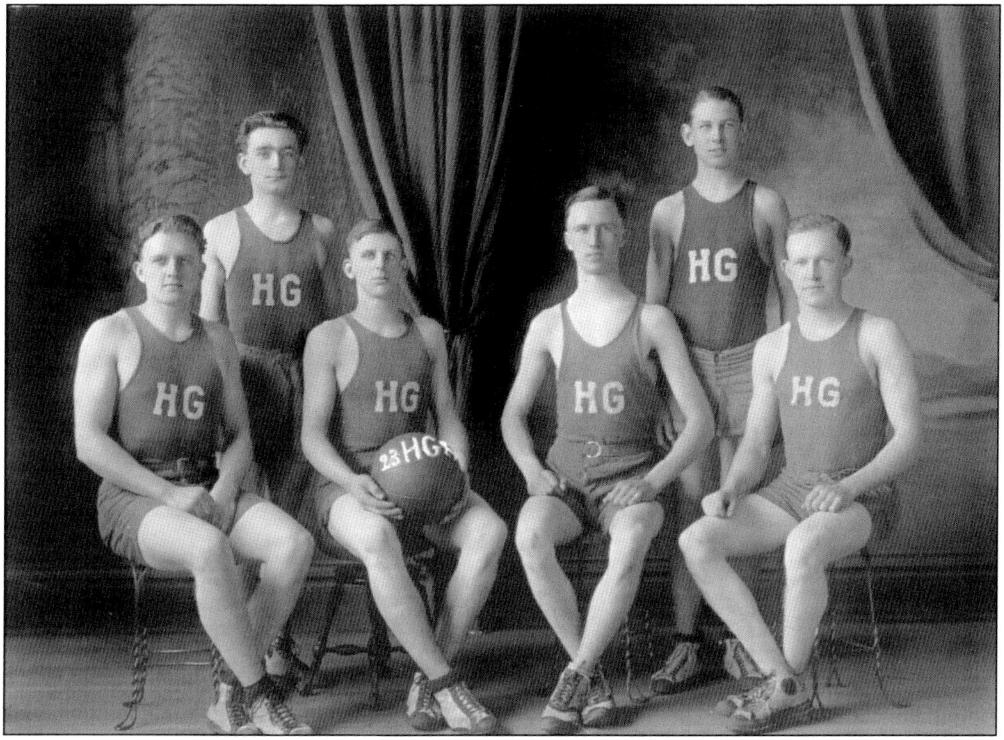

The photograph above shows the 1923 Harlem boys' basketball team. The only identified players are Ralph Schoonmaker (far left in the first row), and David Schoonmaker (far right in the first row). The 1914 photograph at right is of the first girls' basketball team at Harlem Consolidated School. Pictured are, from left to right, (first row) Freda Larson, Frances Miller, and Bess McFarland; (second row) Nell Conklin and Irene TenEyck. Other sports offered at HCS included track, baseball, and—later—football.

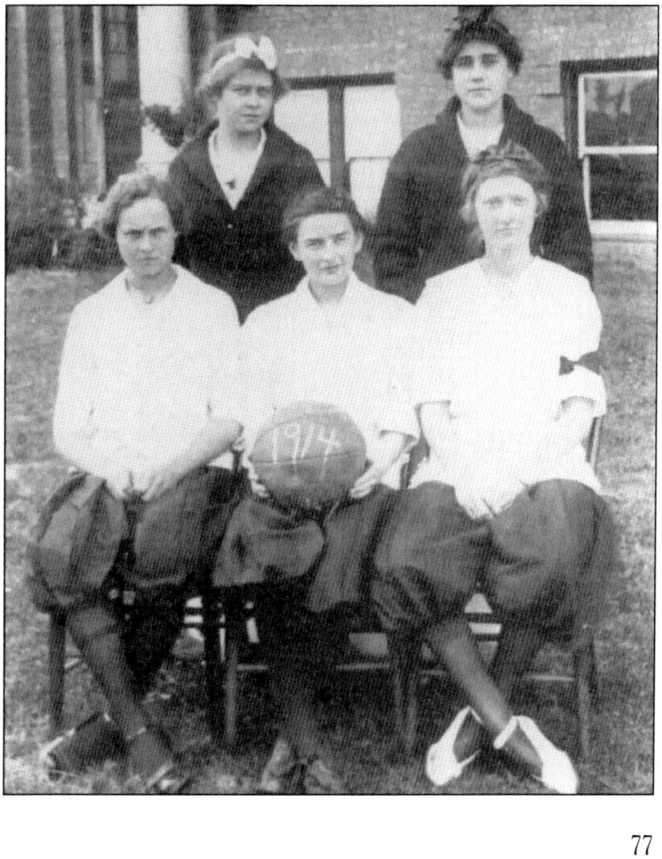

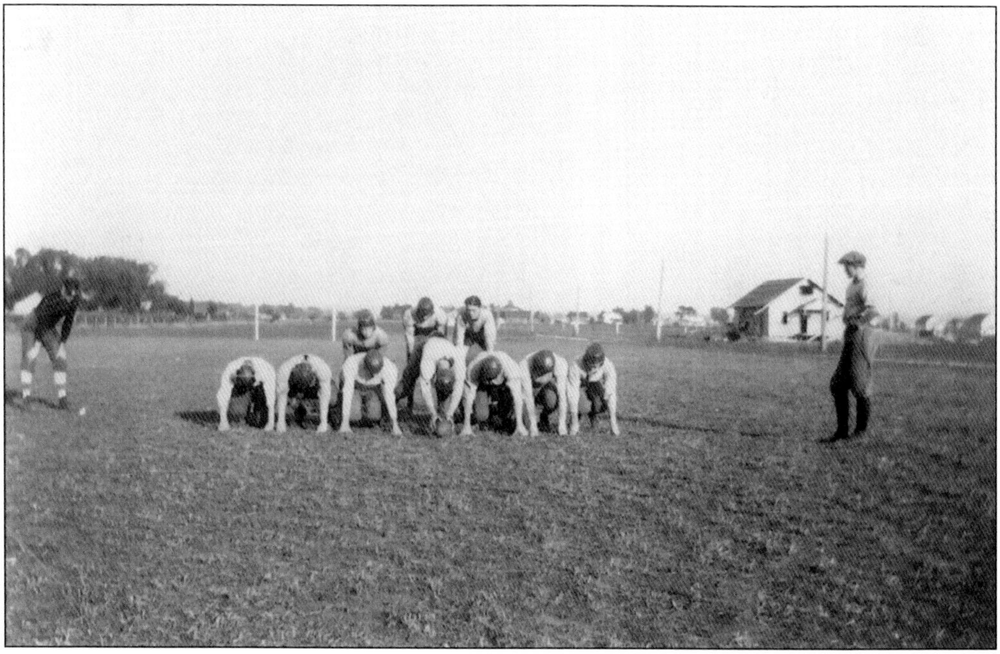

Above is a team shot of the Harlem Consolidated School football team at one of its practices. Although the date is unknown, is believed to be sometime in the 1930s, and none of the individuals are identified. Below is a team picture of the HCS track team, which won the Winnebago County Track Championship in 1927. The coach is David Schoonmaker, but the rest of the individuals are unidentified. Track was one of the first sports organized after the Harlem Consolidated School opened in 1911. The Harlem Athletic Association established two track teams, along with a girls' basketball team and a baseball team.

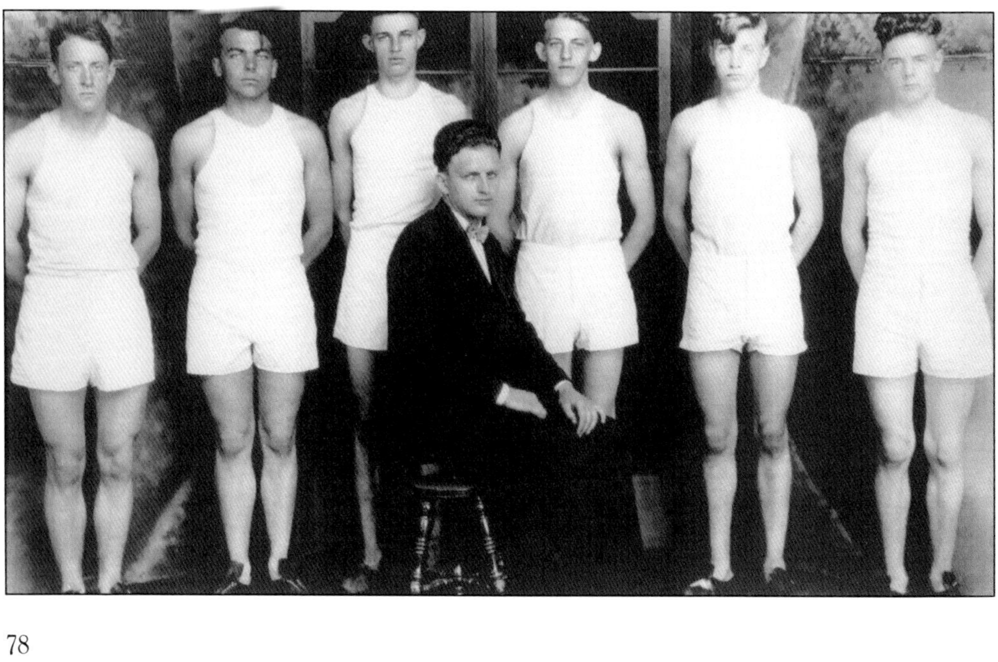

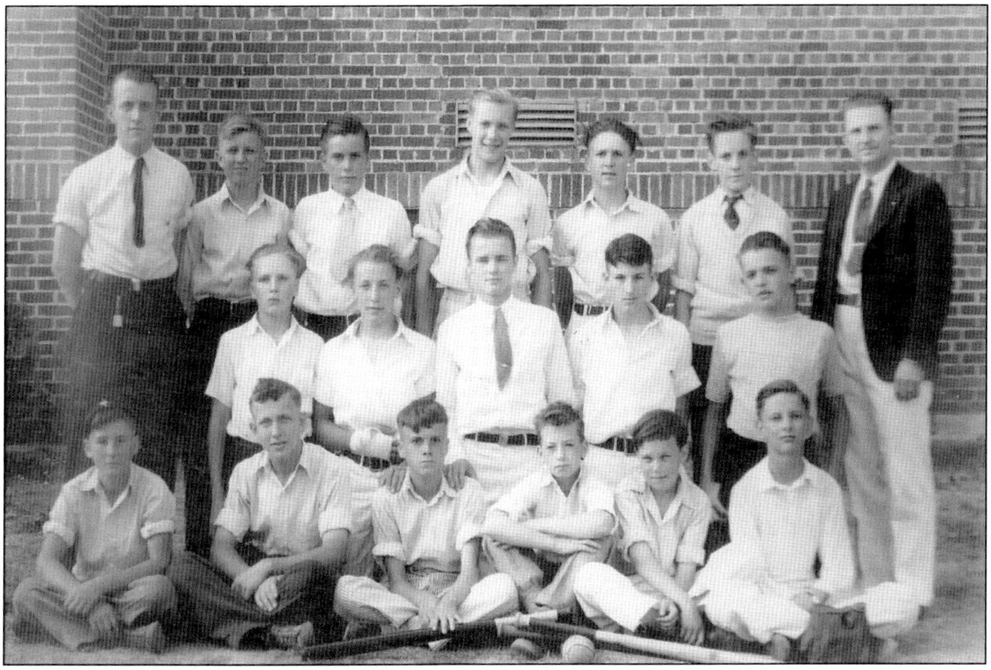

The baseball team posed for the above photograph in front of the Loves Park Grade School at 344 Grand Avenue during the 1933–1934 school year. The man standing at right is principal Russel Hovey. The only players identified are Al Turney (far left in the first row) and John "Jack" Kasper (second from left in the first row). Note the skinny tie the man at far left in back is wearing. The photograph below, which was taken at Harlem High School, shows Nellie Olson and Hovey, who had then been promoted from principal to superintendent. Olson served as Hovey's secretary from 1941 to 1945. Note the telephone, typewriter, and planner on the desk.

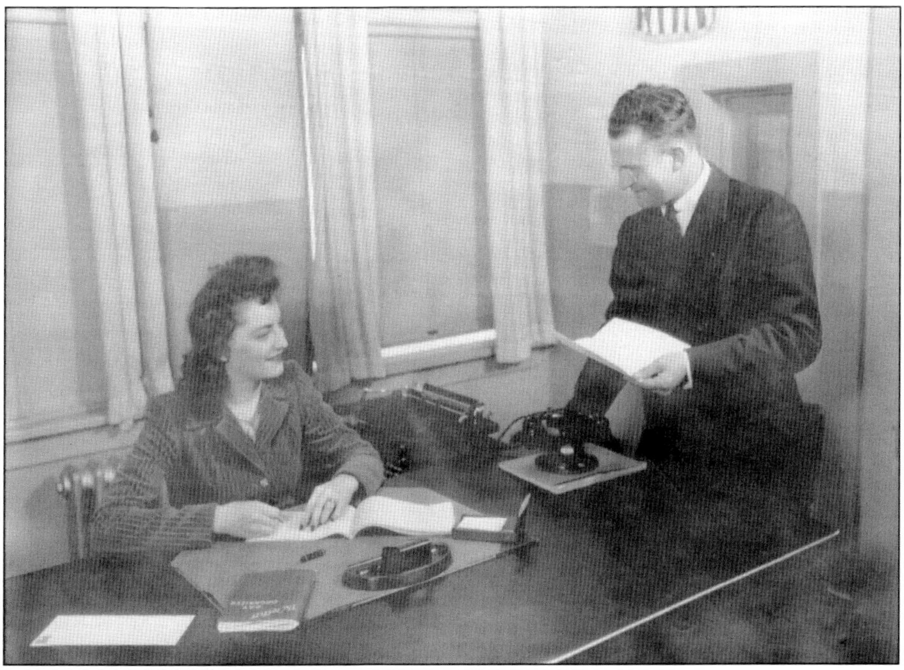

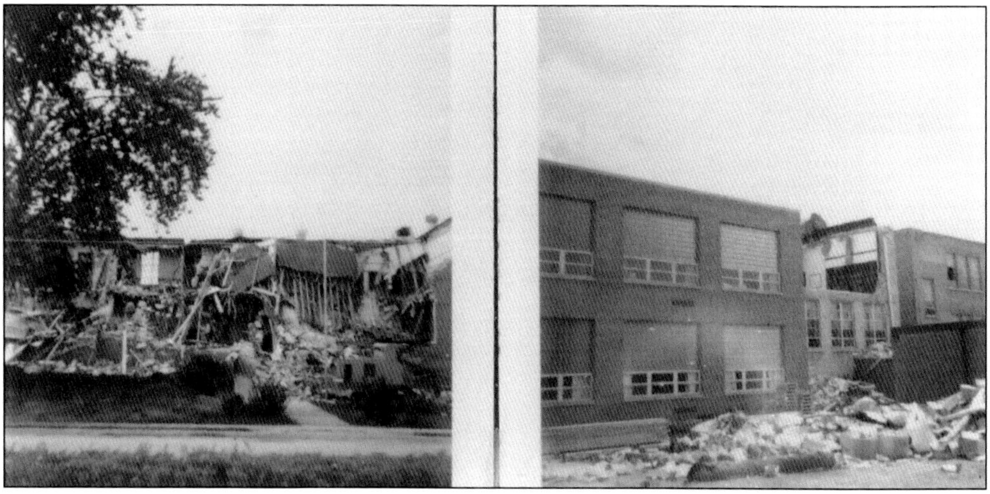

The images above show two phases of the demolition of Loves Park Grade School at 344 Grand Avenue on June 16, 1973. A new Loves Park Elementary School was constructed in its place. The images below capture two phases of the demolition of Harlem Consolidated School, which was located at the intersection of Harlem Road and North Second Street, on April 16, 1970. The current Harlem School District has one early learning center, eight elementary schools, one middle school, and one high school—all of which are shared by Loves Park and Machesney Park. Enrollment continues to grow as the population expands in both cities.

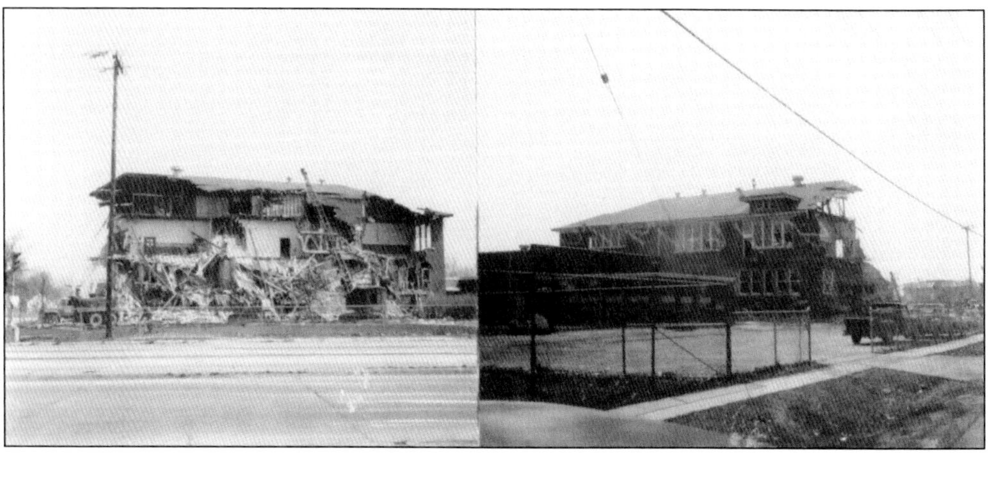

Six

PLACES OF WORSHIP

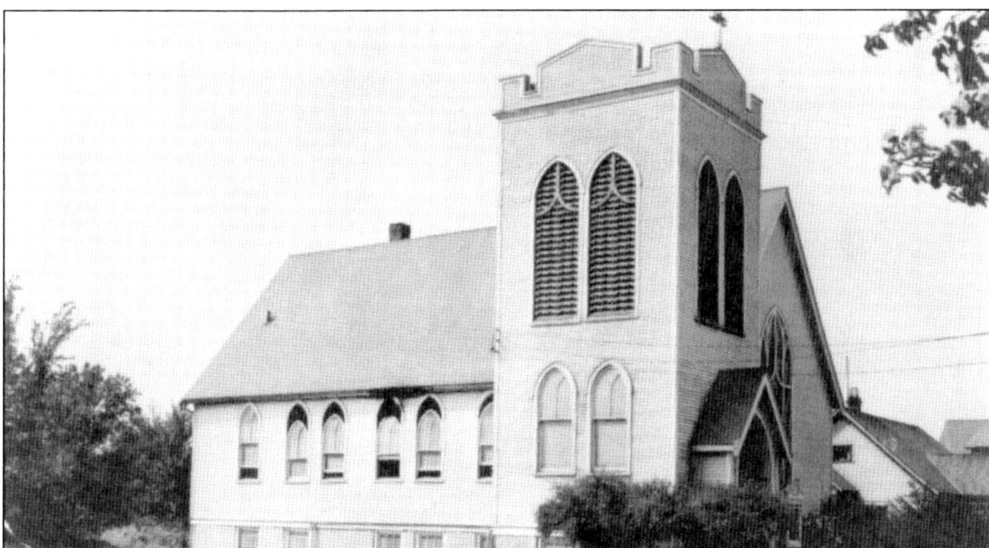

Grace Lutheran Church, located at 343 Grand Avenue, is pictured here in 1924. Prior to its completion, the church held services in the Loves Park Grade School on River Park Road. The church was dedicated on Christmas Day in 1924, and total construction costs were $18,575.68. Note that the windows could be opened.

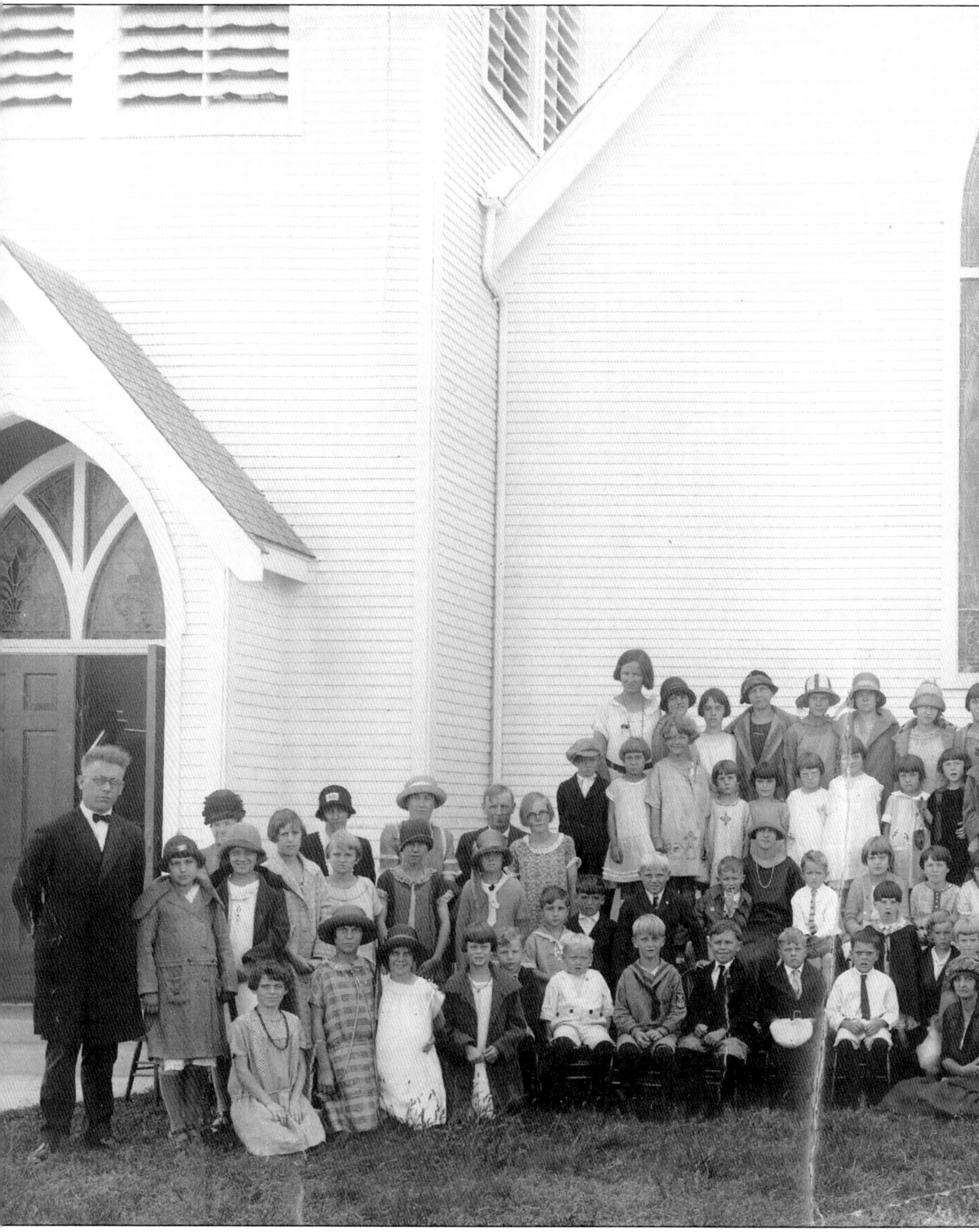

The Sunday school class of 1924–1925 is pictured here in front of the new Grace Lutheran Church. None of the individuals in the photograph are identified. Services during these years were led by Paul V. Randolph, a seminary student. He worked as the church's secretary and had helped raise funds for the construction of the new church. The vice pastor at this time was Dr.

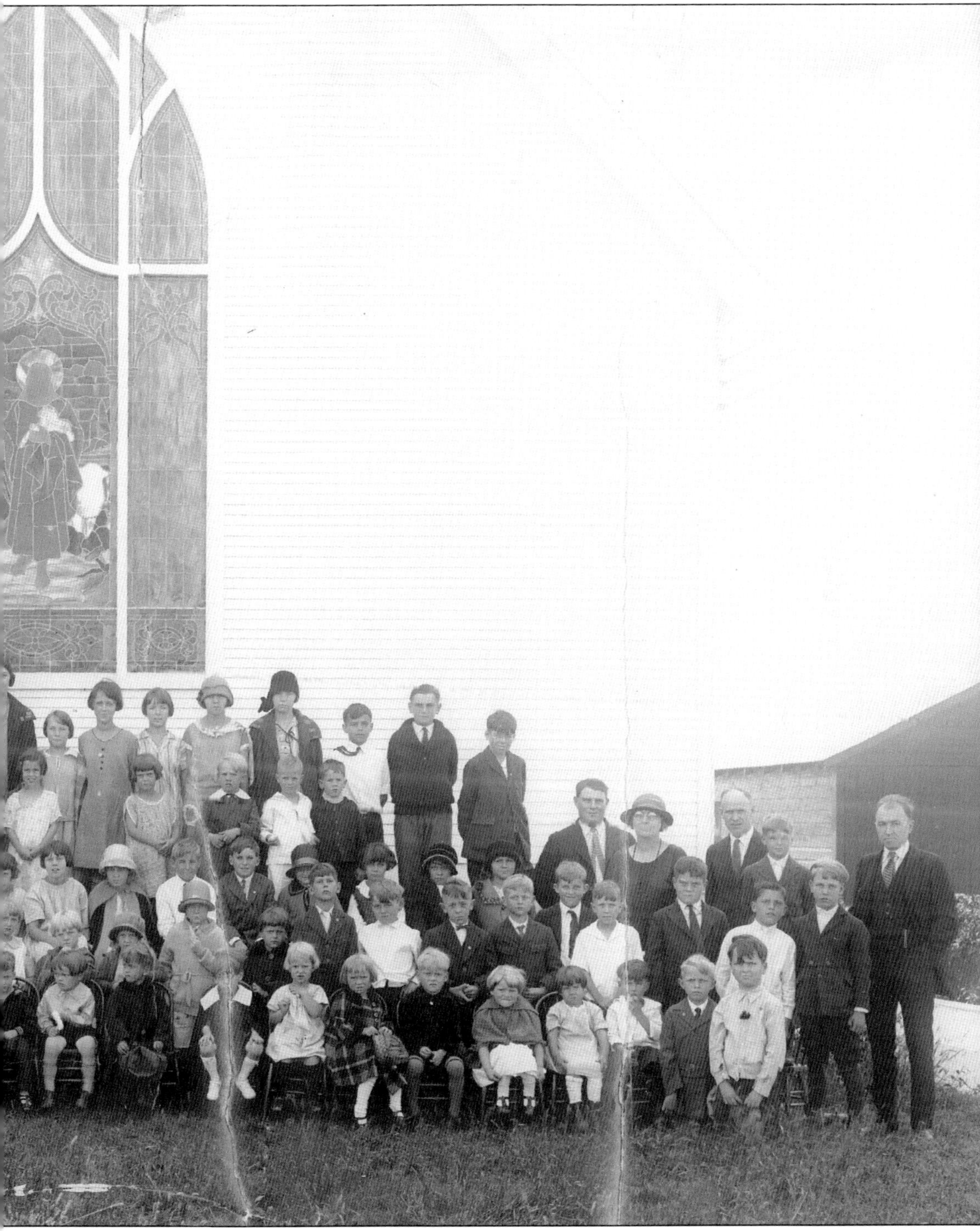

J.A. Benander. Randolph was later ordained, and his first official sermon was held on Sunday, June 28, 1925. Grace Lutheran Church was a member of the Illinois Conference of the Augustana Synod. (Courtesy of Grace Lutheran Church.)

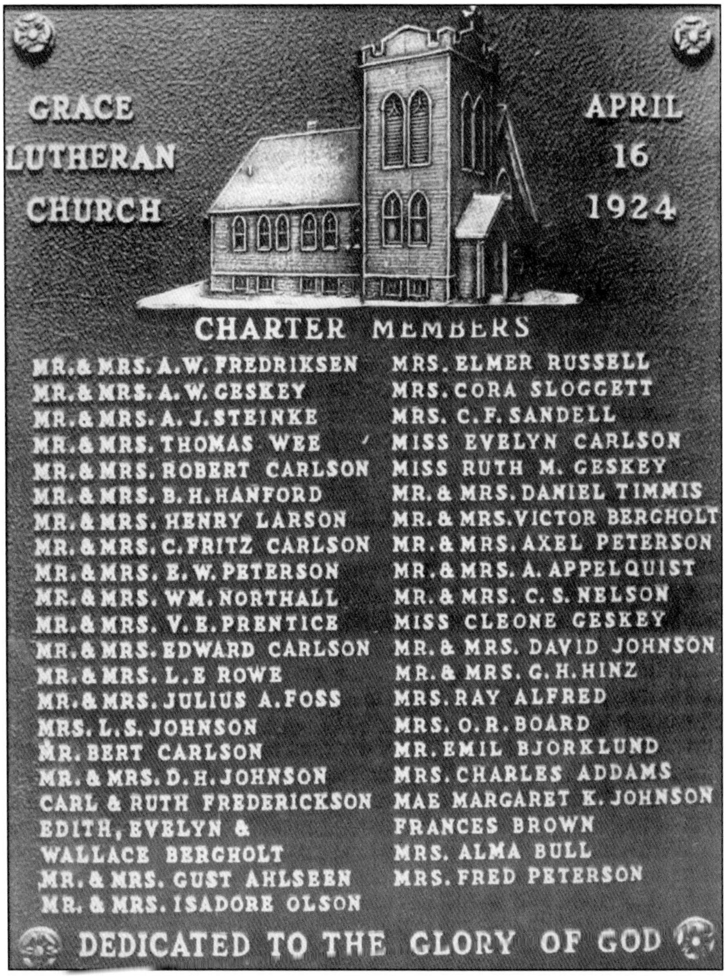

The plaque shown at left, dated April 16, 1924, commemorates the charter members of Grace Lutheran Church. The plaque is still displayed in the church today. The charter membership list was officially closed on January 1, 1925, a date that had been decided upon at one of the church's first meetings. The photograph below shows the interior of Grace Lutheran Church as it looked in the early days. The church could seat 200 people. Rev. Paul V. Randolph worked to organize the church and grow the membership, but he eventually left in December 1927 for a position in Long Beach, California. (Both, courtesy of Grace Lutheran Church.)

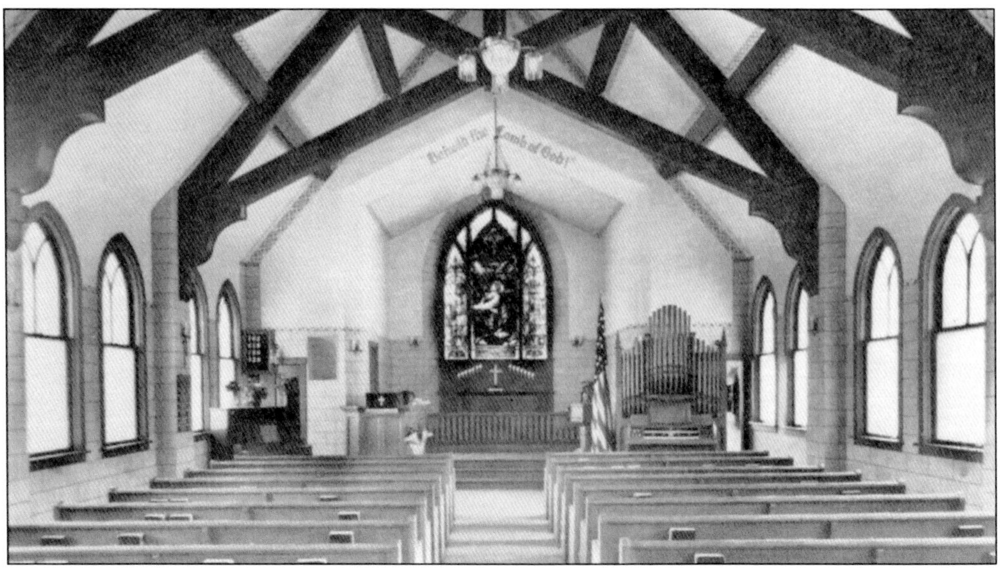

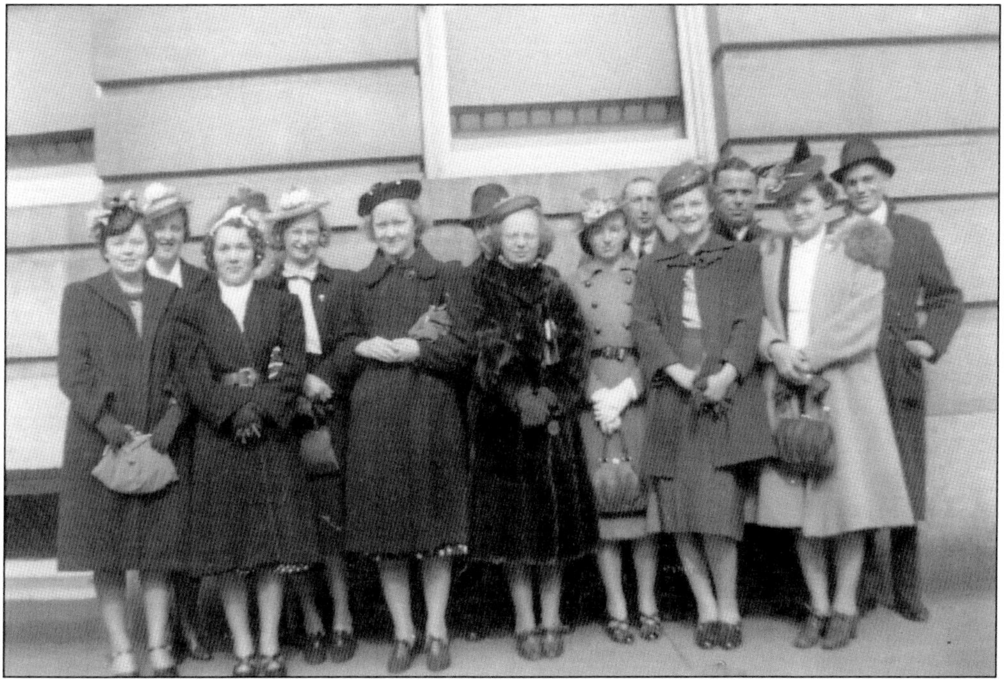

The Grace Lutheran Church Choir is pictured above at an unnamed location on May 13, 1939; the only members identified are Nellie Oswald (second from the right in the first row), Edith Carlson (wearing what appears to be a fur coat in the center of the first row), and Beverly Evans (second from left in the first row). The photograph below shows Grace Lutheran Church as it appeared in 1963 after the construction of the first youth center and a gymnasium. Renovations in the 1950s and in 1963 gave the church a more modern look while also incorporating the church's original building. (Above, courtesy of Gayle Englof.)

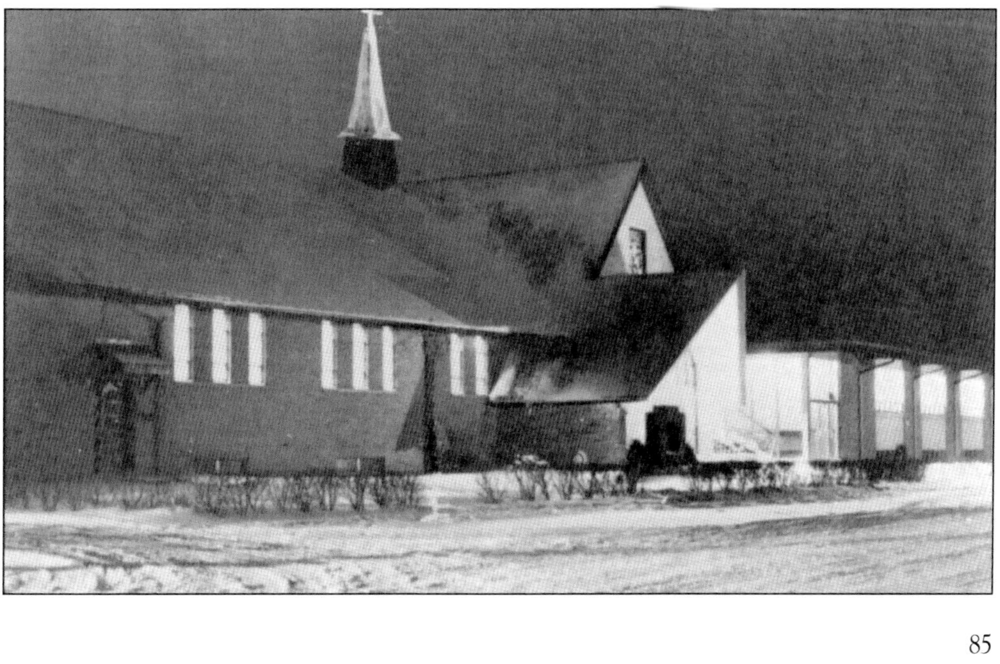

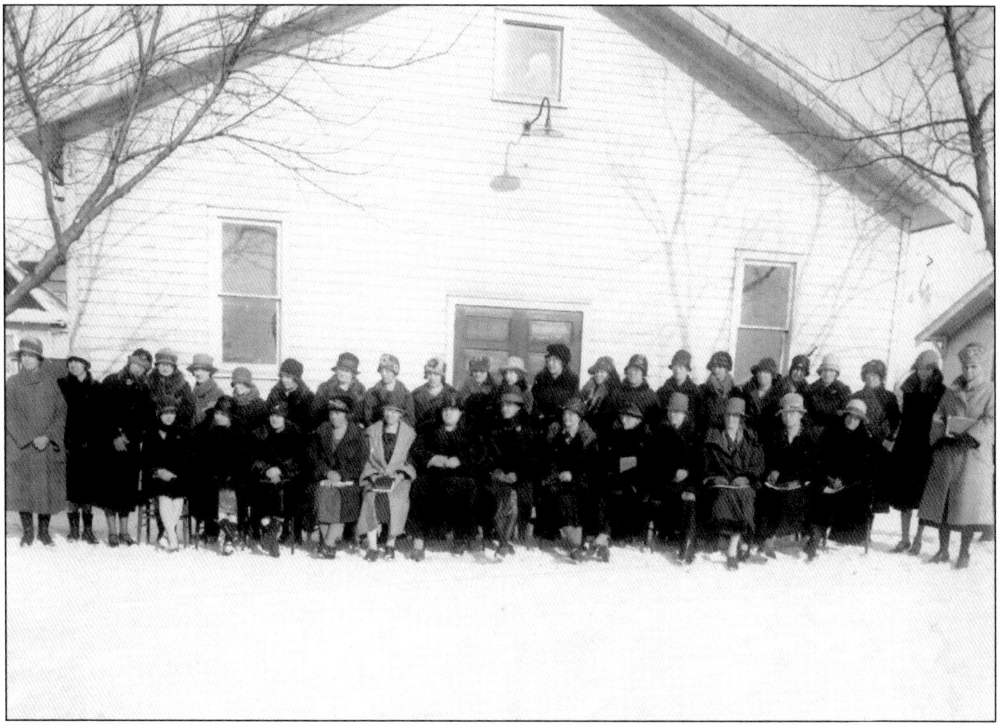

A large group of unidentified ladies poses in front of the Bethany Union Presbyterian Church tabernacle, which was located near the rear of the church's current location at 5403 North Second Street. The tabernacle was built from an old Fort Grant Quonset hut in 1917 with the use of donated labor. The hut was 36-by-60 feet with a black tar paper exterior and cement floor. Benches were used as pews, a basement was also dug, and two furnaces were installed. Although it is undated, this photograph was taken after 1921, when white siding was installed over the tar paper. In the c. 1928 photograph below, Russ Reichenbach is at the construction site of the new church. (Above, courtesy of Bethany Church.)

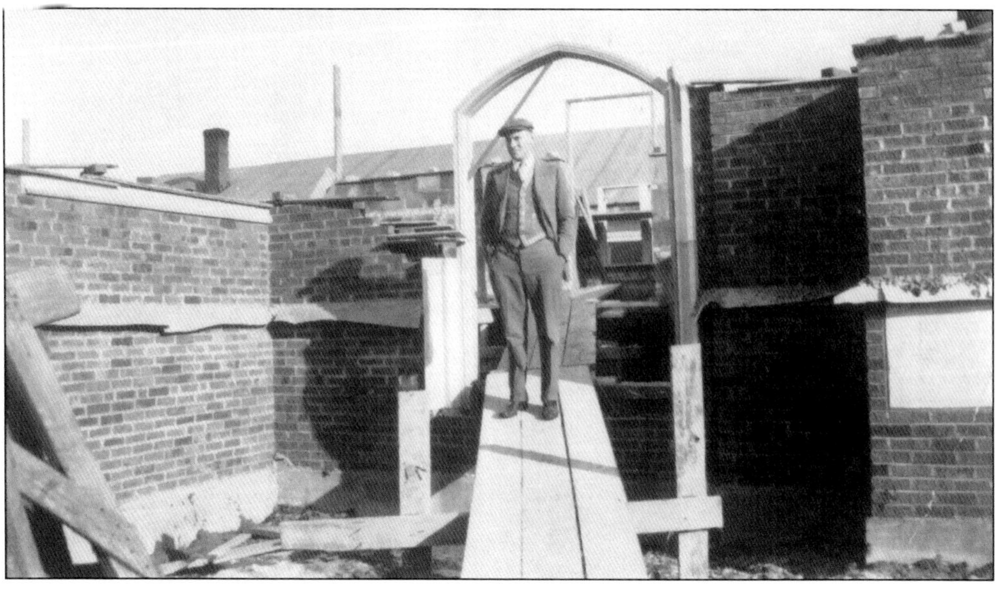

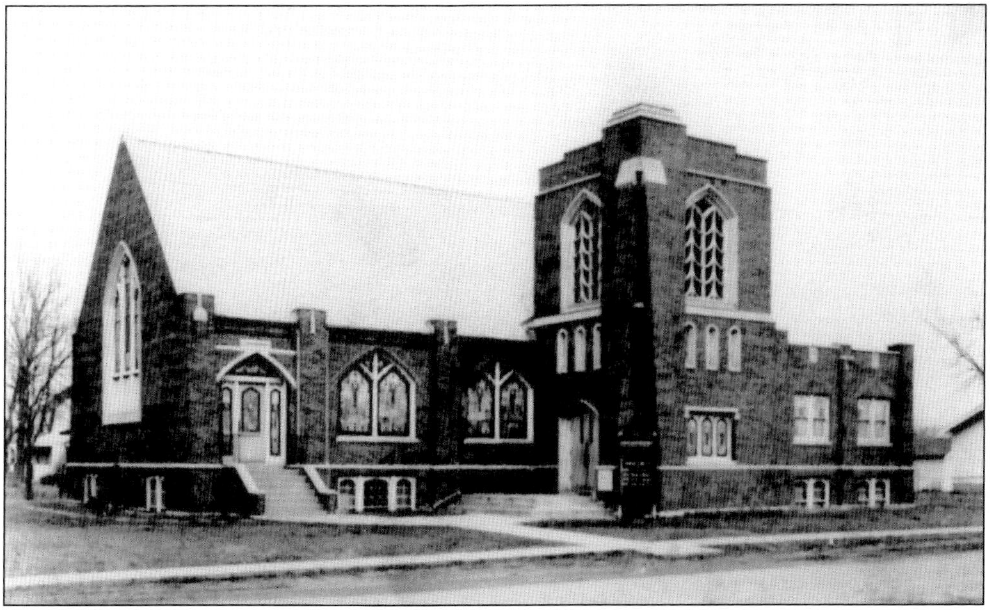

The image above shows Bethany Presbyterian Church as it appeared in February 1934. The name had been changed in 1929 from Bethany Union Presbyterian Church to Bethany Presbyterian Church because Grace Lutheran Church was formed in 1924, and many members with a Lutheran background left to join their own denomination. The photograph below shows the interior of the church as seen from the altar. It is believed that the service is being conducted by Rev. Marvin A. Weishaar in the mid- to late 1950s. Under Rev. Weishaar, attendance nearly doubled, and the church held two Sunday services. In this photograph, extra chairs are visible at the back of the room. (Both, courtesy of Bethany Church.)

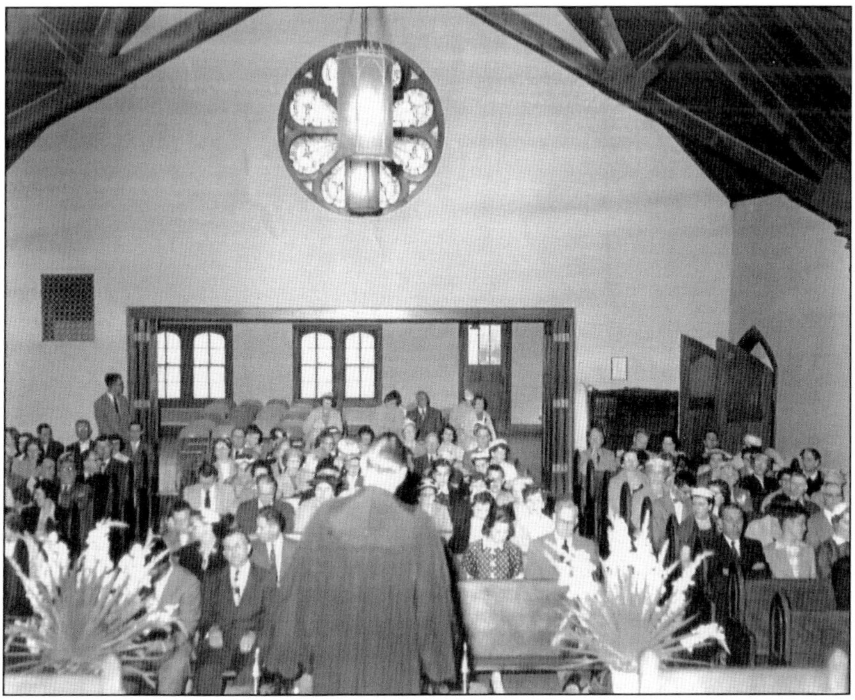

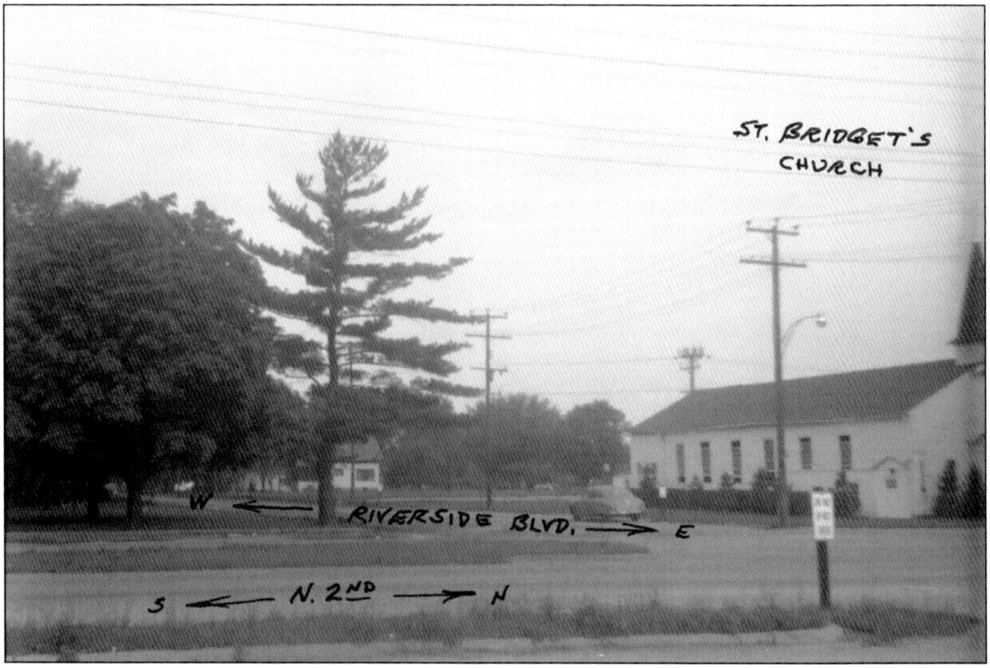

Services at St. Bridget Catholic Church started in a circus tent that was erected at the corner of Riverside Boulevard and North Second Street in 1946. Rev. Raymond P. Gordon was appointed by Bishop John J. Boylan to be the pastor of the church. The church purchased a building known as Post Chapel No. 1 from Camp Grant for $1,075 and had it dismantled, moved, and then rebuilt at the same intersection where the tent was erected. In the undated photograph above, the church is at right. The road from left to right is North Second Street, and the road intersecting it is Riverside Boulevard. The 1988 image below shows construction of the new church at 600 Clifford Avenue.

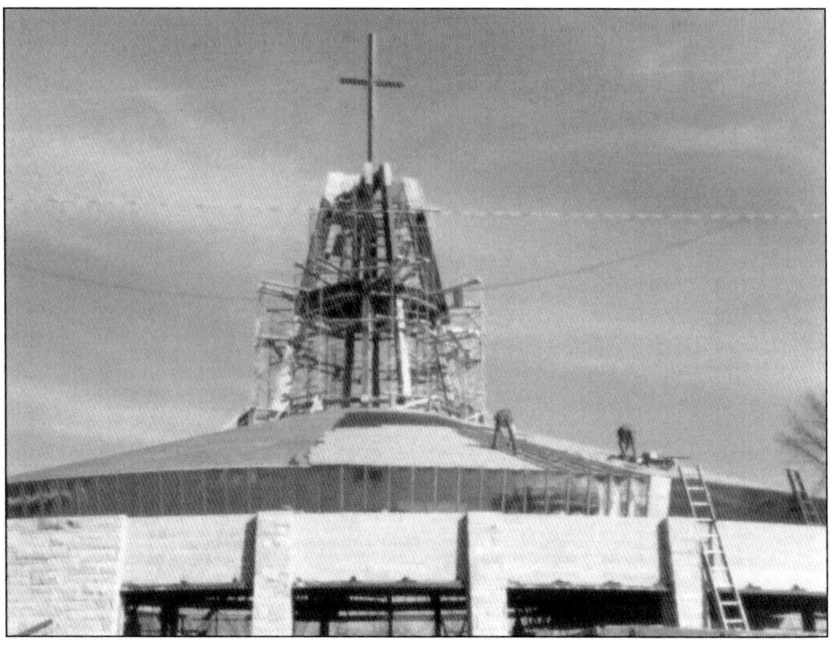

The first Forest Hills Evangelical Free Church, pictured in 1948, was located near the intersection of North Second Street and Pennsylvania Avenue. The current Forest Hills Evangelical Free Church is located at 5183 Pebble Creek Trail—the former site of Peace Evangelical Lutheran Church, which relocated in 2009.

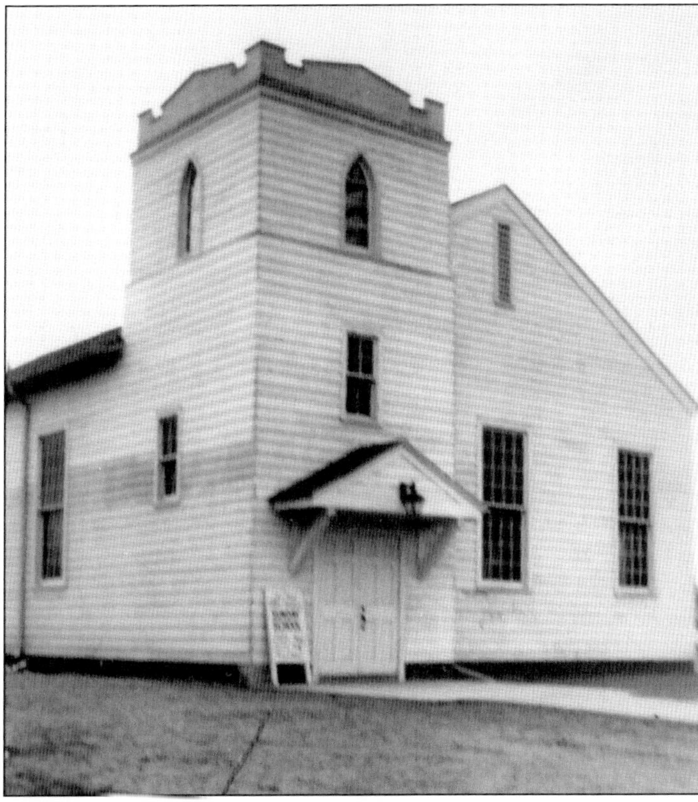

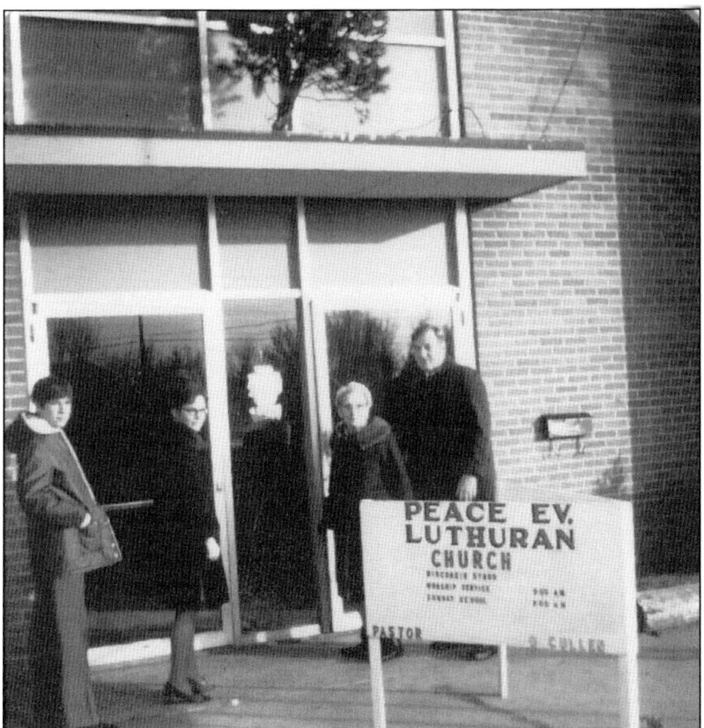

In the early years of its organization, from 1971 to 1975, Peace Evangelical Lutheran Church held services at the Harlem Boys Club near the corner of Elm and Evans Avenues. Pictured here in front of the Harlem Boys Club building are, from left to right, Tom Kissinger, G. Peterson, Elsie Geyer, and Charles Kissinger. The pastor was Oral Cullen. (Courtesy of Peace Evangelical Free Church.)

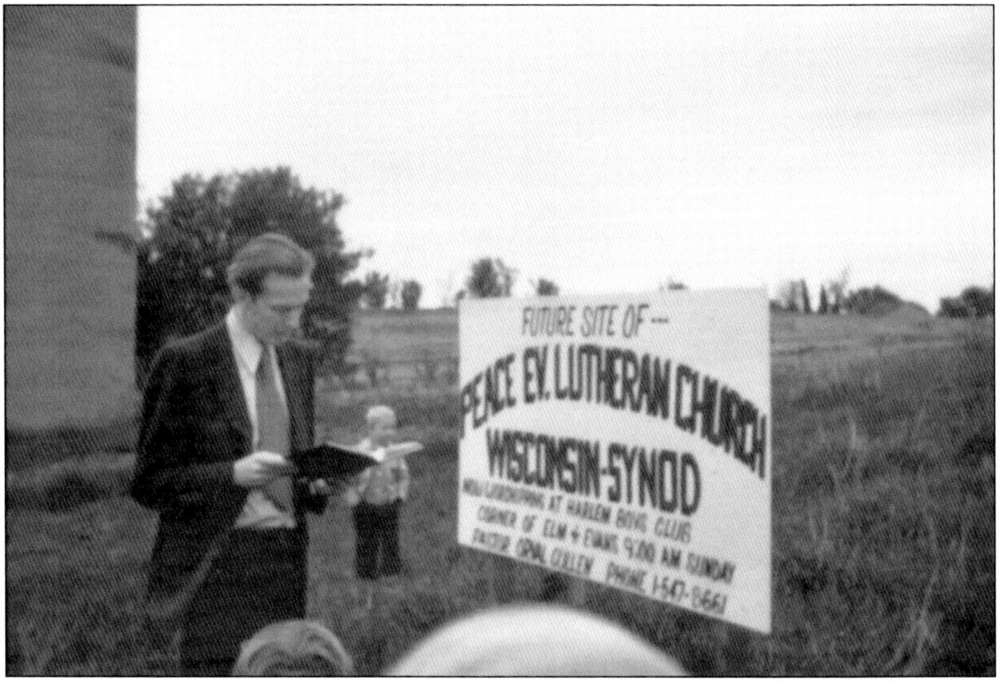

On May 10, 1981, a ground-breaking ceremony was held for the new Peace Evangelical Lutheran Church at 5183 Pebble Creek Trail. Pastor Oral Cullen is pictured above at the ceremony. The church was dedicated on October 18, 1981—the 10th anniversary of the congregation's formation. At the time, the church had 97 baptized members. As the sign says, the church was a member of the Wisconsin Synod. The image below shows the nearly completed church building. This structure was occupied from 1981 until 2009, when Peace Evangelical Lutheran Church moved to its current location, at 502 Orth Road, and Forest Hills Evangelical Free Church moved into this building. (Courtesy of Peace Evangelical Free Church.)

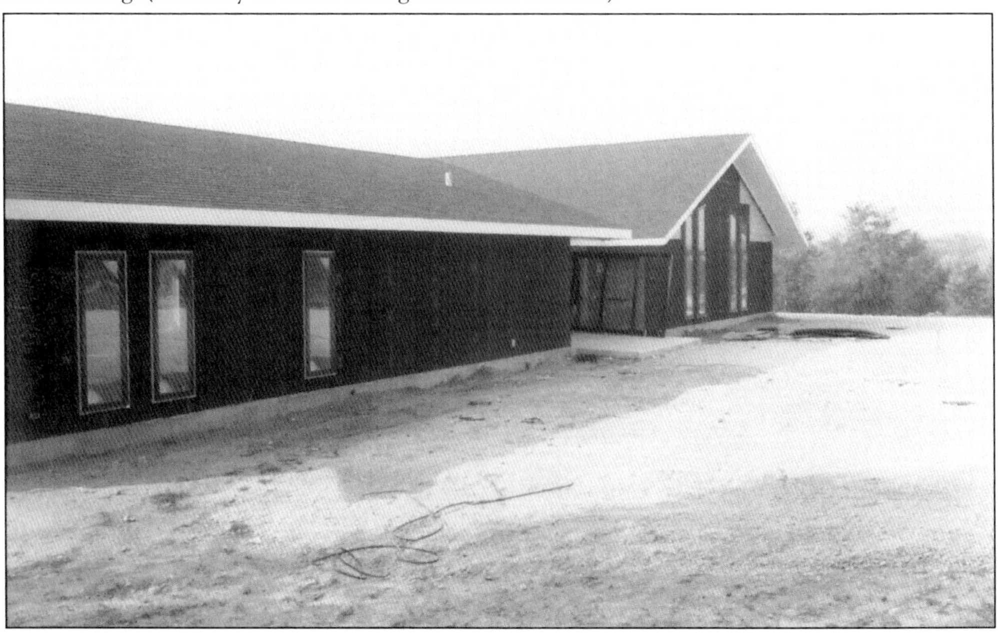

Seven

PARKS, RECREATION, AND ENTERTAINMENT

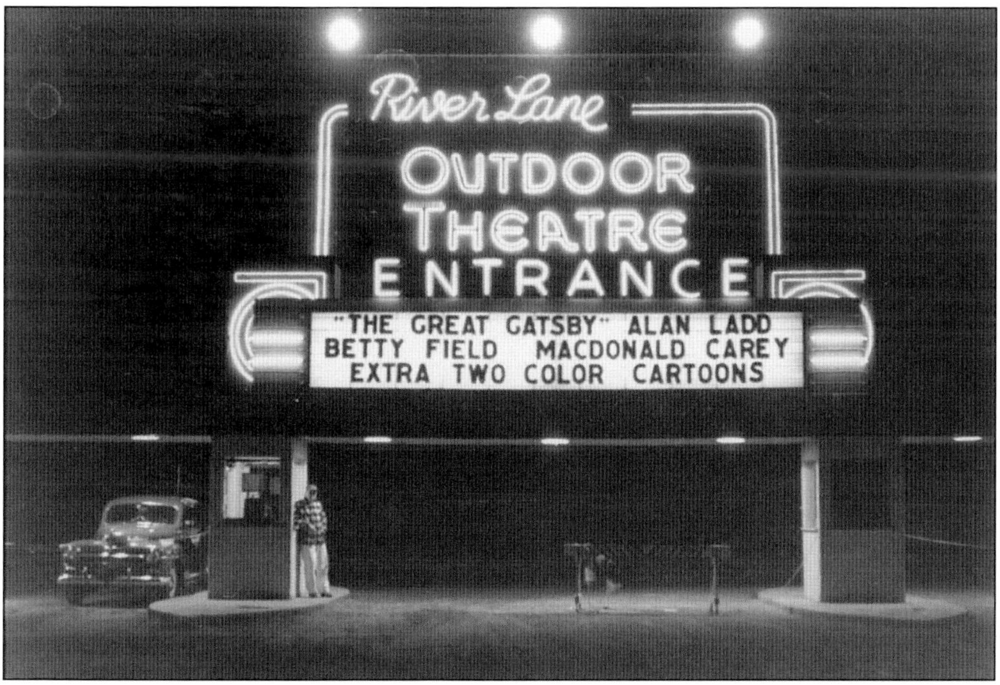

This 1949 image shows the River Lane Outdoor Theatre lit up for a showing of *The Great Gatsby*, starring Alan Ladd. The theater opened in May 1948 at 1000 River Lane and had a 750-to-1,000 car capacity, an 80-foot-wide screen, and a concession stand. It closed in the fall of 1984 and was demolished in March 1987.

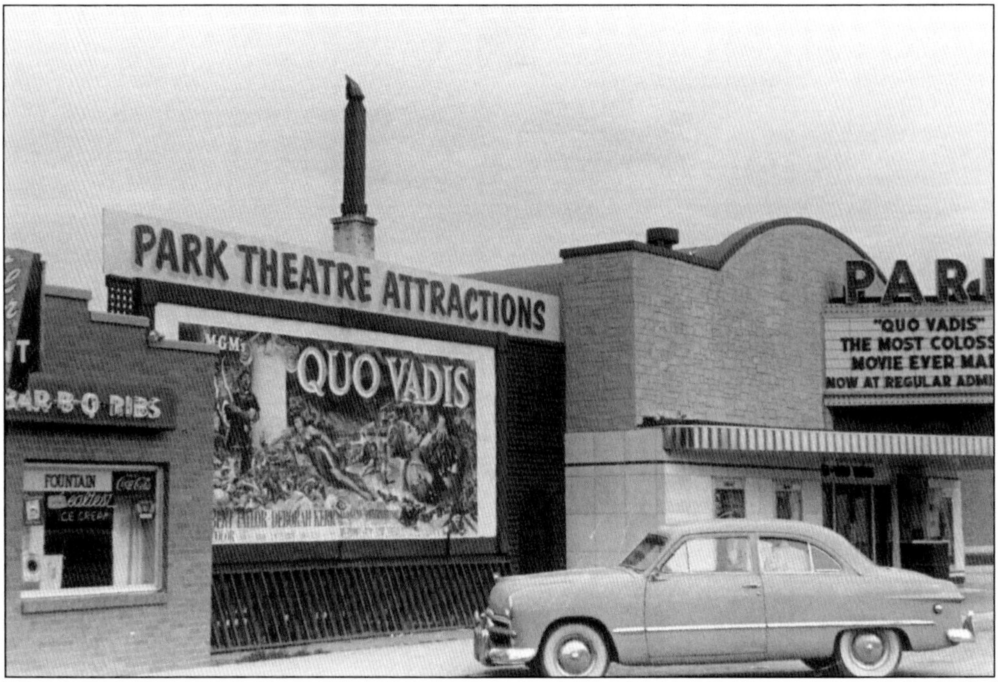

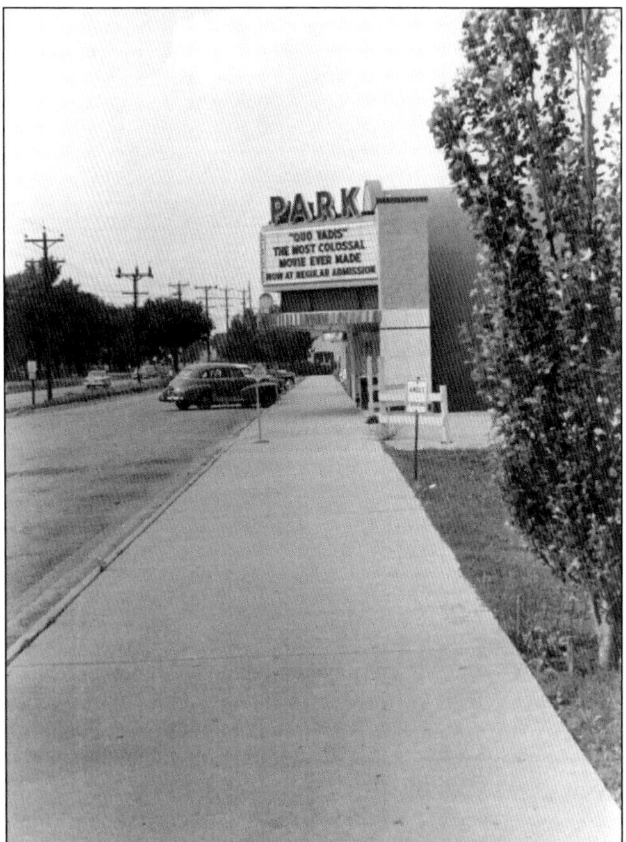

These 1952 photographs of the Park Theatre at 5723 North Second Street were taken when the theater was showing the movie *Quo Vadis*, starring Robert Taylor and Deborah Kerr. The theater opened on May 20, 1948, with the film *They Become Restless.* The screen was 15 feet tall and 20 feet wide, and the theater included a party room and "children's cry room." The image at left shows a side view of the Park Theatre's neon marquee. The theater was owned by J. Albert Johnson and built by Tolan Engineering Company-Theatre Builders out of Chicago. The theater closed in 1978, and the building now houses Crafts Plus.

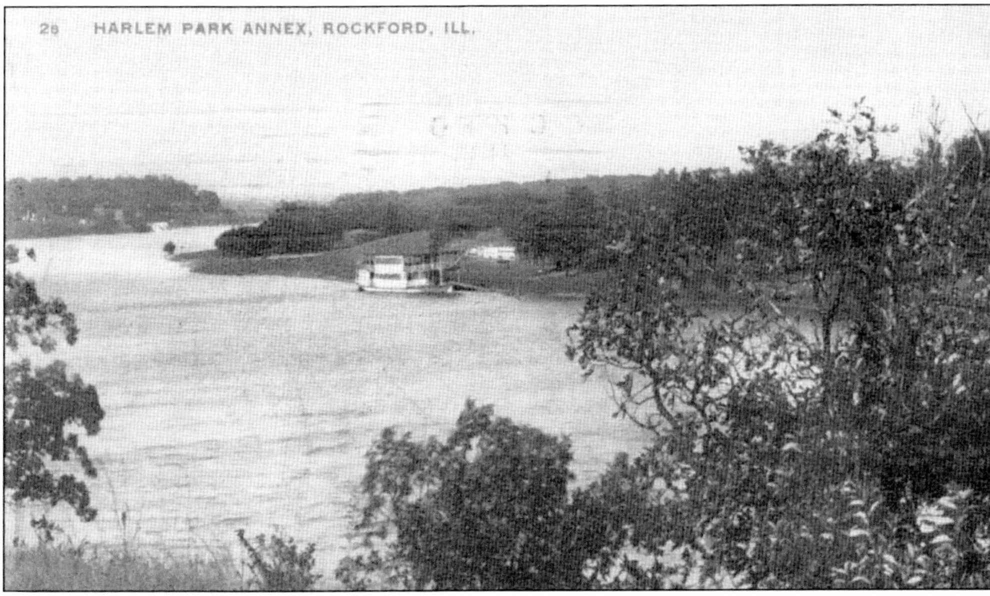

In this vintage postcard, the Harlem Park Annex is shown on the east side of the Rock River. The property belonged to Malcolm A. Love, and a ferry shuttled passengers between the annex and Harlem Park on the west side of the river. The ferry was 60 feet long by 18 feet wide and could carry approximately 200 people. (Courtesy of Nicole C. Lindsay.)

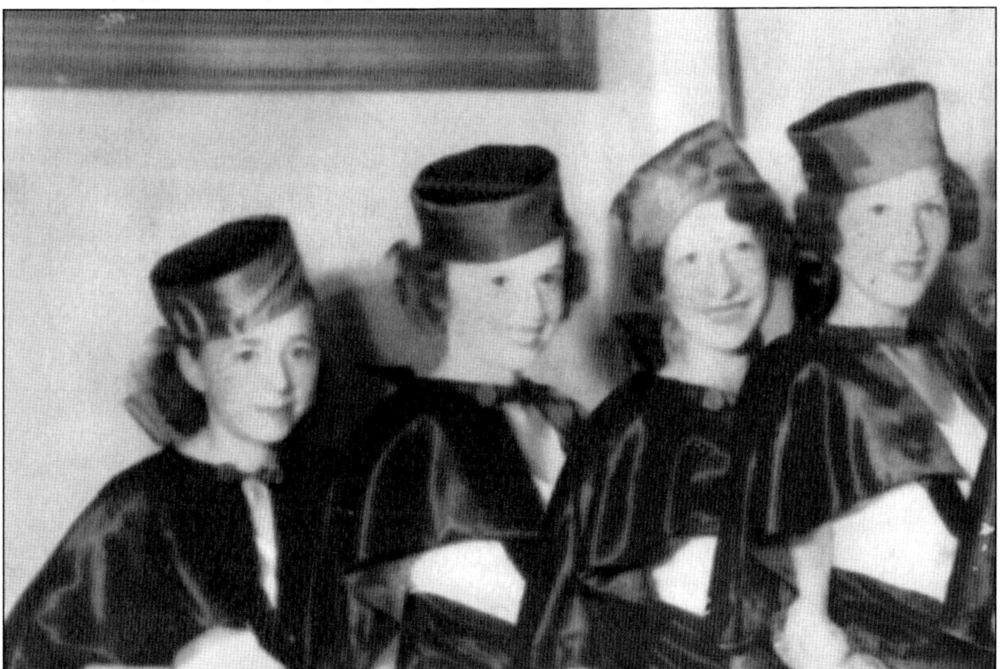

This June 11, 1936, photograph shows four members of the Loves Park Broadway Steppers dance troupe during a recital. The women pictured are, from left to right, Helen Hull, Selma Bocelik, Marjorie Reed, and Jean Skar. Members of the troop not included in this picture were Juanita Juhlin, Genevieve Garavalia, Jean Hoffman, Helen Trosper, and Betty Peltier. (Courtesy of Warren Paulson.)

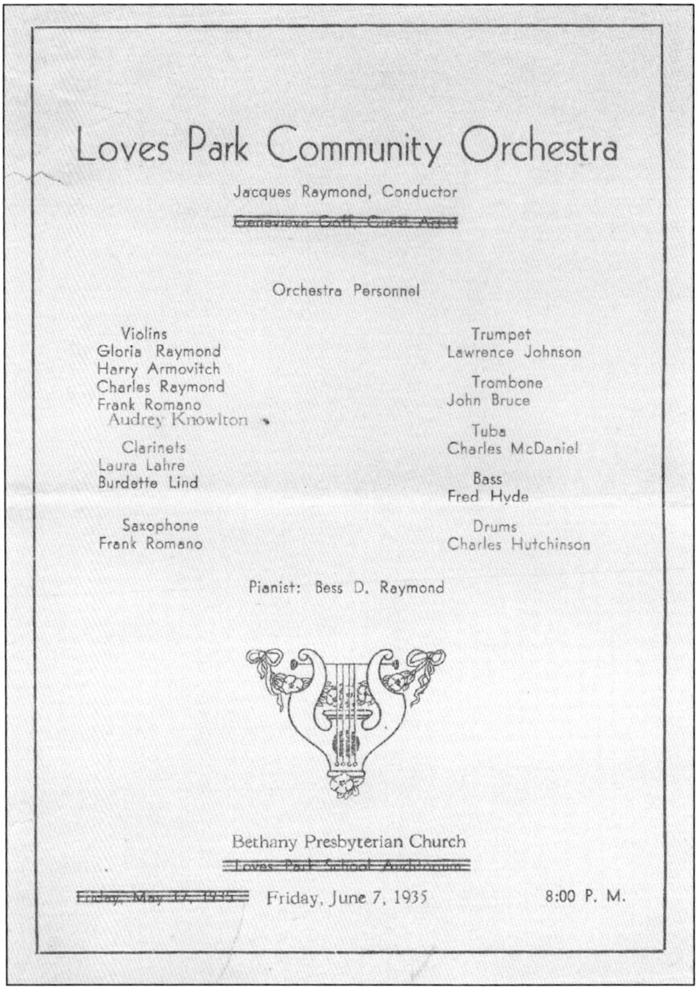

Loves Park Community Orchestra

Jacques Raymond, Conductor

~~Genevieve Goff, Guest Artist~~

Orchestra Personnel

Violins
Gloria Raymond
Harry Armovitch
Charles Raymond
Frank Romano
Audrey Knowlton

Clarinets
Laura Lahre
Burdette Lind

Saxophone
Frank Romano

Trumpet
Lawrence Johnson

Trombone
John Bruce

Tuba
Charles McDaniel

Bass
Fred Hyde

Drums
Charles Hutchinson

Pianist: Bess D. Raymond

Bethany Presbyterian Church
~~Loves Park School Auditorium~~

~~Friday, May 17, 1935~~ Friday, June 7, 1935 8:00 P. M.

This program from a Loves Park Community Orchestra performance held on Friday, June 7, 1935, at 8:00 p.m. at Bethany Presbyterian Church has survived through the years. As seen in the strike-through markings, some changes were made to the event; it was originally scheduled to take place at the Loves Park School Auditorium. The photograph below shows the orchestra in 1937 at the Loves Park School Auditorium, which is easily recognized by the "LP" above the group. The only members identified are Helen Hull, standing just to the right of the orchestra leader in the center, and Ray Johnson, sitting at far right. (Left, courtesy of Brian Landis; below, courtesy of Warren Paulson.)

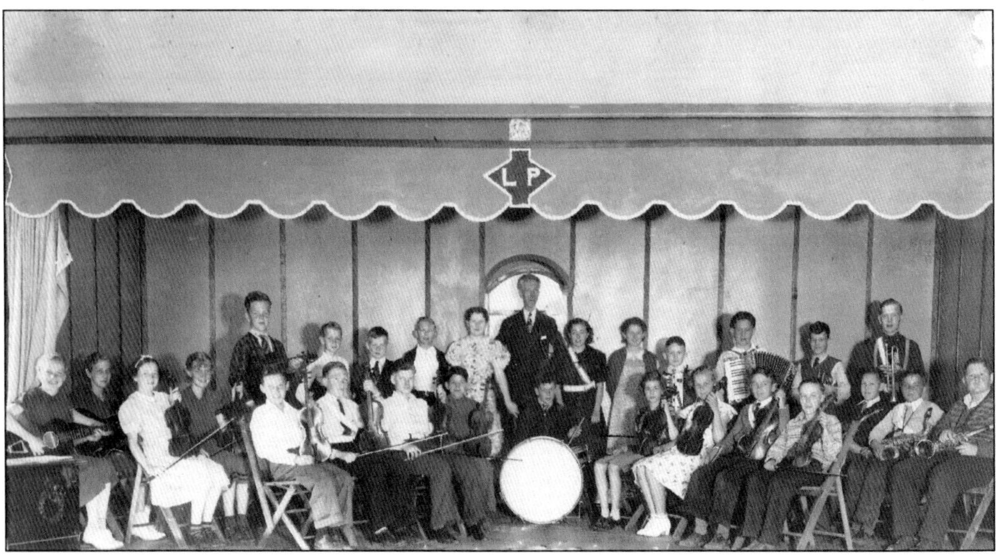

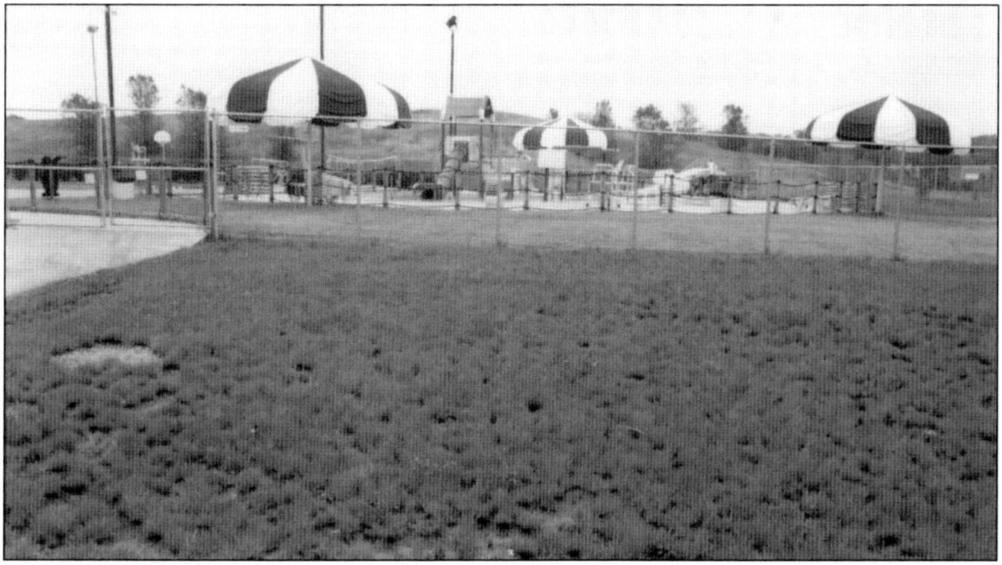

Sand Park Pool, located at 1401 East Riverside Boulevard, is operated by the Rockford Park District. Sand Park was a sand quarry and then the site of a landfill, which closed in 1973 when the park district began to develop the land. The pool features Penguin Pond and a wading pool for younger children.

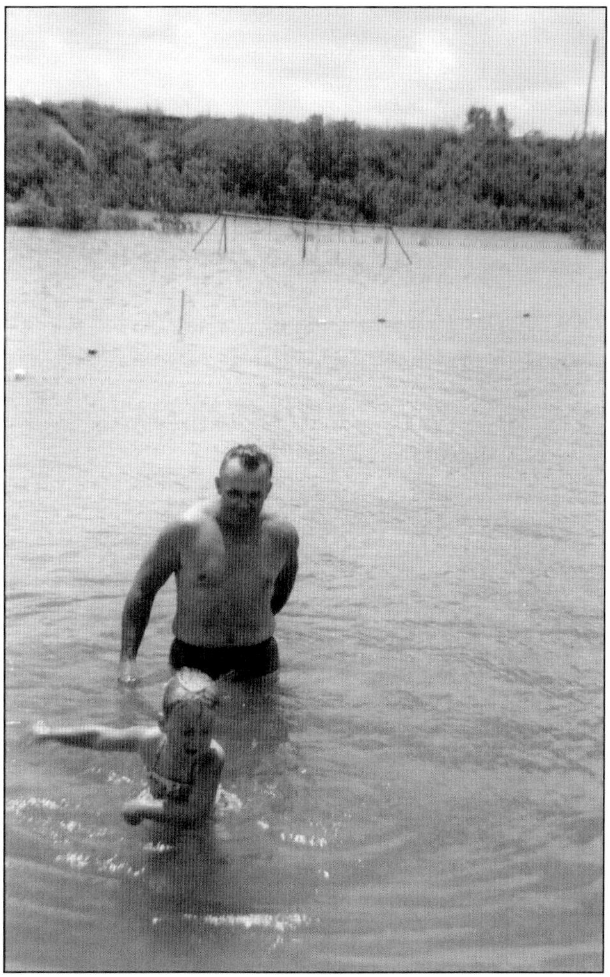

This July 1960 image shows Windsor Lake, located at the intersection of Alpine Road and Windsor Road. The man is unidentified, but the little girl is Paige Ballard. Owner Ed Carlson leased the lake to the Rockford Park District in 2012 for $1 to allow recreation such as fishing and boating.

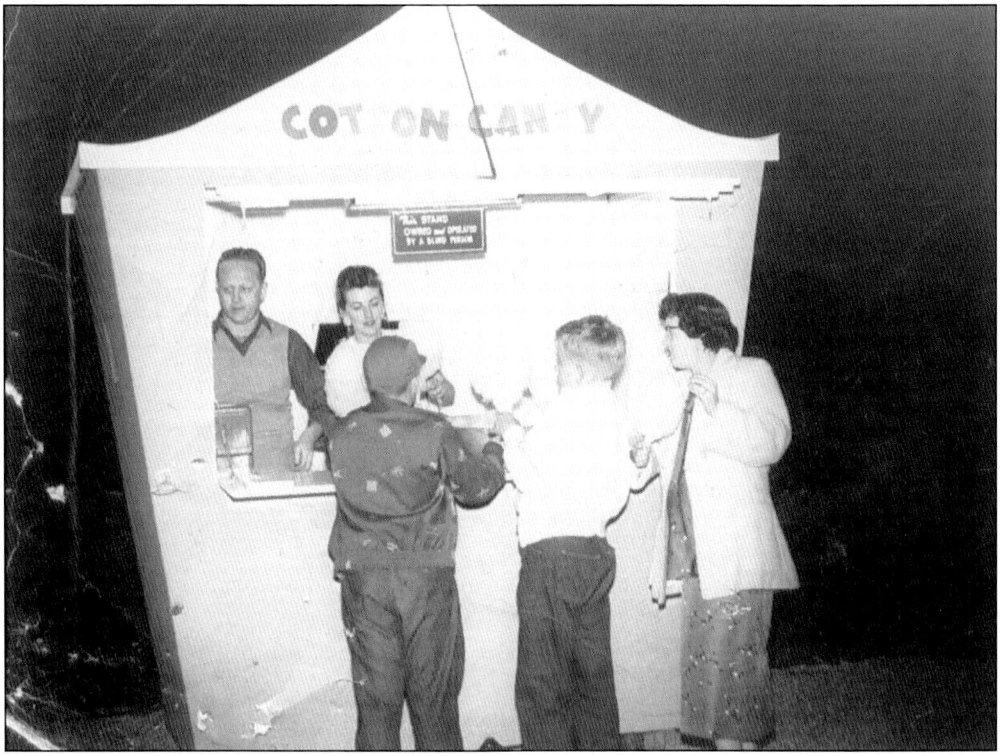

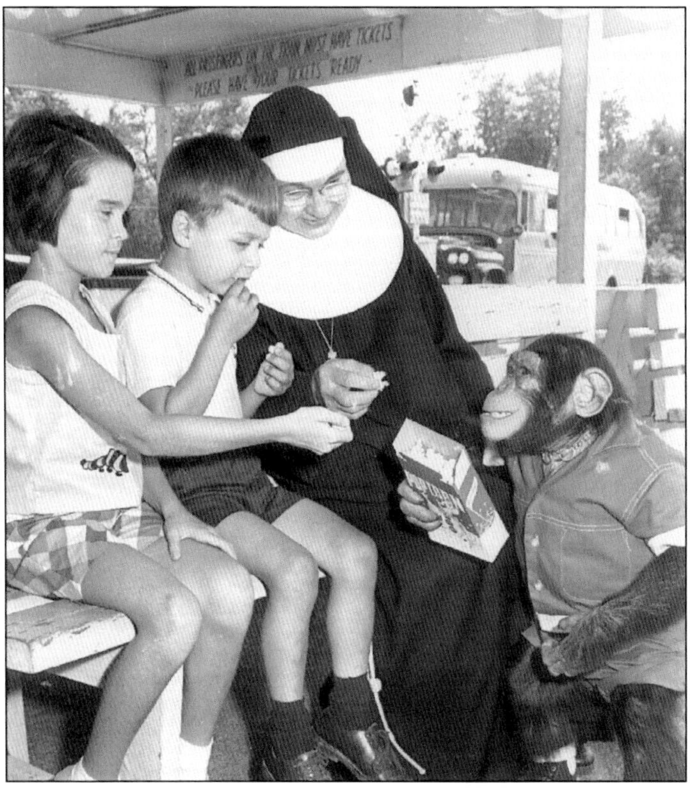

Kiddieland, located at 5810 Forest Hills Road, opened in 1950 near the River Lane Outdoor Theatre in suburban Loves Park. The photograph above shows a cotton candy booth operated by John Goodrich Sr. (left, behind the counter) and his wife, Eileen. The customers are unidentified, and the date the picture was taken is unknown. The Lions Club helped to build the booth. At left, Tico the chimpanzee enjoys some popcorn with an unidentified nun and two unidentified children sometime in the 1950s. Prior to Tico's arrival, the park also had another chimpanzee named Koko.

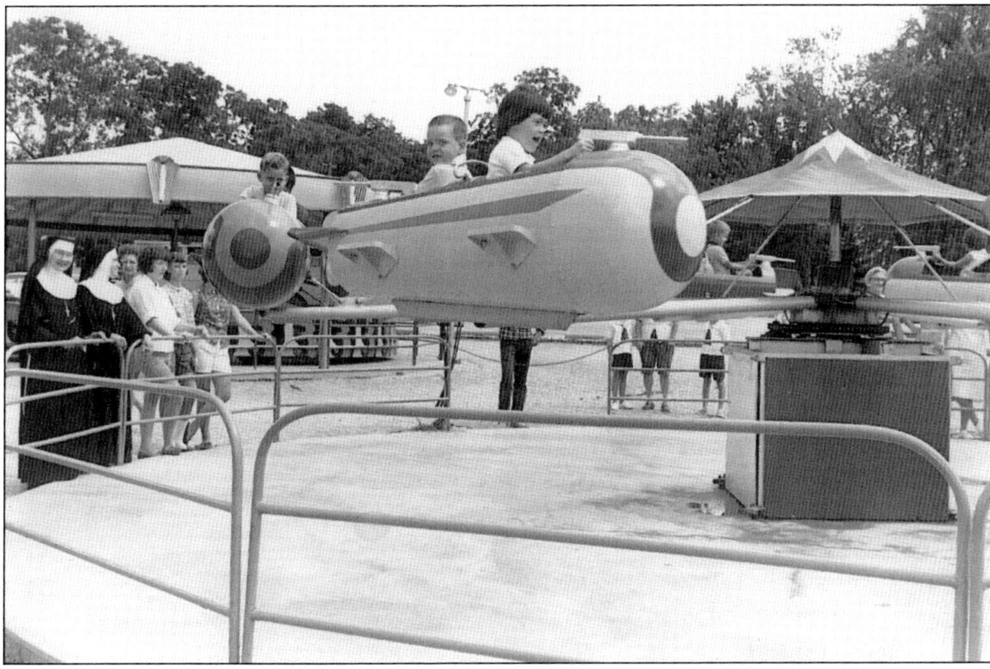

A "futuristic" airplane ride let these unidentified children shoot at each other with toy guns on one of the rides at Kiddieland amusement park, as seen in the 1950s image above. Children could also ride the train around the perimeter of the park; none of the people in the photograph below are identified, but the picture was taken in 1952. Kiddieland contained amusement rides including a roller coaster, Ferris wheel, and carousel; refreshment stands; and two chimpanzees and ponies. In the 1950s, tickets for rides were 15¢ per ticket, seven for $1, or 30 for $4. The park closed in 1977.

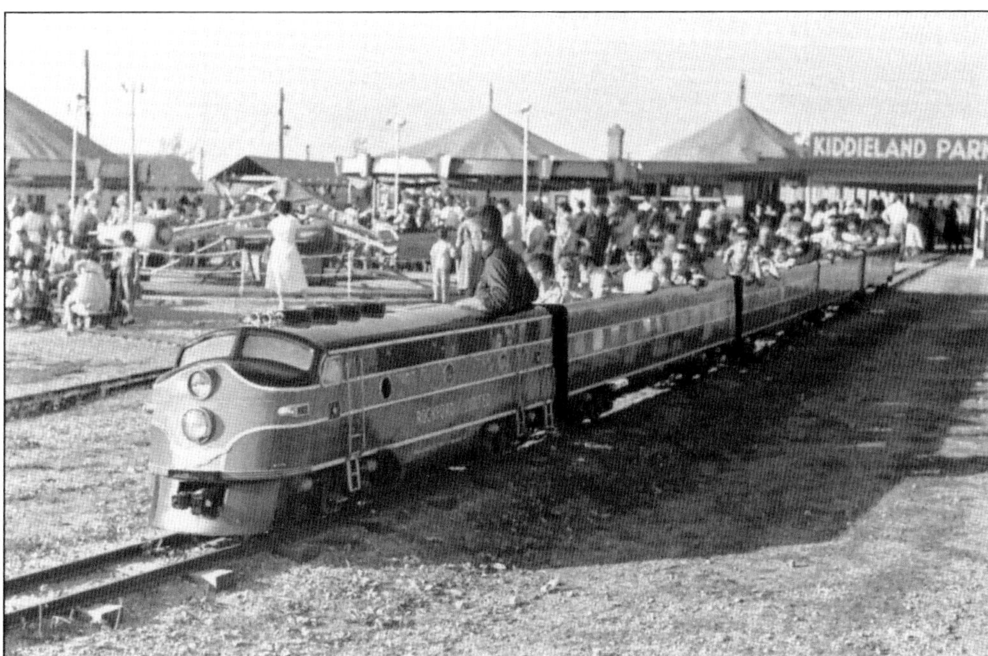

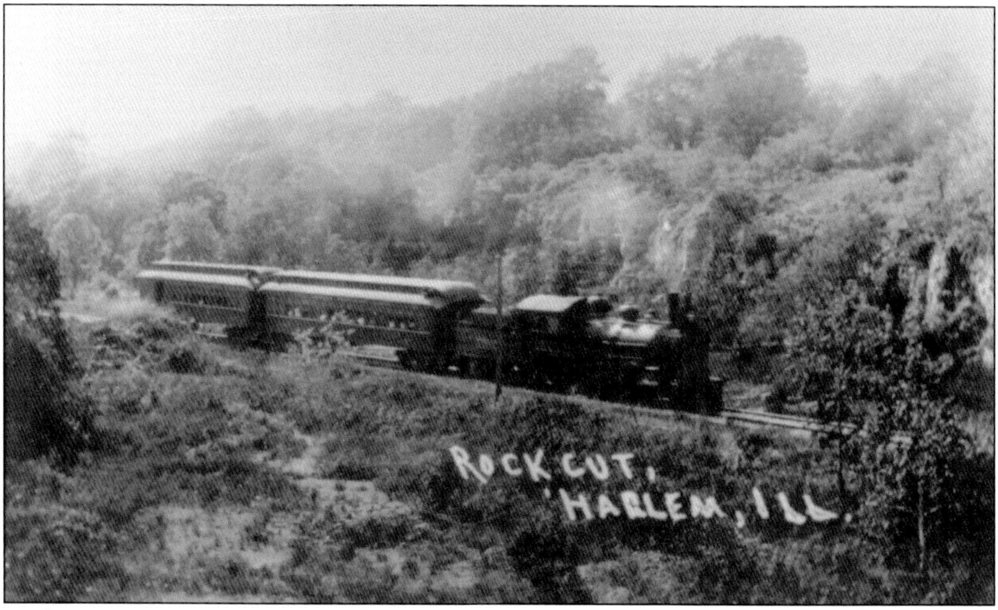

In the c. 1910 image above, a Chicago & North Western passenger train travels through Rock Cut, located about eight miles outside of Rockford. Before the area was a state park, it was a forest preserve in the 1930s. The name Rock Cut comes from the limestone rock that crews had to cut through in order to build the railroad line; they blasted through the massive area in 1858. Today, most of the rail bed is covered by Pierce Lake, but portions of it are still visible at Willow Creek just below the spillway. Below, construction proceeds during the creation of Pierce Lake. (Both, courtesy of Rock Cut State Park.)

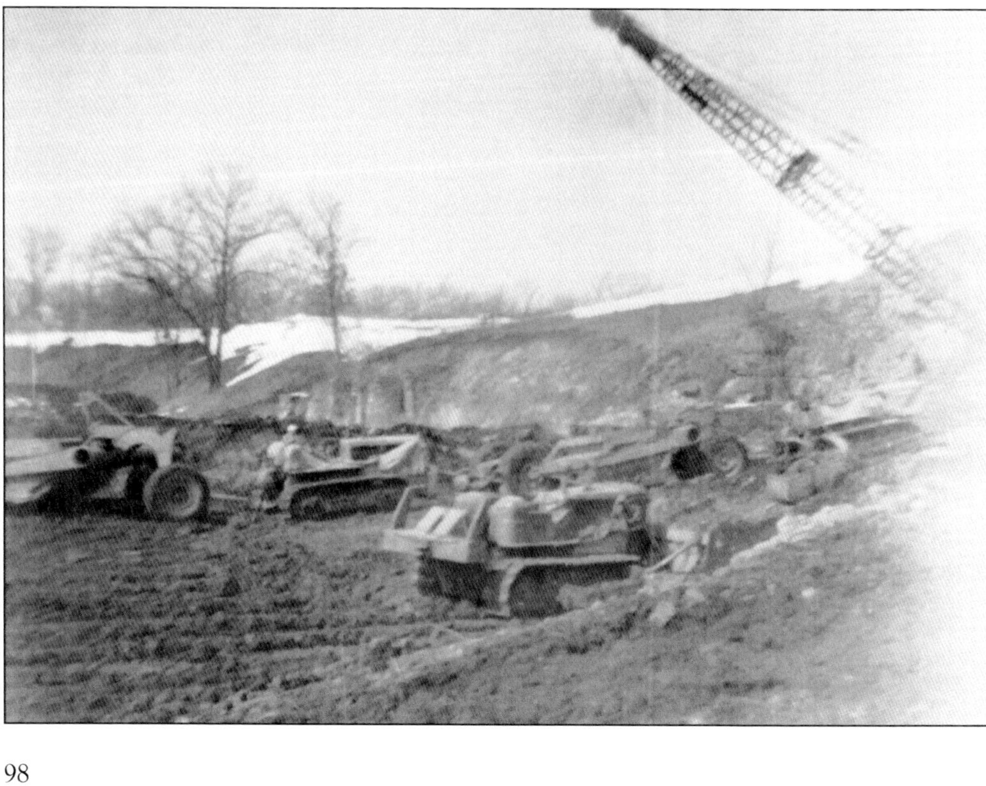

Rockford state representative William Pierce, for whom Pierce Lake in Rock Cut State Park is named, poses at the park in the undated photograph at right. Below, a vintage postcard shows sailboats on a sunny day at Pierce Lake. The postcard reads "In a rolling wooded countryside just outside of Rockford, the 162 acre Pierce Lake and 267 acre Rock Cut State Park has year round recreational facilities. Fishing, camping, picnicking, hiking trails, and boating are available. Winter sports include ice-skating, ice fishing, cross country skiing, and sledding." The park also includes the 50-acre Olson Lake, named for Loves Park residents Roland and Gladys Olson, which is used exclusively for swimming. (Right, courtesy of Rock Cut State Park; below, courtesy of Nicole C. Lindsay.)

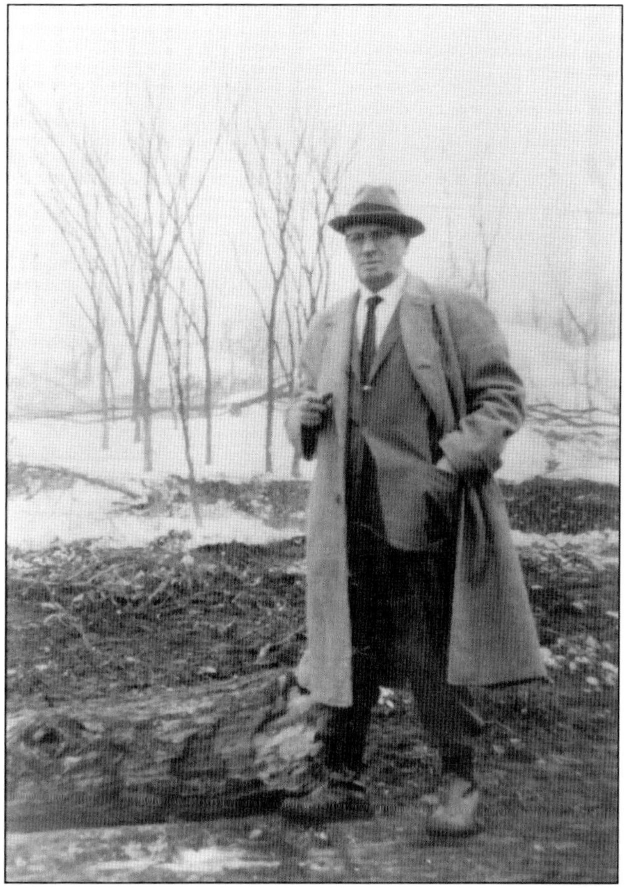

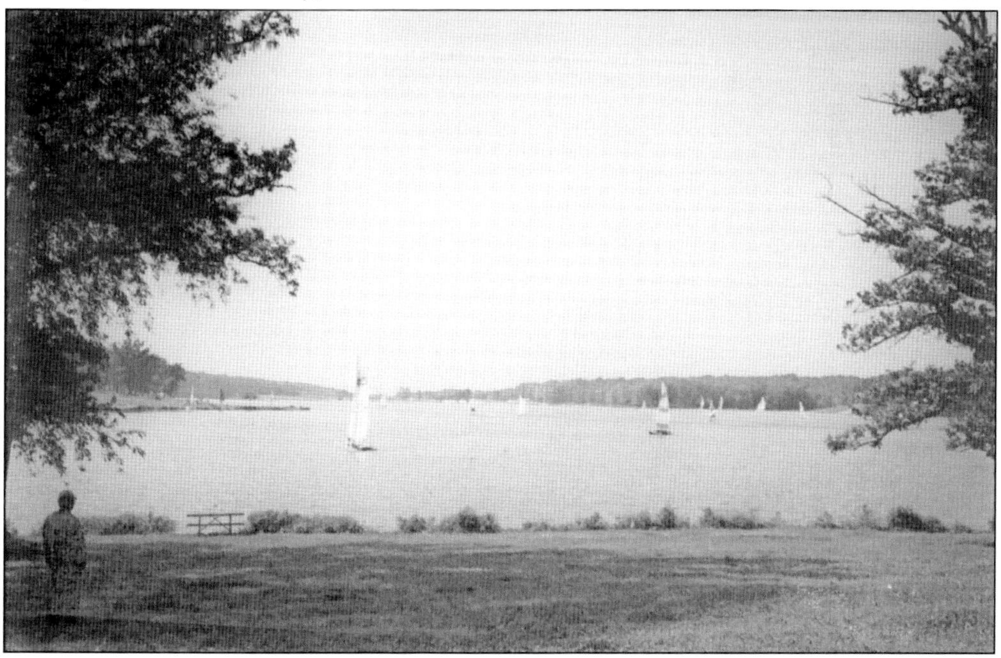

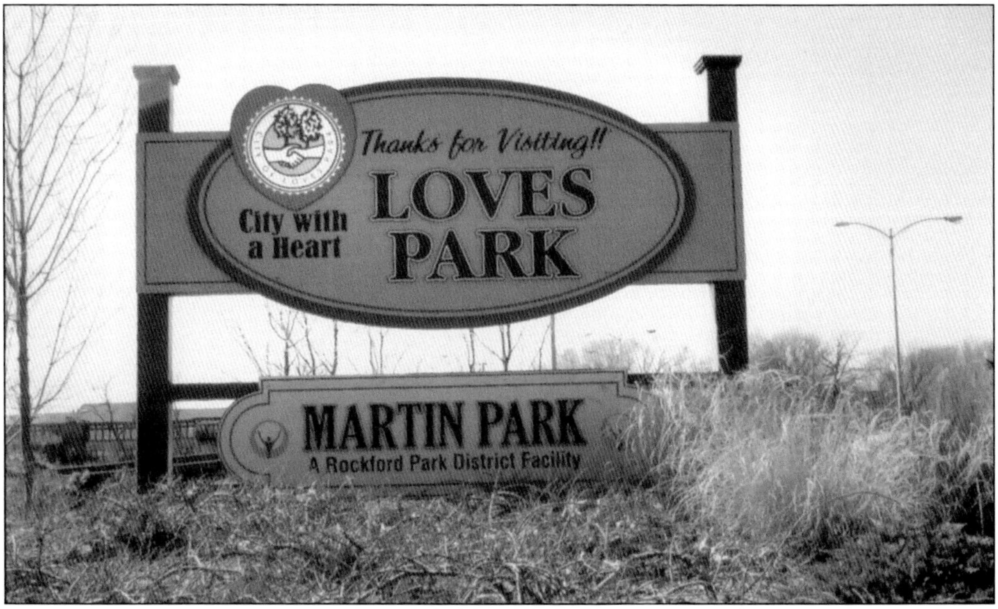

The sign shown above welcomes visitors to Martin Park along the east banks of the Rock River, just west of East Drive. The area was a landfill until Loves Park mayor Frank S. Larson closed it and worked with the Rockford Park District to redevelop it as a park. On July 23, 1958, Martin Memorial Park was officially dedicated. It was named after Charles Woodward Martin, the son of Mr. and Mrs. Irl C. Martin, who died at the young age of 13. The c. 1960 photograph below shows a parking lot full of cars as visitors enjoy the park's many amenities. (Both, courtesy of Rockford Park District.)

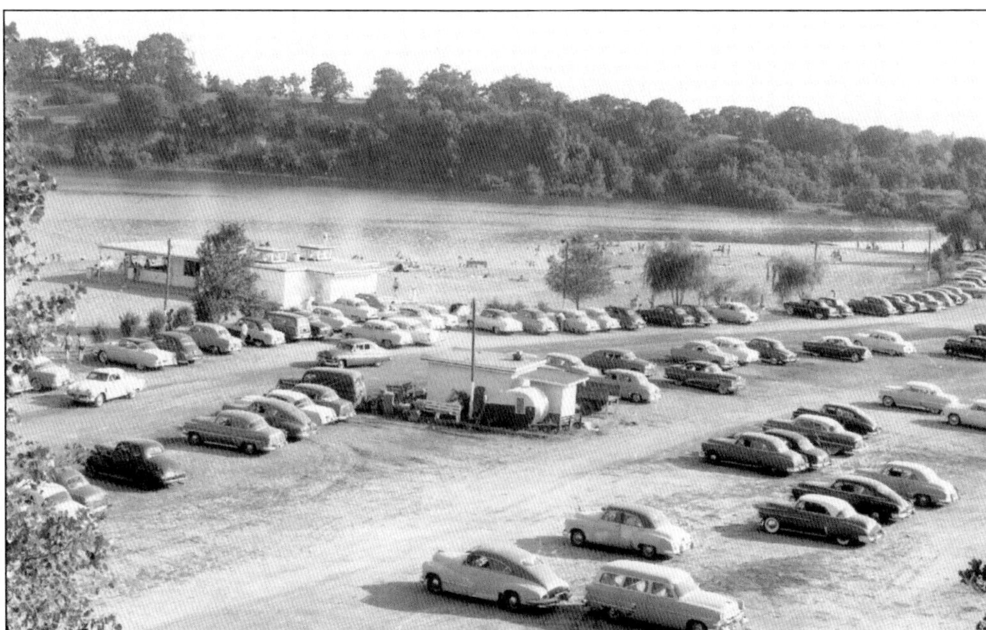

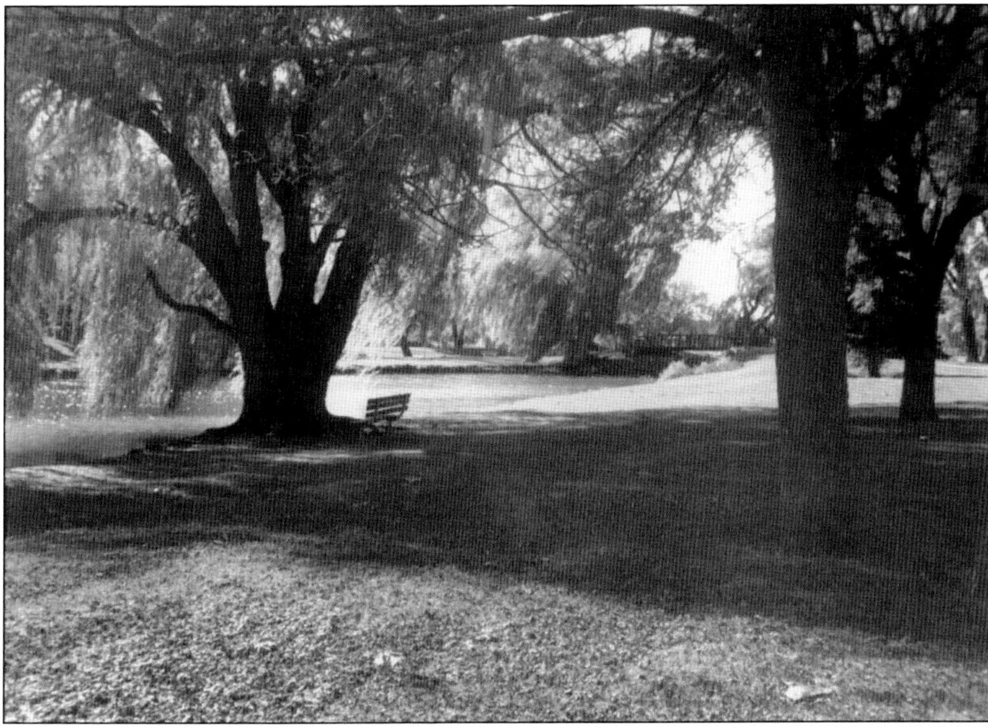

Martin Park includes 12 acres for fishing, picnicking, and other recreational activities. The lagoon is famous for the ducks and geese that frequent the area, and in the winter, it makes the perfect place for ice-skating or ice fishing. Boaters can use the boat ramp to set off into the Rock River, and children can play on the playground. The shelter house at the park was originally built using $25,000 donated by Woodward Governor Company (now Woodward, Inc.). Martin Park was the site of the annual Loves Park Young at Heart Festival until recently, when the festival moved to the Loves Park City Hall grounds. (Both, courtesy of Rockford Park District.)

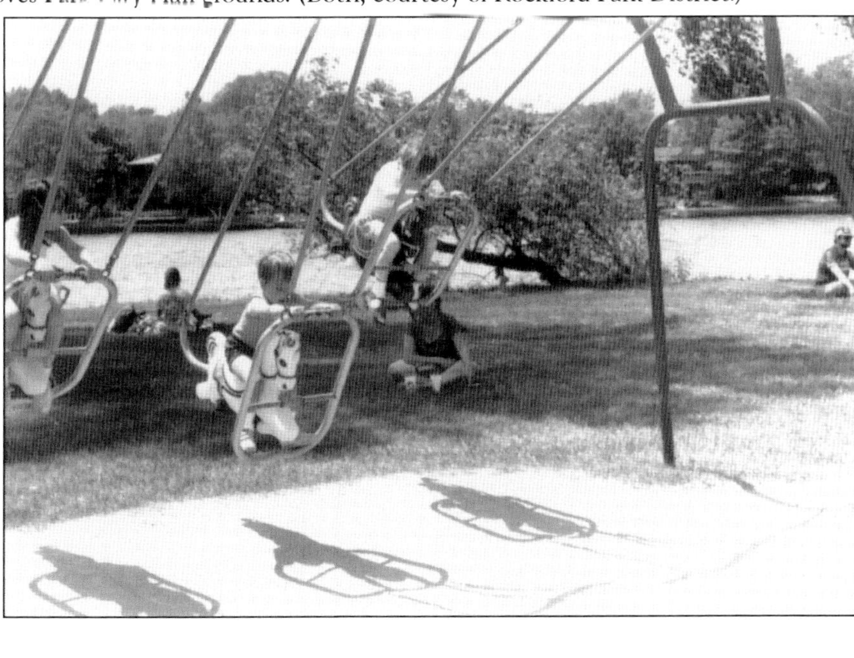

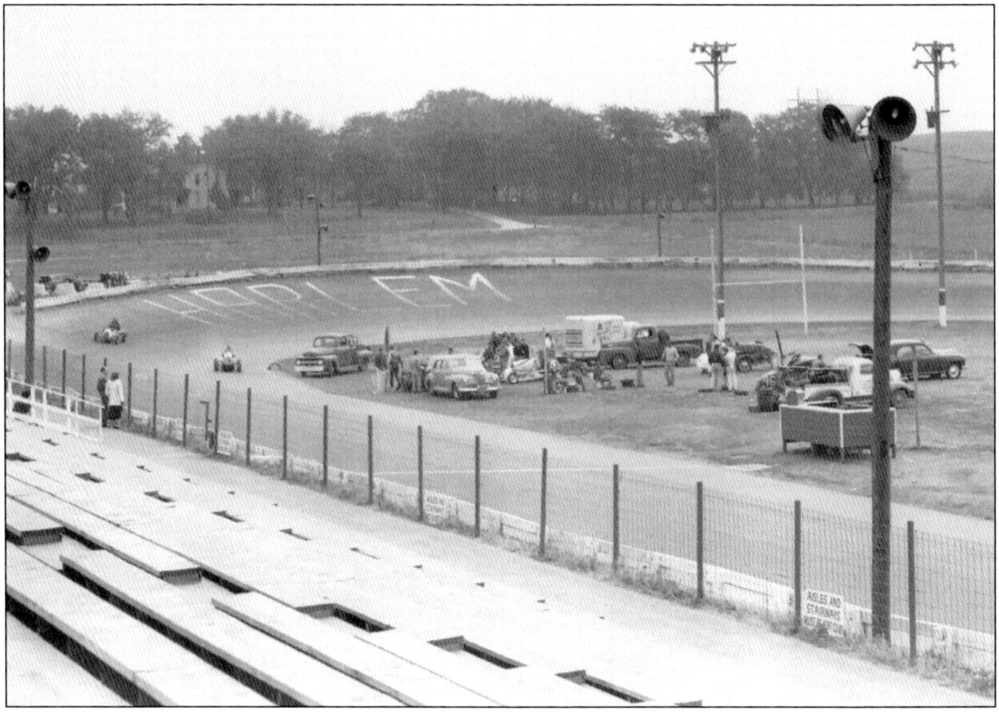

Before it had its own field, the Harlem High School football team used the inner grass of the Rockford Speedway, located at 1601 West Lane Road, as a playing field. The 1952 image above clearly shows the word *Harlem* written in the dirt of the racetrack along with a goalpost at right. On the track, midget cars are practicing for an upcoming 400-lap race. Below, a large crowd gathers at the speedway's original ticket office around 1949. An advertisement for Blue Star Potato Chips, made in Loves Park, is visible just above the booth for Sections C and D. (Both, courtesy of Rockford Speedway.)

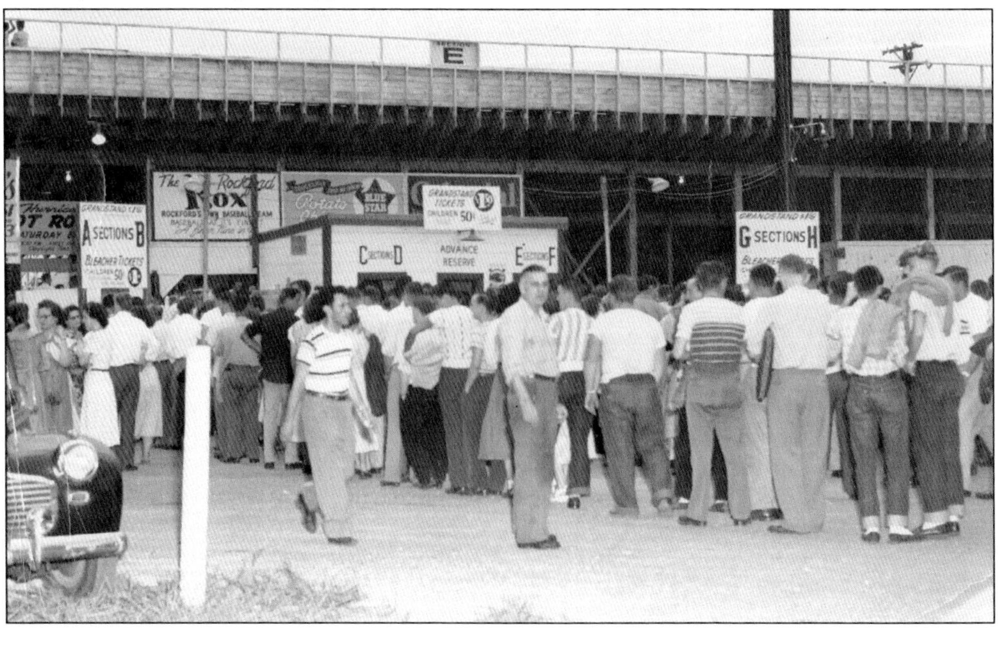

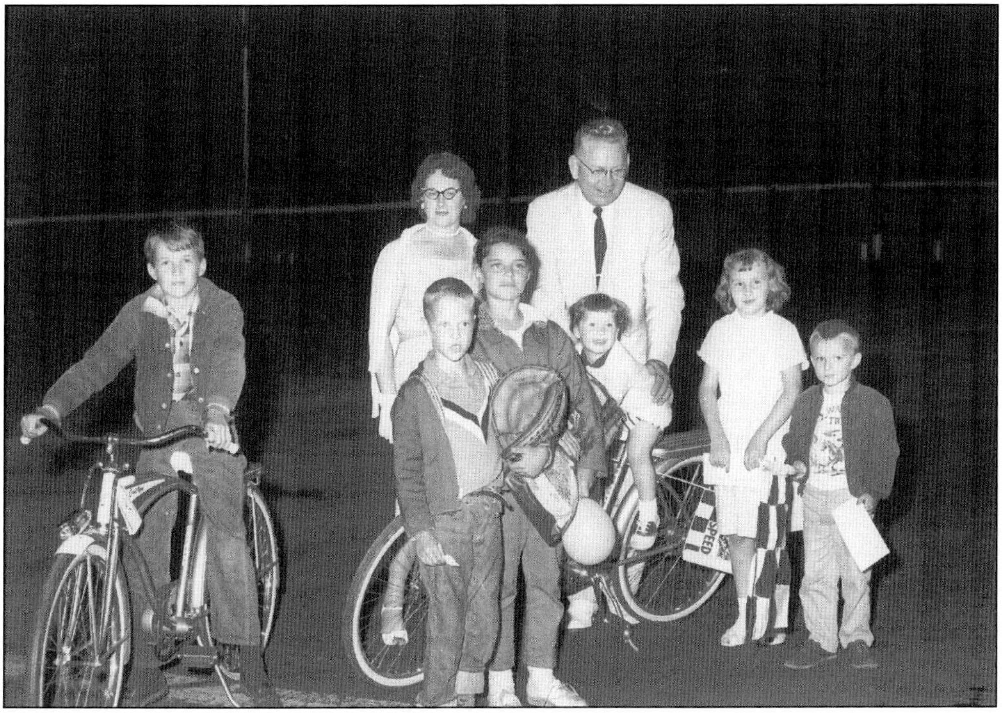

The original decal below advertises Saturday night races at the Rockford Speedway. Above is a group of children who won prizes on Kid's Night—none of the individuals are identified, and the date of the photograph is not known. The speedway often gave away prizes such as bicycles and baseball gloves. The Rockford Speedway, originally started for the Rockford Midget Auto Racing Association, celebrated its 65th season in 2012. Racing is the only organized sport that has continuously existed in the Rockford area for that many years. (Courtesy of Rockford Speedway.)

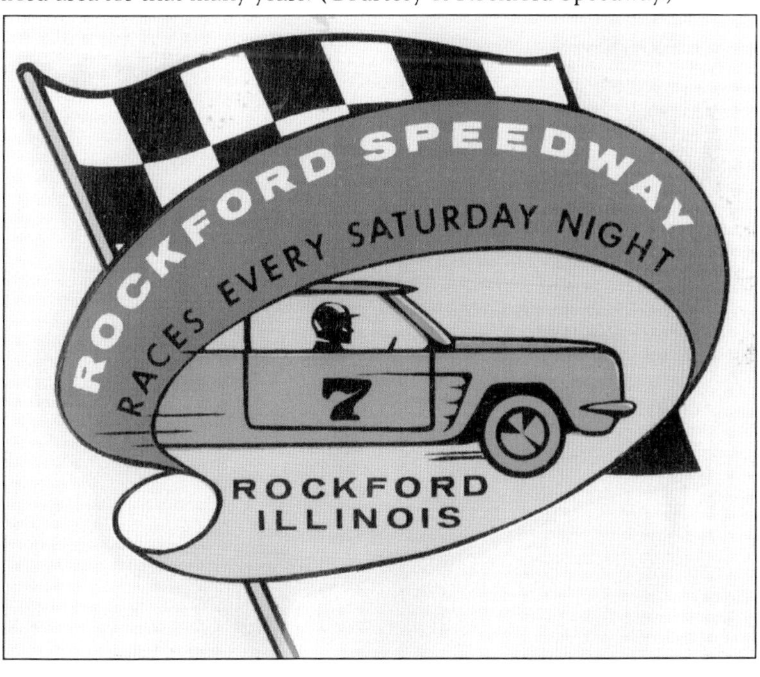

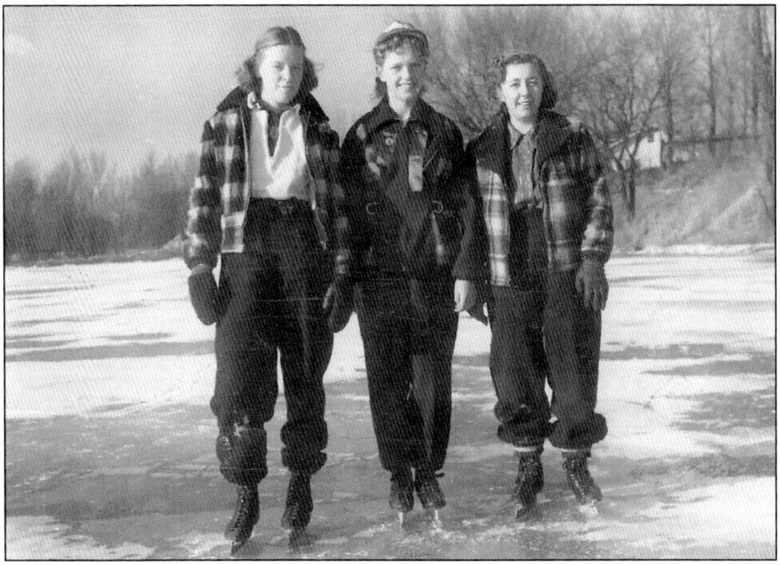

In this early-1930s photograph, Mary Timmis (left), Dorothy Alfred (center), and Helen Hull pose during a break in ice-skating on the lagoon that is now part of Martin Park. The Timmis family lived at 5540 East Drive, and the lagoon was practically in their backyard. (Courtesy of Mary Timmis Miller.)

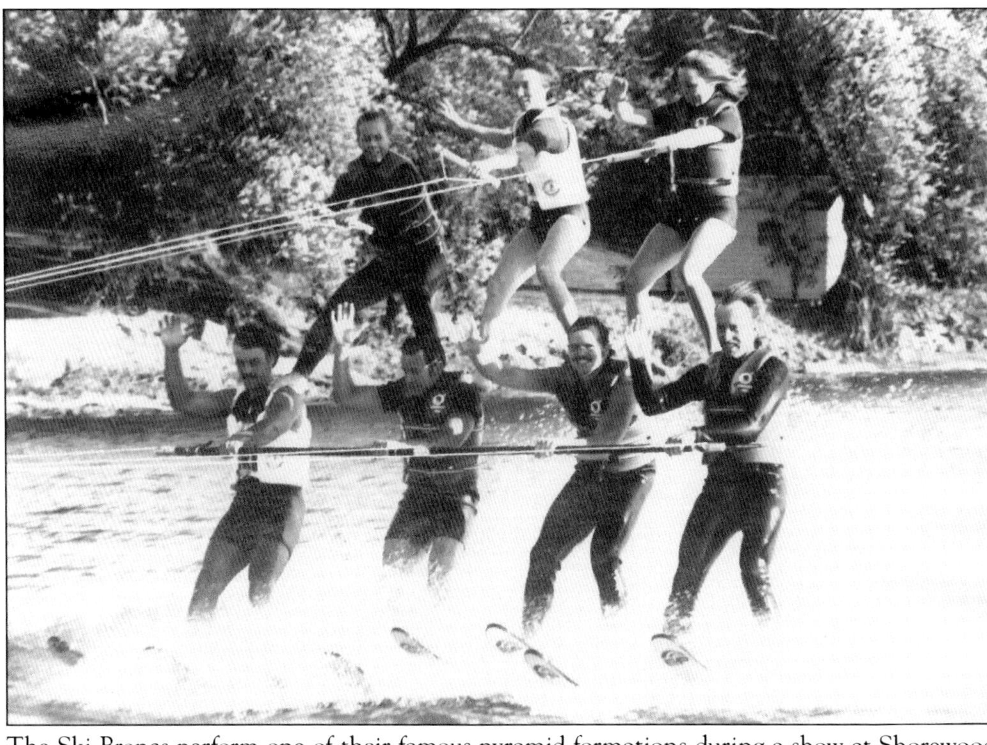

The Ski Broncs perform one of their famous pyramid formations during a show at Shorewood Park, which is located on the east bank of the Rock River just west of Forest Grove Street. The skiers are unidentified, but the photograph was taken on July 4, 1976. The present-day group's pyramid formation includes four levels. (Courtesy of Ski Broncs.)

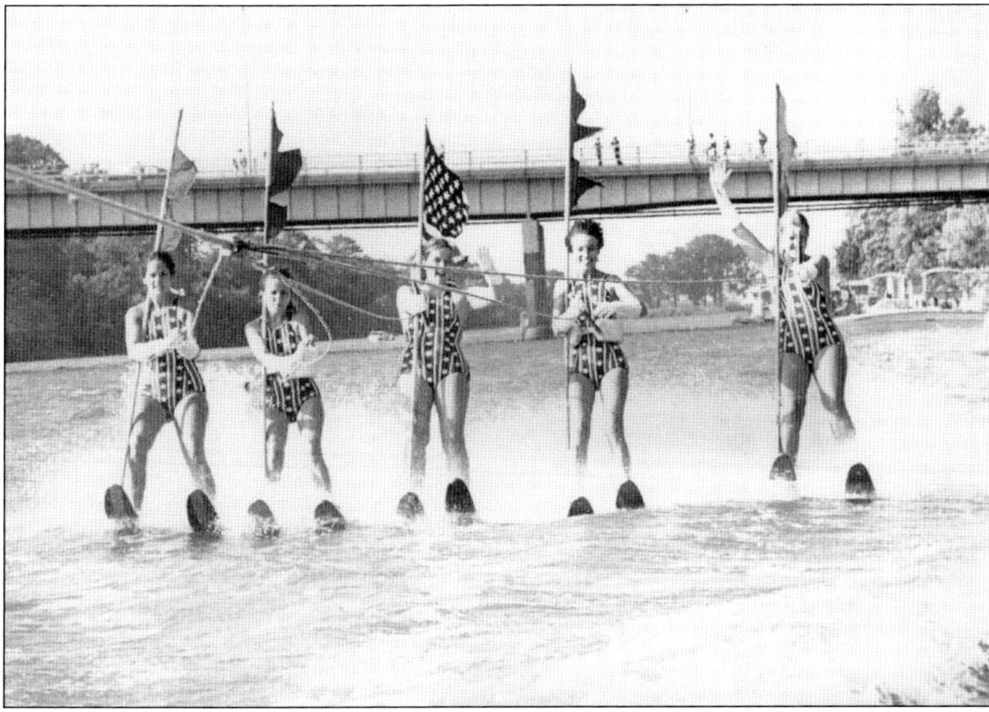

Above, a group of five unidentified women with patriotic swimming suits and flags performs a chorus line formation during the Ski Broncs show on July 4, 1976. At right, two unidentified men perform a trick using ladders during the same show. The Ski Broncs were formed in April 1967 by four area families—the Littles, the Oxleys, the Browns, and the Augensens. The ski club built its first ski jump and performed its first show in 1968. In 1975, its started performing in the Rock River at Shorewood Park. The Ski Broncs perform on Wednesday and Friday nights from the end of May through Labor Day and also participate in numerous regional and national tournaments. (Both, courtesy of Ski Broncs.)

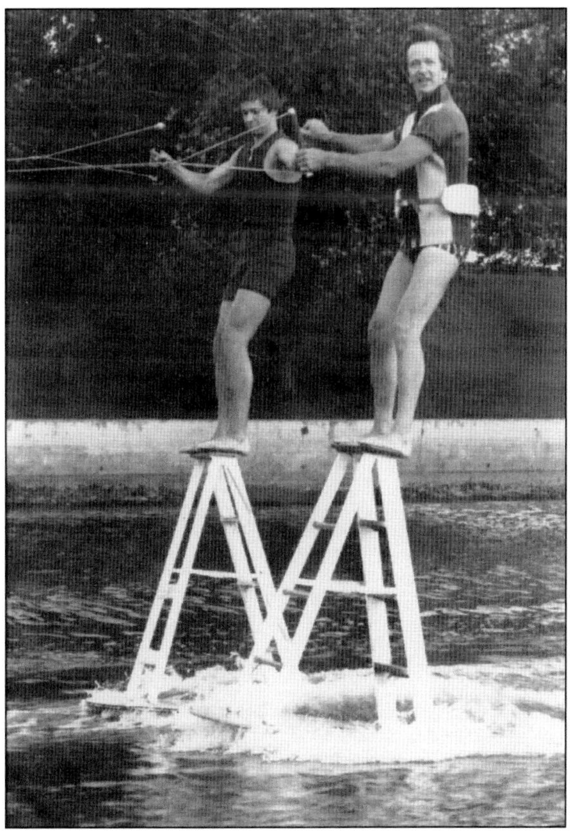

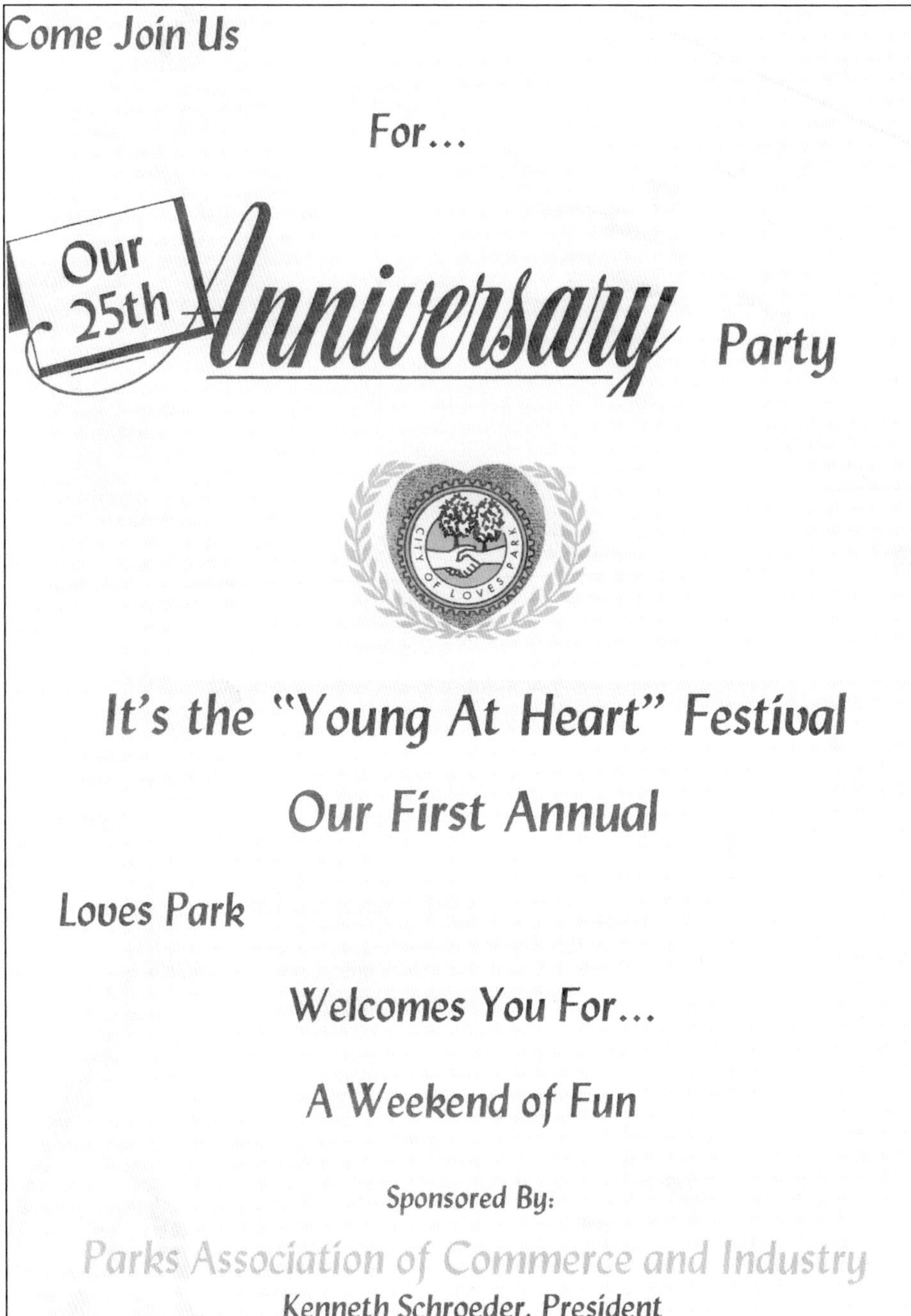
Come Join Us

For...

Our 25th Anniversary Party

It's the "Young At Heart" Festival

Our First Annual

Loves Park

Welcomes You For...

A Weekend of Fun

Sponsored By:

Parks Association of Commerce and Industry

Kenneth Schroeder, President

The Young at Heart Festival was first held August 25 through 27 in 1972 as a way to celebrate the 25th anniversary of the incorporation of Loves Park. A contest was held to name the event, and the winner was Patricia Kelley, who received a commemorative plaque. The first Miss Loves Park was 17-year-old Cyndi Oyen, a junior at Harlem High School. This original program shows the schedule for the three-day event, which ran from Friday through Sunday. The festival included a parade, musical performances, carnival rides, a baseball tournament, a ski show, boat races, a talent show, and an ice cream social.

Program

Friday, August 25, 1972

7:30 P.M. – Harlem High School Auditorium
Musicale Extravaganza and Grand Opening

Featuring . . .

Loves Park Festival Queen – Cyndi Oyen and her Court

Sweed Adelines

Harlem High Band

Barber Shop Singers

Local Welcoming Committee

Admission – Adults $1.00, Children (under 16) 50c

9:00 P.M. – Meadowmart Shopping Center

FREE STREET DANCE

Featuring . . . *TWO* Bands
Dave Remington, Aristocrat of Jazz
And . . . Missing Links , No. Illinois best of Rock

Admission – FREE

Try the Balloon Walk, in the area

Concessions, Courtesy Harlem Fan Club,
Carl Nelson, President

Saturday, August 26, 1972

3:00 P.M. – North on N. Second Street (Hwy 51) to . . . Harlem High Schoo

Parade – Northern Illinois' Greatest

Featuring . . .

Geri's Float with Loves Park Festival Queen,
Cyndi Oyen and her Court

7 of the TOP Drum and Bugle Corps in the USA
plus . . . Many exciting entries

The first page of the inaugural Young at Heart Festival program details the kick-off events held on Friday, August 25, 1972. It began with a musical "extravaganza" at the Harlem High School Auditorium and continued with a street dance at the Meadow Mart Shopping Center. The festivities began on Saturday, August 26, 1972, with a parade.

Program

7:30 P.M. — Harlem High School Stadium

Drum and Bugle Corp Competition

Seven qualifying Corps in competition

Admission — Adults $2.00, Children (under 16) $.75

Sunday, August 27, 1972

1:00 P.M. — Martin Park, on Rock River

Water Ski Show — Courtesy Bronc's Ski Inc.,
Phil Salmons, President

Admission — FREE
Parking at No. Town Shopping Center

2:30 P.M. — Band Concert — Courtesy Harold Luhman, Music Director
Harlem School District

4:00 P.M. — Championship Boat Races —
Courtesy Richard Ingebretsen and Terry Leatherby

5:15 P.M. — Torch Parade on Rock River with Surprise displays

5:30 P.M. — Fast Pitch Women's Soft Ball Exhibition

Loves Park Cougars vs. a Challenging Team

While at Martin Park, plan to partake in the . . .
Old Fashioned Ice Cream Social,
Courtesy Loves Park Volunteer Fire Dept.,
Marlyn Ryall, Assistant Chief

7:30 P.M. — Harlem High School Auditorium

Grand Finale and Awards Presentation and Talent Show
Featuring the top talent from Northern Illinois
Talent Show — Courtesy Francis School of Dance

Admission — Adults 50c, Children (under 16) 25c

TICKETS for all 3 BIG EVENTS are available in book form

	Adults	Children under 16
Musicale	$1.00	$ .50
Competition	2.00	.75
Talent Show	.50	.25
Book Prices	$3.50	$1.50

Purchase tickets from any Committee member or ticket booths, as announced.

The Parks Association of Parks and Industry gratefully acknowledges the support of the Park State Bank and the creative assistance of their advertising agency.

The second page of the inaugural Young at Heart Festival program outlines the events scheduled for Saturday, August 26, and Sunday, August 27, 1972. A drum and bugle competition was held at Harlem High School Stadium. The last day of the festival featured a water-skiing show, boat races, a softball game, and a talent show.

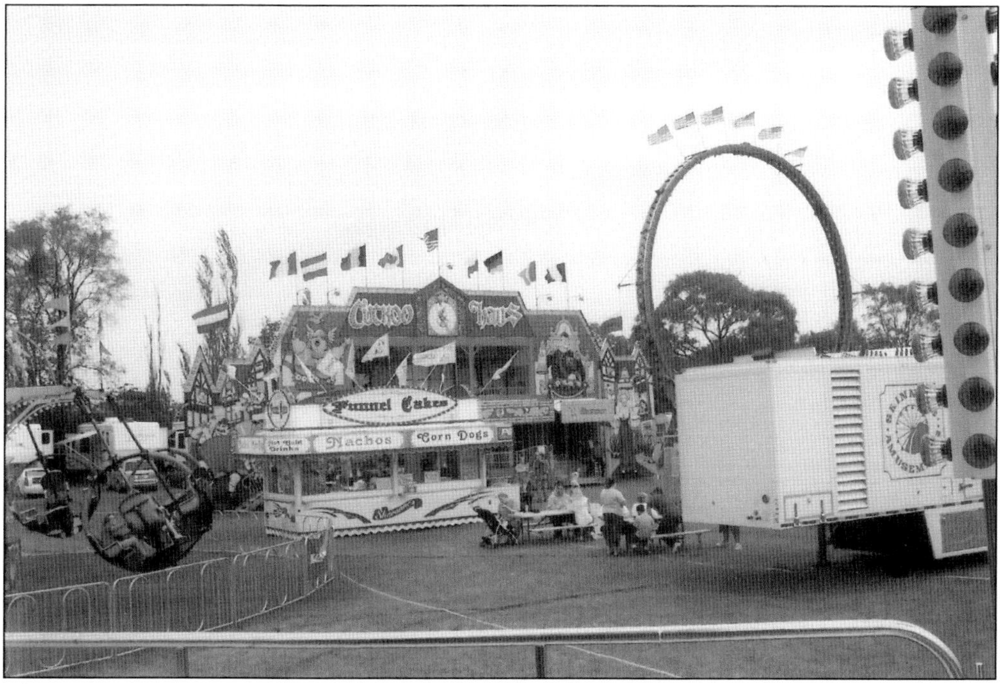

The Young at Heart Festival is still held to this day and attracts people from across northern Illinois. The carnival rides and concession stands for all ages are still a popular part of the festival, as are the parade and musical entertainment. The pageant portion has expanded, and fireworks are now a part of the events. The festival is now held at the end of May, and events are also held on the Monday following the weekend (Memorial Day). The festival is organized by the Parks Chamber of Commerce and, in recent years, has moved from Martin Park to the Loves Park City Hall grounds at 100 Heart Boulevard. (Both, courtesy of Parks Chamber of Commerce.)

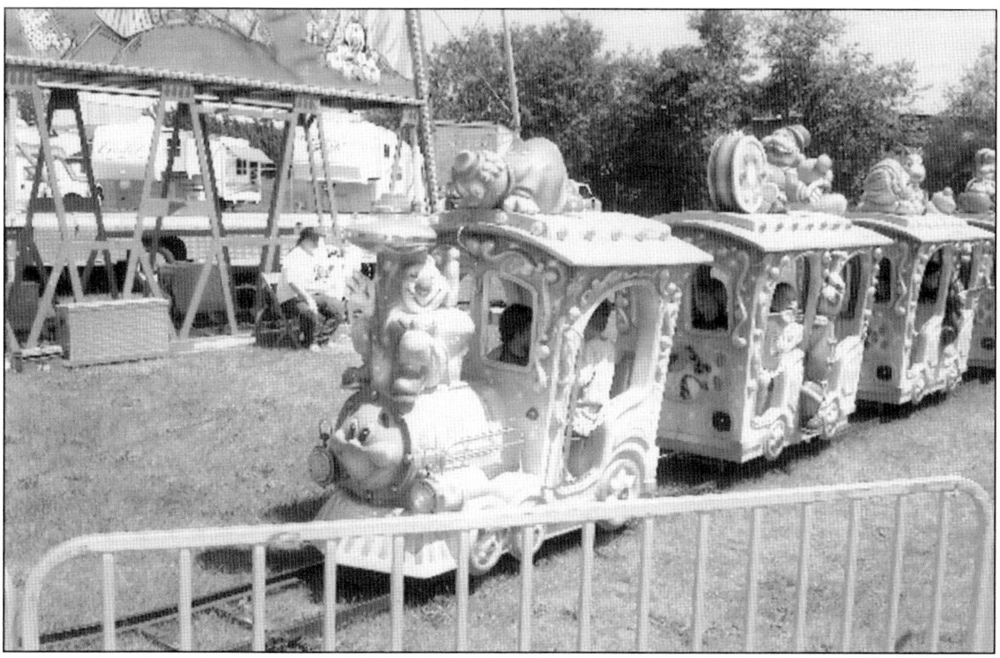

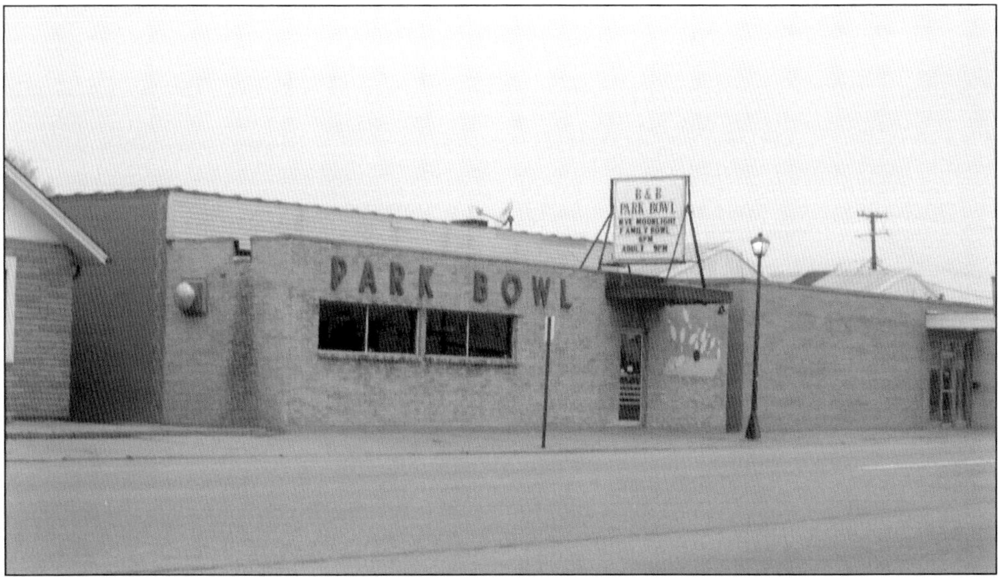

B &B Park Bowl, located at 5626 North Second Street, has been a popular bowling spot for decades. It has remained in the same location since it opened and is currently owned by Butch Olson. Other bowling facilities in Loves Park include Park Bowl (at 5318 North Second Street) and Forest Hills Lanes (at 7742 Forest Hills Lane).

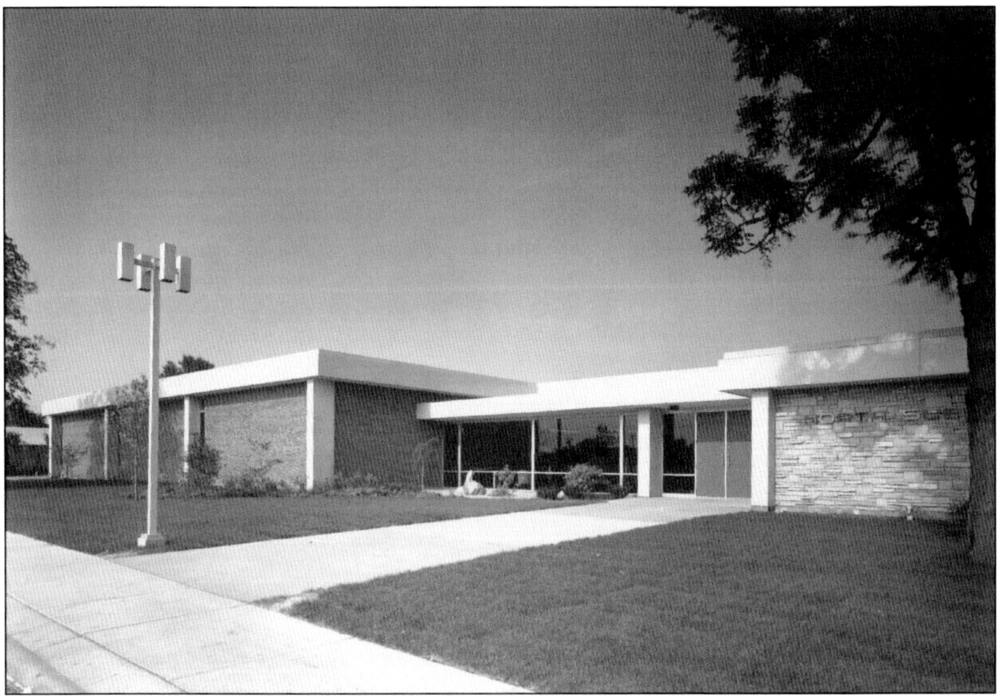

North Suburban Library District first opened on April 15, 1944, at 5426 North Second Street. The project of establishing a library was sponsored by the North Suburban Woman's Club. In 1950, the library was moved to 515 Loves Park Drive, and in 1960, it was moved to 535 Loves Park Drive. In 1970, the library was moved to its current location at 6340 North Second Street. The Loves Park location is shown here. The other location is in Roscoe, Illinois.

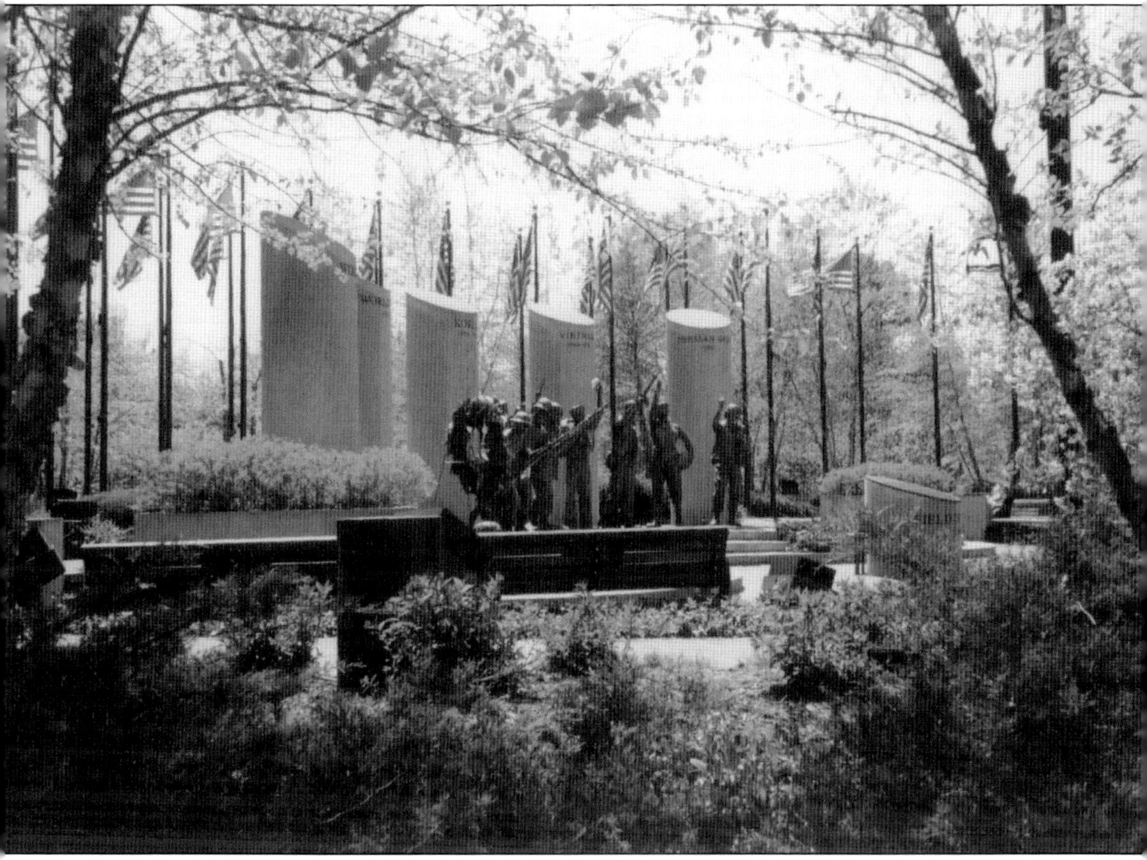

Just north of the Loves Park City Hall is the Sand Park Field of Honor Veterans Memorial. The idea for the memorial started with Arthur W. "Art" Anderson, but it became a community project that united the Field of Honor Veterans Memorial Committee, the City of Loves Park, the Village of Machesney Park, the Veterans of Foreign Wars Post No. 9759, the Rockford Park District, the Rockford Park District Foundation, and numerous individual contributors. The memorial was dedicated on November 10, 1995. It consists of five limestone columns, which represent the five wars of the 20th century: World War I, World War II, the Korean War, the Vietnam War, and the Persian Gulf War. The eight bronze statues represent each branch of the US Armed Forces and include an infantry soldier, sailor, nurse, paratrooper, pilot, medic, tank battalion solder, and support personnel. The memorial is surrounded by American flags.

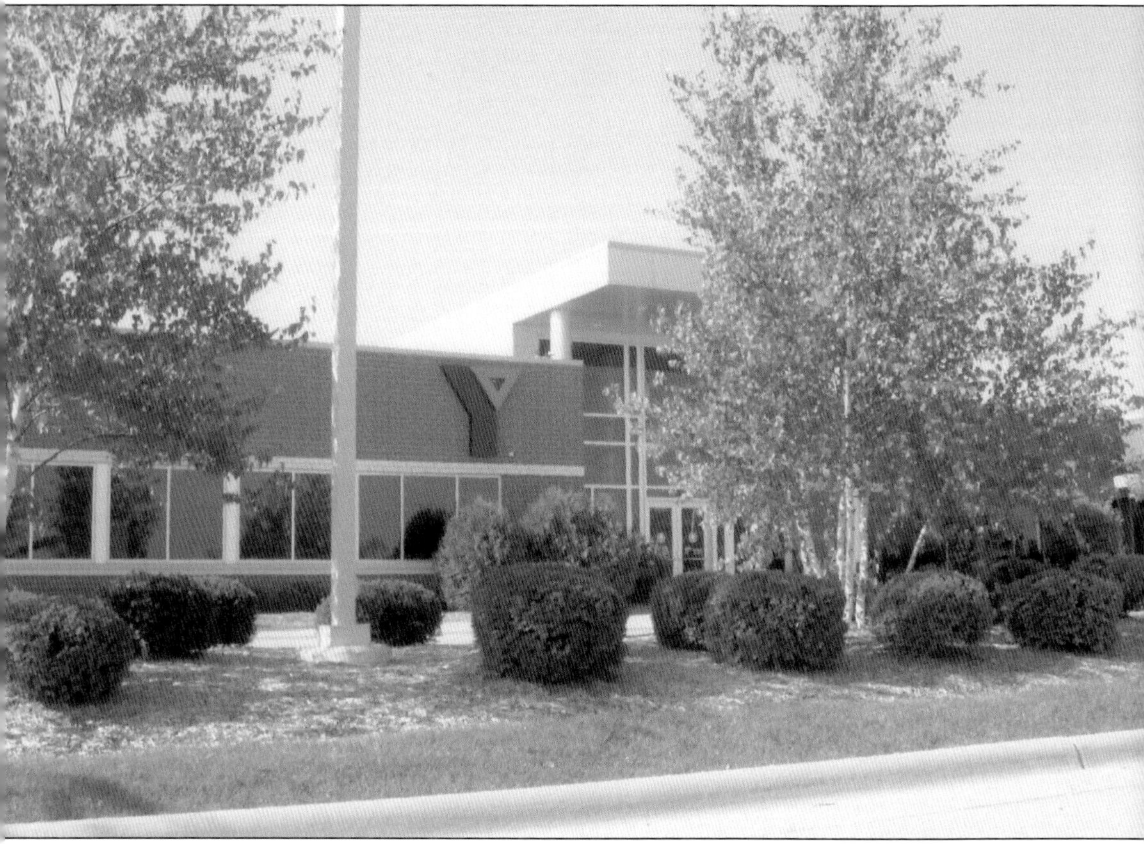

The Northeast Branch of the Rock River Valley YMCA, located at 8451 Orth Road, opened in 2007. The building cost approximately $12 million to construct and is 65,000 square feet in size. The YMCA partnered with SwedishAmerican Hospital in Rockford to offer physical therapy and rehabilitation services at this new location. The YMCA also has three exercise and dance rooms, a swimming pool, a weight room, locker rooms, a youth and family center, a youth fitness center, a child-care center, and a recreational path. Some of the sports offered include basketball, dance, gymnastics, soccer, volleyball, cheerleading, swimming, yoga, Zumba, and karate. The facility is open seven days a week. (Courtesy of Nicole C. Lindsay.)

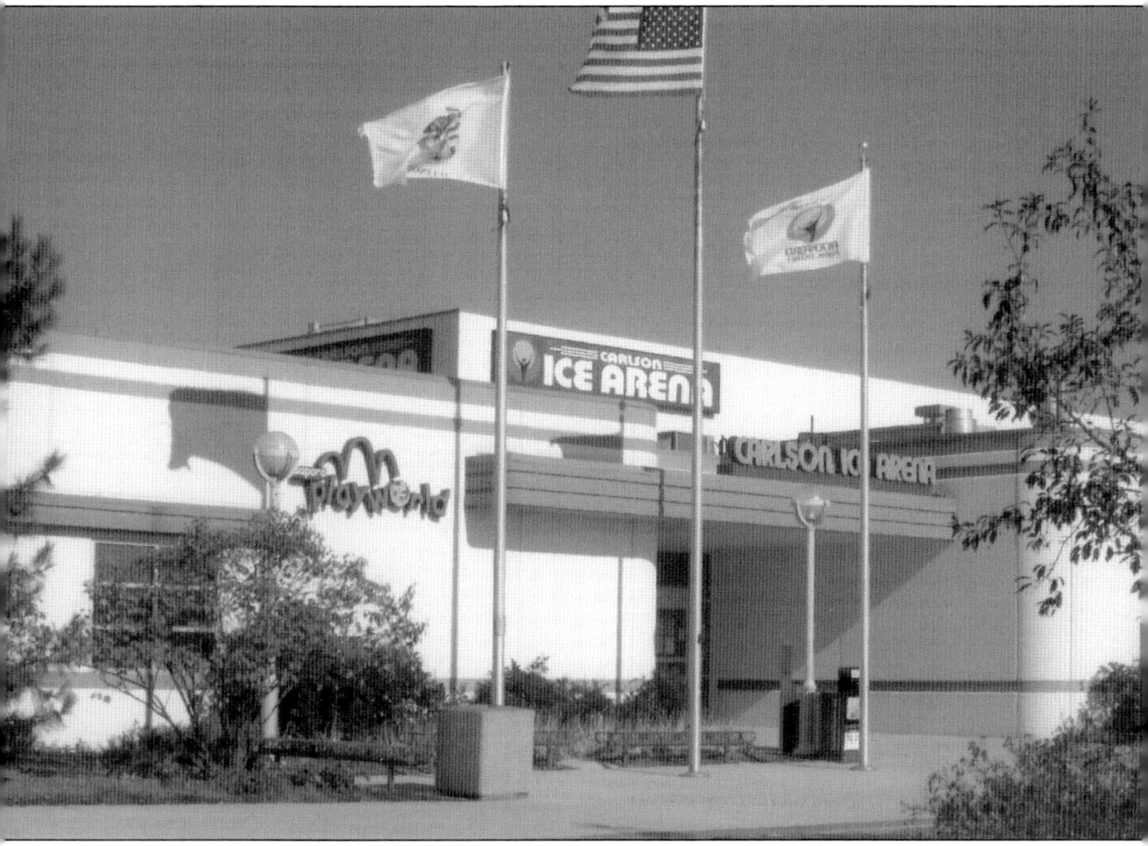

In August 1996, ground was broken for a new skating rink in Loves Park. Rockford Park District's Carlson Ice Arena, located at 4150 North Perryville Road, officially opened in 1998. Kurt Carlson, an area businessman, donated the land for the building, which cost approximately $7 million to construct and includes a 200-by-85-foot ice-skating rink and seating for 600 people. The facility also has the Sapora Playworld, a three-level soft play structure for school-age children, and the Tiny Tots Playspace for children four years old and younger. The facility is open six days a week. (Courtesy of Nicole C. Lindsay.)

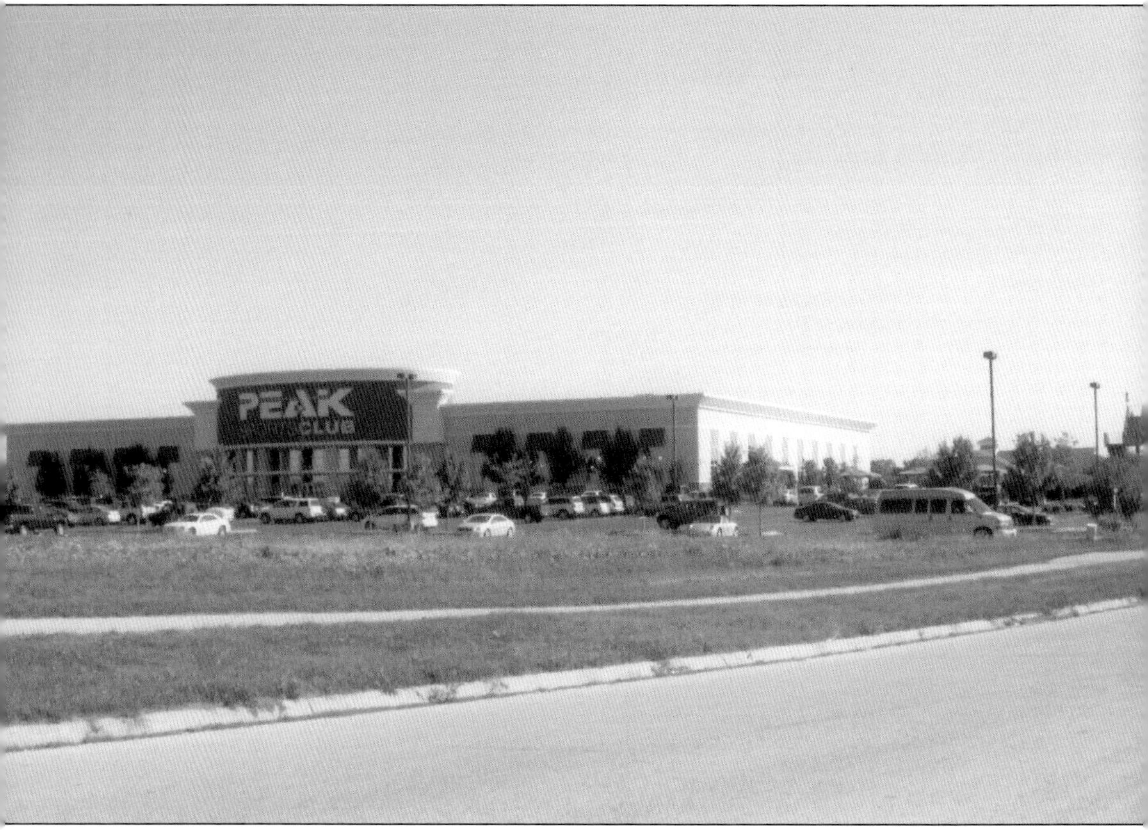

In 2007, Peak Sports Club opened a new Loves Park location at 4401 Peak Drive. The new facility is 80,000 square feet in size. Amenities include a steam room; a sauna; a whirlpool; a basketball court; a rock-climbing wall; a game room for children seven years of age and older; two indoor pools with a four-lane lap pool and a warm-water pool; an outdoor pool featuring a six-lane lap pool, cabanas, and concessions; a birthday party room; a ladies-only workout area; swimming lessons; and certified trainers. A salon and spa are also located in the facility. The Peak Sports Club is open 24 hours a day. (Courtesy of Nicole C. Lindsay.)

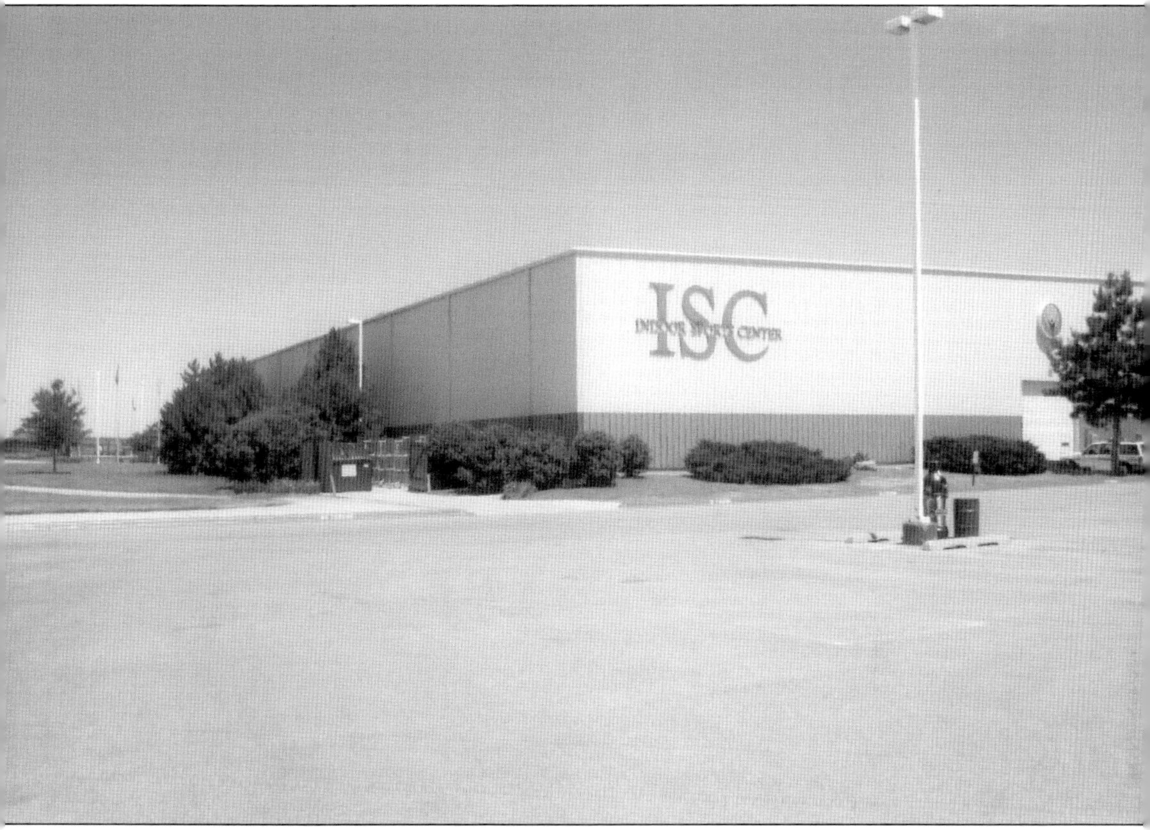

In 2001, the Rockford Park District purchased the Indoor Sports Center at 8800 East Riverside Boulevard from Donald "Doc" Wedgbury. The facility became part of Sportscore Two's 124-acre site. The building itself is 60,000 square feet in size. The entire facility consists of 19 soccer fields, 5 sand volleyball courts, 3 multisport indoor fields, locker rooms, a sports equipment store, a restaurant and sports bar called SkyBox, and Wedgbury Stadium, which seats 2,000. Sports played here include soccer, volleyball, rugby, football, golf, softball, basketball, Wiffle ball, dodgeball, Frisbee, badminton, in-line hockey, and wheelchair sports. The center also hosts conventions, car shows, and other large events. (Courtesy of Nicole C. Lindsay.)

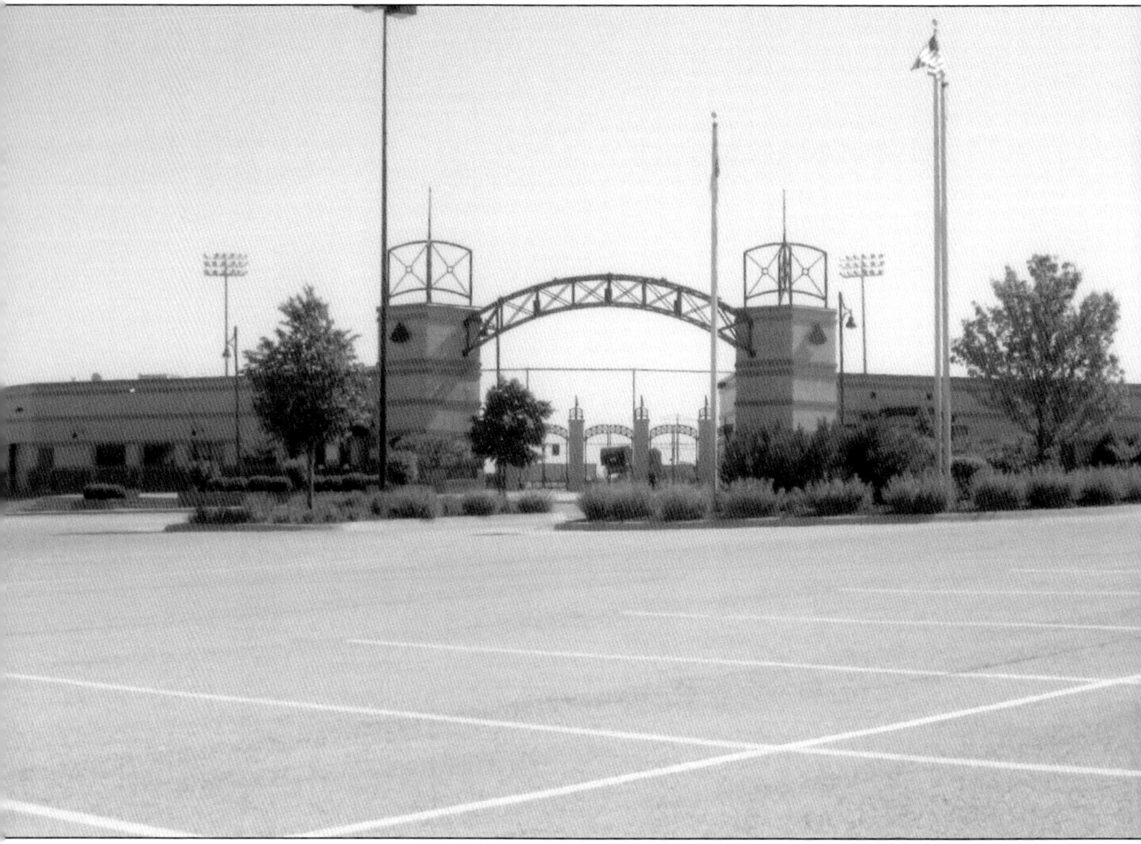

The Rockford RiverHawks Stadium at 4503 Interstate Boulevard is home to the Rockford RiverHawks Frontier League baseball team. The team moved here in 2006 from its former location at Marinelli Field in Rockford. The team originated in Portsmouth, Ohio, where it played as the Portsmouth Explorers from 1993 through 1995; then moved to Springfield, Illinois, where it was the Springfield Capitals from 1996 through 2001; and came to Rockford in 2002 and became the RiverHawks. The RiverHawks stadium can seat over 4,200 people and center field stretches 380 feet. The Frontier League is an independent, professional baseball league based in Sauget, Illinois. (Courtesy of Nicole C. Lindsay.)

Eight

Natural Disasters

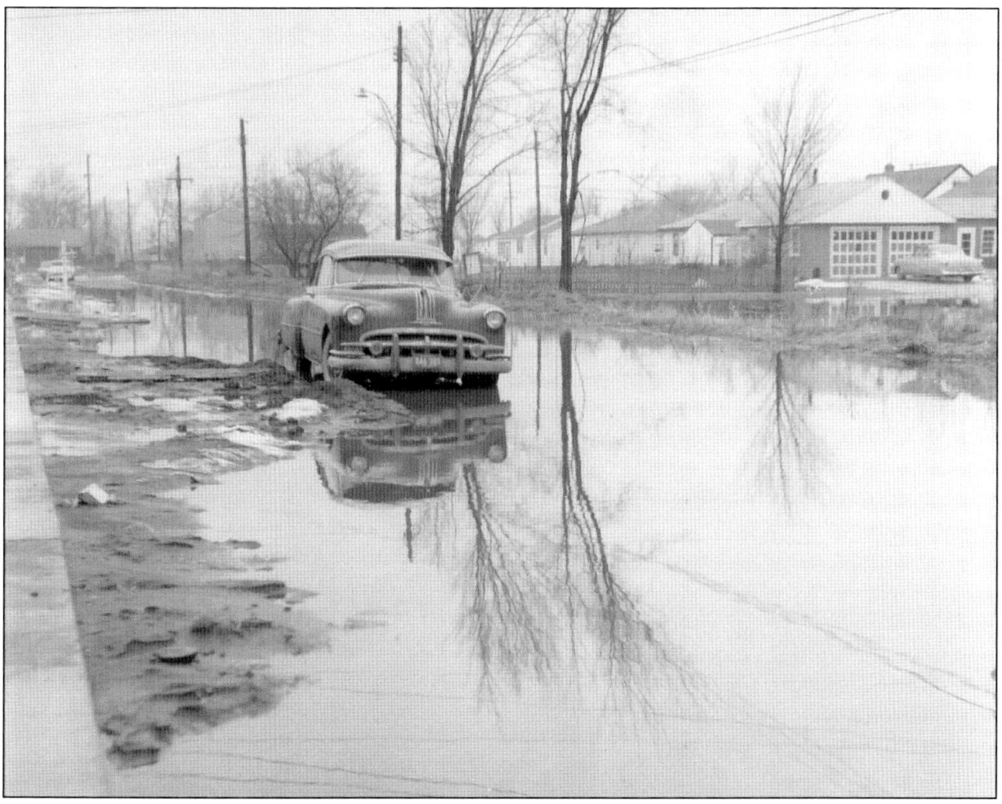

This car is stuck in the mud and debris caused by flooding that hit the Loves Park area in January and February 1957. The location where this car is stuck is around 609 East Hosmer Street, in front of the home of Gene and Alice Duclon. The photograph was taken looking west towards First Street.

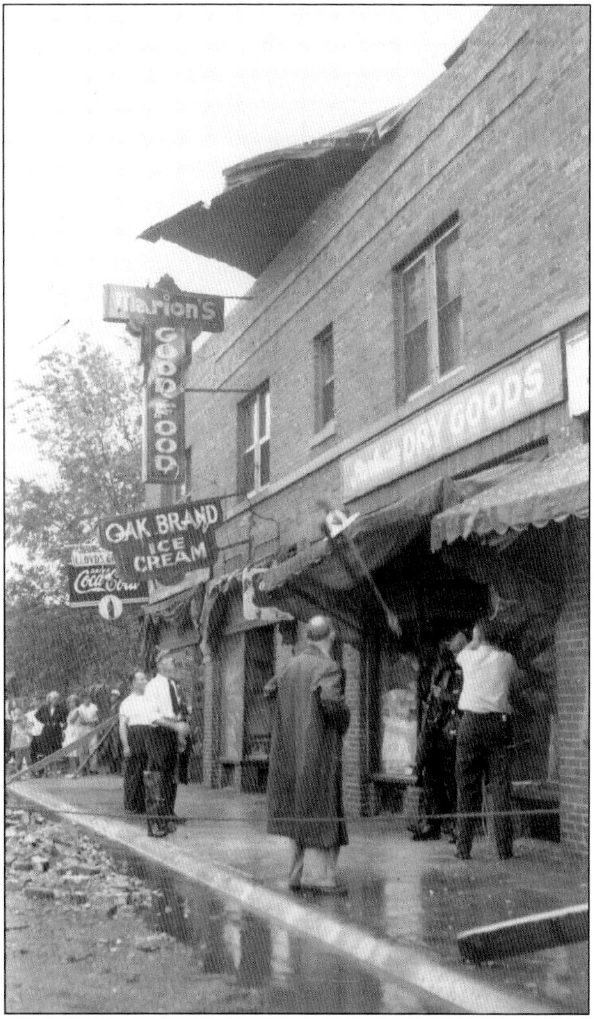

A tornado struck Loves Park on Thursday, July 22, 1948. The photograph at left shows the damage at Parkside Dry Goods (5422 North Second Street), Marion's Good Food Restaurant (5420 North Second Street), and Lloyd's Grocery (5418 North Second Street). The image below offers a wider view showing the damage to Haddon Floor Company (5424 North Second Street), North Suburban Library District (5426 North Second Street), and Ancona's Orthopedic Shoes (5428 North Second Street). A Loves Park fire truck and a state police car are on the street as official inspect the damage to the sides and roofs of the businesses. Numerous residents also gathered to view the damage.

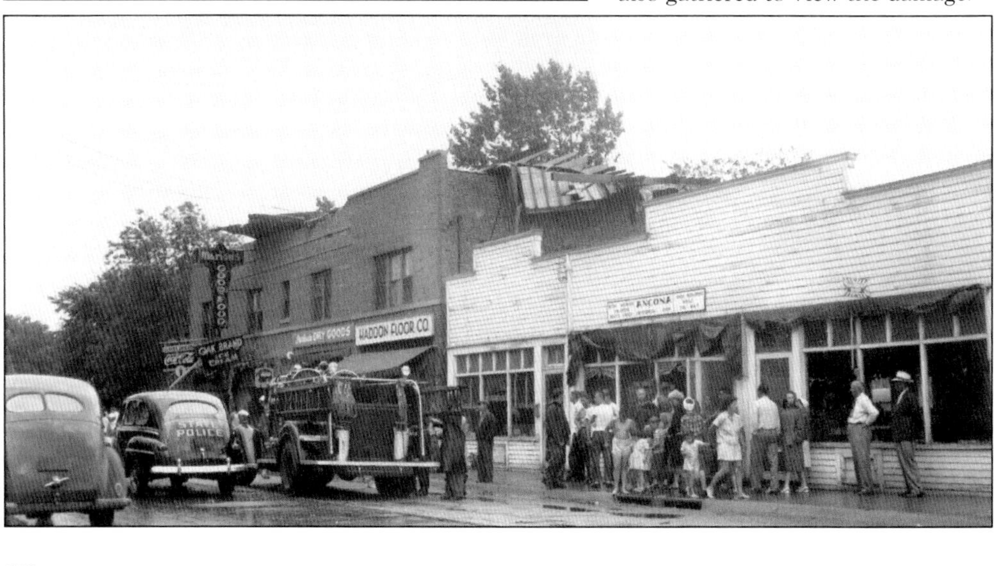

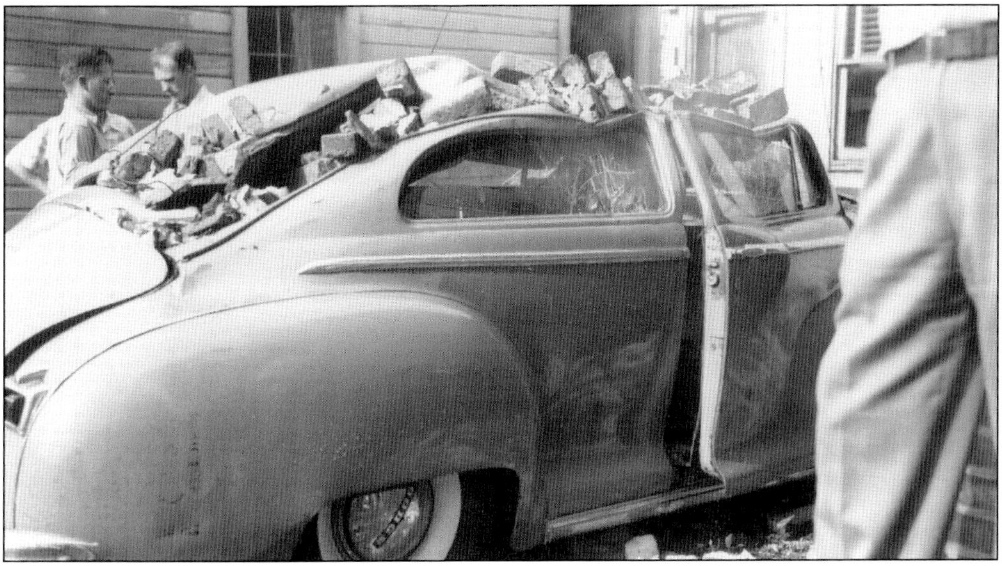

Nicholas Ancona (believed to at far left), the owner of Ancona's Orthopedic Shoes at 5428 North Second Street, and other area residents inspect the damage to Ancona's Dodge that was caused by falling bricks and other debris thrown about in the July 22, 1948, tornado. Ancona's car was parked to the west of North Second Street—behind his business—when the tornado struck. The photograph below shows the back of Ancona's Orthopedic Shoes (the wooden building) and the neighboring businesses (brick buildings), with most of the damage occurring on the roof and second floor.

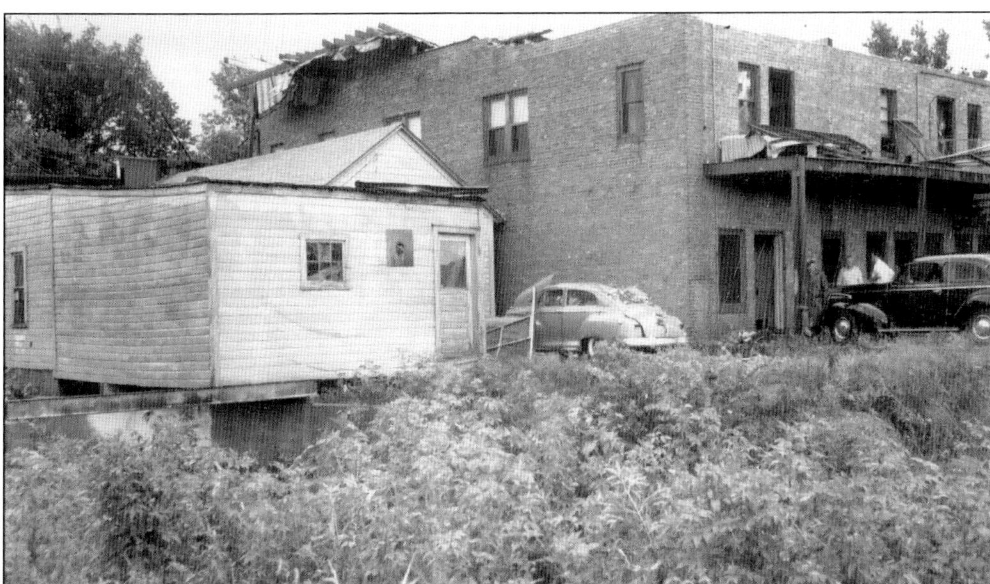

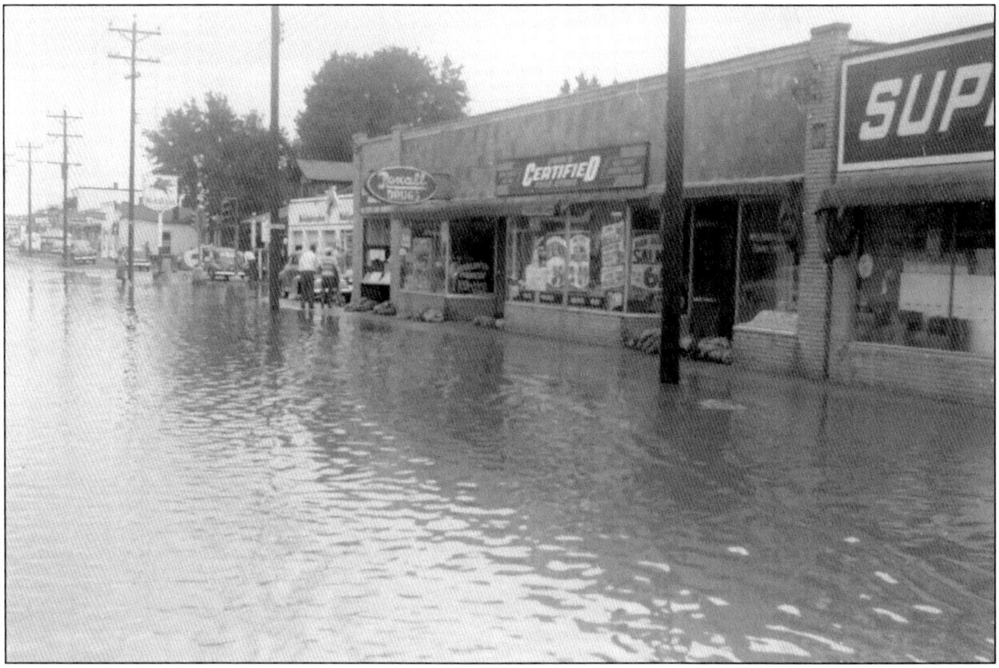

These photographs show flooding that occurred on July 18 and July 19, 1952, in the 5400 block of North Second Street. Records indicate that over 11 inches of rain fell during the two days, and the city's drainage system failed to clear the water. The photograph above shows Rexall Drugs in the center and a Mobilgas station farther to the north. The photograph below shows more of the extent of the flooding and includes the Piggly Wiggly and both sides of North Second Street. At right is a Keep to Right sign that shows where traffic should be; instead, the street is covered in water.

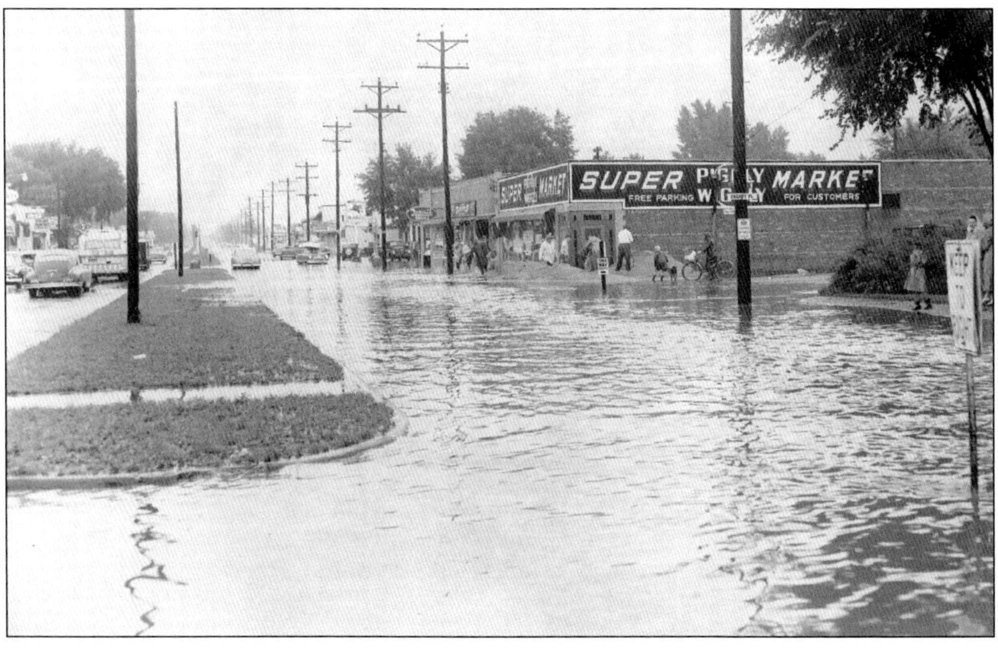

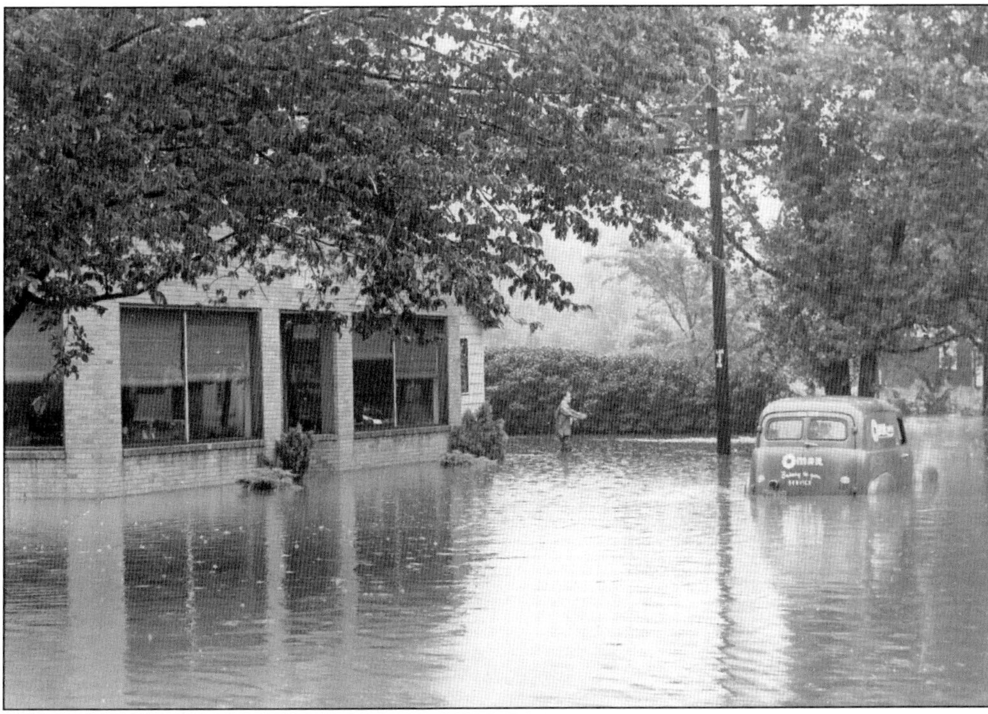

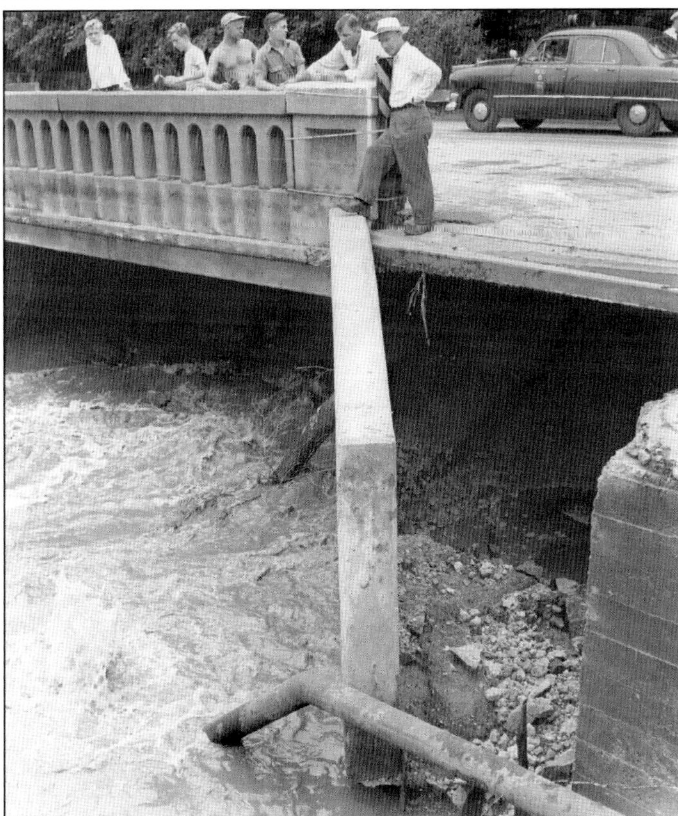

These images offer another view of the flooding on July 18 and July 19, 1952, in the 5400 block of North Second Street. The photograph above shows the Post Publishers newspaper building; the stranded vehicle is a car belong to Omar bakery. The man in front of the building is unidentified. The photograph at right shows damage and debris, including a large tree limb, in the storm drain at 518 Merrill Avenue, near the intersection of North Second Street, during the floods. None of the individuals in the photograph are identified, and an Illinois State Police car is visible in the background.

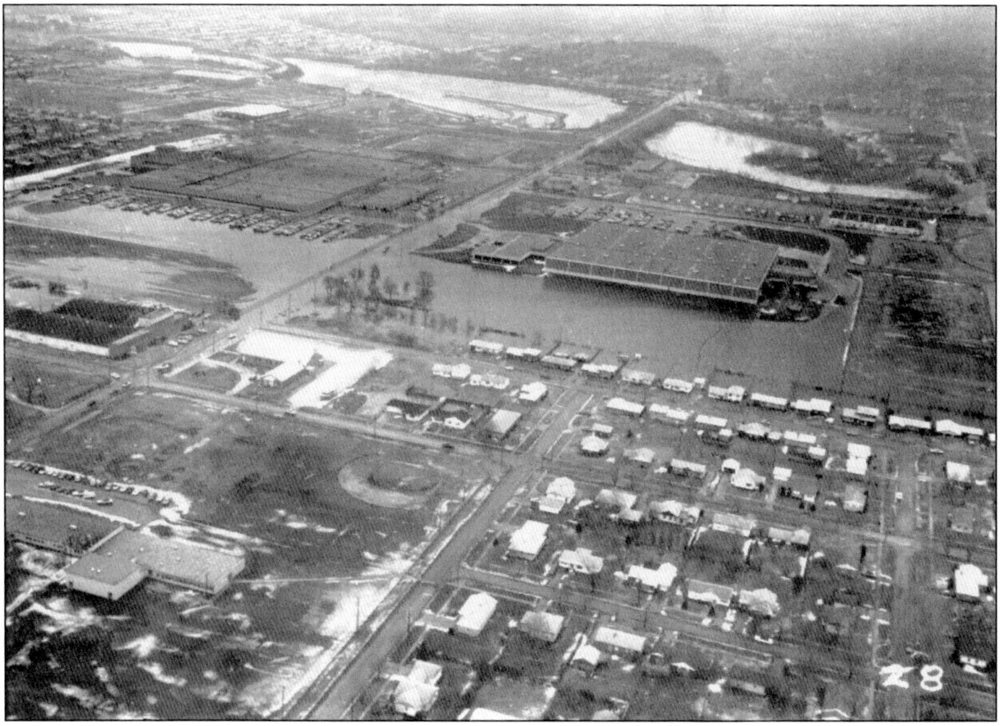

These aerial images show the extent of the damage caused by the flooding that occurred in February 1971. The photograph above shows the intersection of Windsor Road and Elm Avenue at center left. Blue Star Foods and Rockford Clutch are at left, and Barber-Colman is at right. At the top of the photograph, Windsor Road divides Windsor Lake. The photograph below shows flooding near the intersection of Riverside Boulevard and North Second Street. Riverside Boulevard runs diagonally from the left to the right of the photograph. North Second Street intersects it near the top of the photograph.

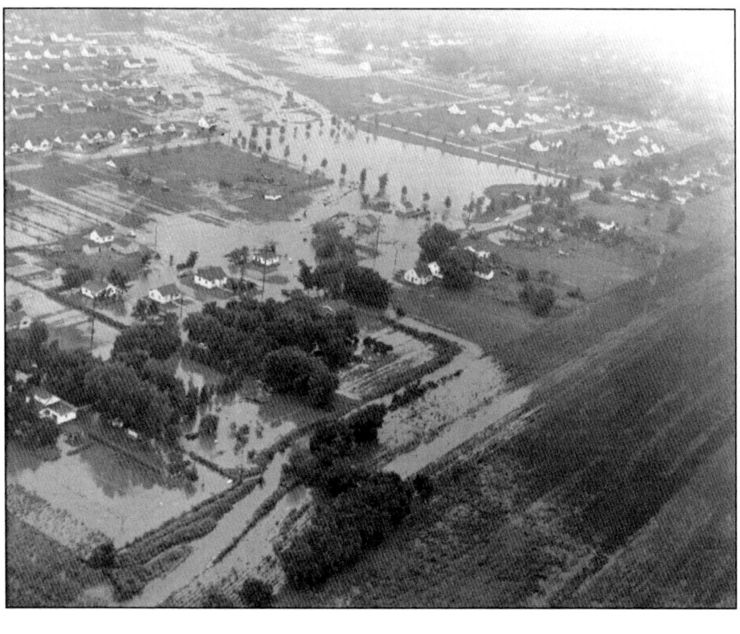

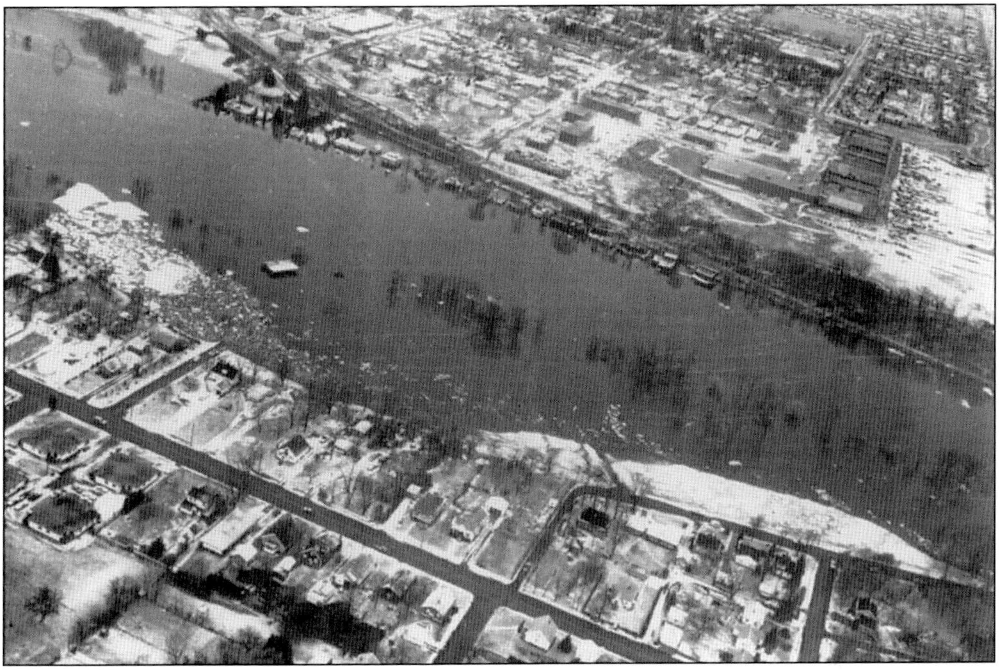

Looking west across the Rock River just south of the Riverside Boulevard Bridge, this aerial view shows Martin Park. The shelter house and the trees along the banks of the river are completely surrounded by water.

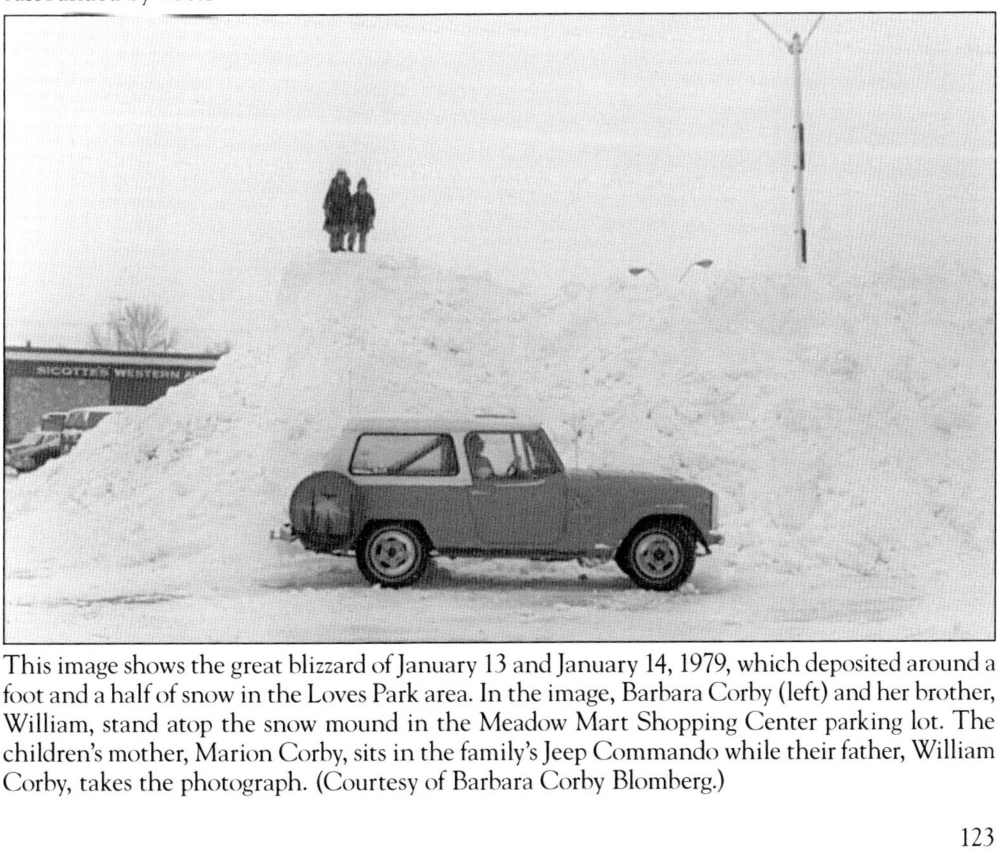

This image shows the great blizzard of January 13 and January 14, 1979, which deposited around a foot and a half of snow in the Loves Park area. In the image, Barbara Corby (left) and her brother, William, stand atop the snow mound in the Meadow Mart Shopping Center parking lot. The children's mother, Marion Corby, sits in the family's Jeep Commando while their father, William Corby, takes the photograph. (Courtesy of Barbara Corby Blomberg.)

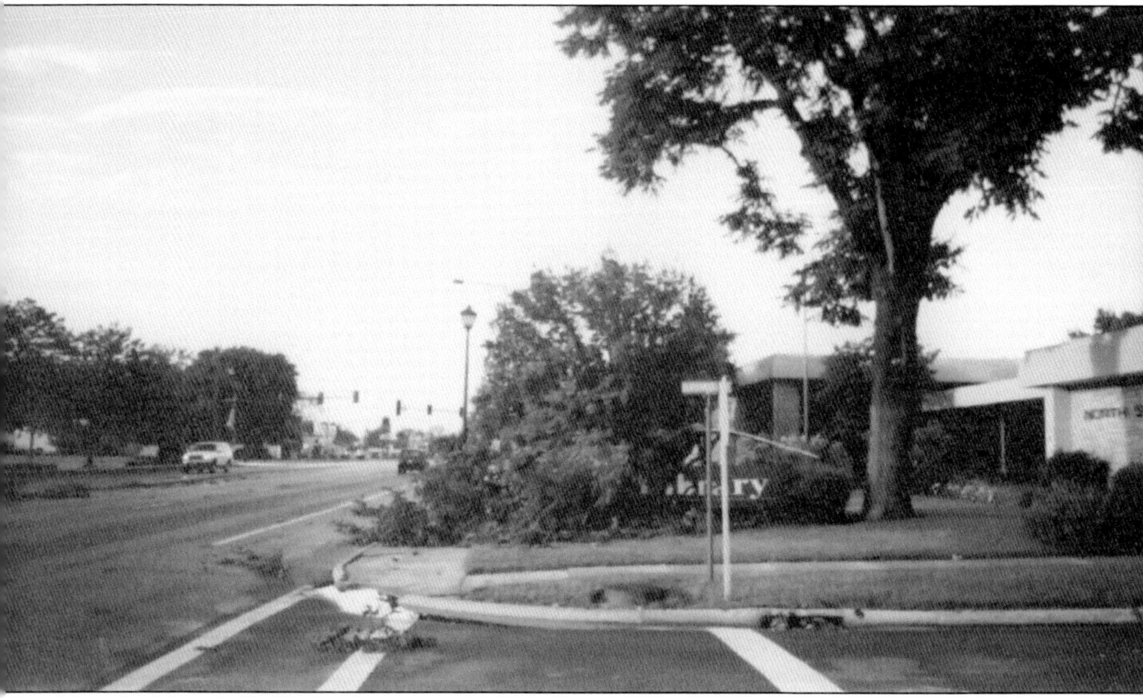

On Saturday, July 5, 2003, at around 4:00 a.m., a microburst hit the Rockford and Loves Park area, knocking down thousands of trees and cutting off power to thousands of area residents. This photograph shows a tree that was knocked down on the North Suburban Library District sign. Some residents were without power for up to a week, and the cleanup took months. (Courtesy of Brian Landis.)

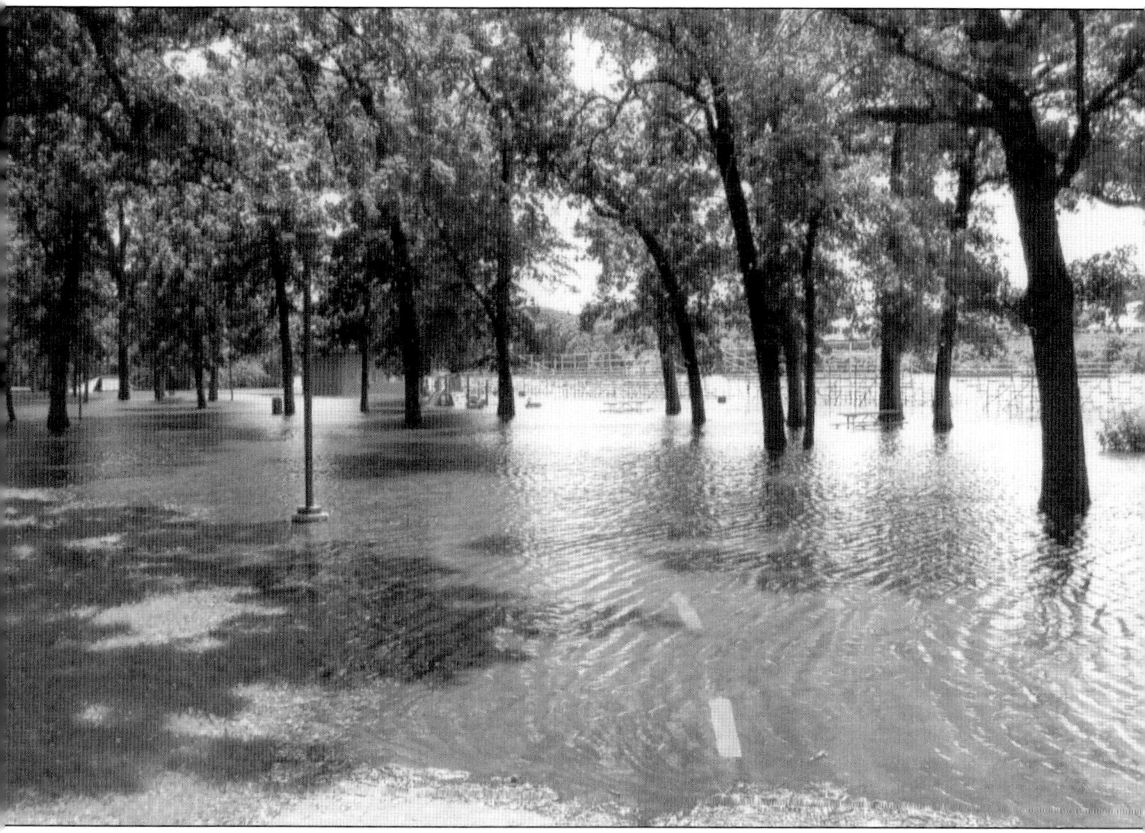

This photograph shows flooding at Shorewood Park in June 2008, when heavy rains caused the Rock River to flood many Rockford and Loves Park neighborhoods. The bleachers used for the Ski Broncs shows are partially underwater in the background. (Courtesy of Brian Landis.)

Bibliography

Campbell, Craig G. *History of Loves Park, Illinois*. Rockford, IL: C.G. Campbell, 1998.
Combined Atlas of Winnebago County, Illinois 1871, 1892, 1905 and Atlas of Boone and Winnebago Counties, Illinois 1886. Chicago: Warner, Higgins & Beers Publishers, 1905.
Hodge, Bob. *The Woodward Way: A History of the Woodward Governor Company, Rockford, Illinois, USA, 1870–1995*. Rockford, IL: Tan Books & Publishers Inc., 1997.
Johnson, Eric A. *Rockford: 1900 to World War I*. Charleston, SC: Arcadia Publishing, 2003.
———. *Rockford: 1920 and Beyond*. Charleston, SC: Arcadia Publishing, 2004.
Rockford Register Star. *Rockford Memories*. Portland, OR: Pediment Publishing, 2007.
———. *Rockford Through Our Eyes*. Portland, OR: Pediment Publishing, 2010.
Rockford Register Star and Midway Village Museum. *Rockford Memories Volume II*. Portland, OR: Pediment Publishing, 2007.
Schafer, Mike and Brian Landis. *Rockford Area Railroads*. Charleston, SC: Arcadia Publishing, 2010.

INDEX